"An elegant collection that showcases all of Adam Hochschild's singular talents as a master essayist, historian, literary critic, and narrative writer. These pieces are special and enduring—a chronicle of our time, past and present, told always on an intimate human scale."

   — Barry Siegel, Pulitzer Prize winner and Director of the Literary Journalism Program at University of California, Irvine

"An inspiring but clear-eyed perspective on what has been—and what can be—accomplished through resistance, persistence, and vision. A wonderful book for our time."

   — Eric Stover, Faculty Director of the Human Rights Center at the University of California, Berkeley and coauthor of *Hiding in Plain Sight*

"These timely, trenchant essays offer a concentrated sample of Adam Hochschild's unique gift for illuminating the history of present-day moral conflicts. Their range is amazing, from the Congo to Siberia to Berkeley, but they are united by Hochschild's wry, compassionate sensibility and voice."

   — Robert F. Worth, author of *A Rage for Order* and contributing writer at the *New York Times Magazine*

Lessons from a Dark Time

Lessons from a Dark Time
and Other Essays

Adam Hochschild

UNIVERSITY OF CALIFORNIA PRESS

909.82
HOC
461-3629

University of California Press, one of the most distinguished university presses in the United States, enriches lives around the world by advancing scholarship in the humanities, social sciences, and natural sciences. Its activities are supported by the UC Press Foundation and by philanthropic contributions from individuals and institutions. For more information, visit www.ucpress.edu.

University of California Press
Oakland, California

Library of Congress Cataloging-in-Publication Data

Names: Hochschild, Adam, author.
Title: Lessons from a dark time : and other essays / Adam Hochschild.
Other titles: Lessons from a dark time and other essays
Description: Oakland, California : University of California Press, [2018] |
    Includes index. |
Identifiers: LCCN 2018009384 (print) | LCCN 2018012726 (ebook) |
    ISBN 9780520969674 | ISBN 9780520297241 (cloth : alk. paper)
Subjects: LCSH: World politics—20th century—Moral and ethical aspects. |
    Political ethics.
Classification: LCC D443 (ebook) | LCC D443 .H5972 2018 (print) |
    DDC 909.82—dc23
LC record available at https://lccn.loc.gov/2018009384

Manufactured in the United States of America

25 24 23 22 21 20 19 18
10 9 8 7 6 5 4 3 2 1

for Harriet Barlow

CONTENTS

ILLUSTRATIONS

FIGURE 1. Nelson Mandela casts the first ballot of his life, 1994.

Introduction

I DO NOT KNOW HOW THINGS will be by the time you read it, but this book goes to press at a grim moment. After spending much of my life writing either about forms of tyranny that we've seen vanish, like apartheid in South Africa or communism in the Soviet Union, or that belonged to earlier centuries, like colonialism or slavery, it is a shock to feel the ruthless mood of such times suddenly no longer so far away. As I write, much of Europe is awash in a bitter stew of revived nationalism, anti-Semitism, and hostility toward Muslims and refugees. Around the world, many a country that was once a democracy, or seemed on the path to being so, has turned repressive. From Poland to the Philippines, Hungary to India, Turkey to Russia, autocrats with little tolerance for dissent are riding high.

Worse yet is that we Americans have elected a president who makes no secret of his enthusiasm for such strongmen and, with nothing but mockery for his critics and contempt for the constitutional separation of powers, would clearly like to be one himself. Donald J. Trump has bent and twisted the truth like pretzel dough, claimed his predecessor was born in Kenya, likened Africa to a toilet, slammed Mexicans as "rapists" and Haitians as all having AIDS, and included in a reference to "very fine people" the toxic collection of white nationalists, neo-Nazis, and Ku Klux Klan members who gathered in Charlottesville, Virginia, in August 2017. One of these "very fine people" killed a woman and injured many others by ramming his car into a crowd. Almost day by day, Trump's racism becomes more naked and his enthusiasm for torture, the death penalty, and nuclear weapons more strident. He has done his best to undermine the investigation into his Russia dealings and called Democrats who failed to applaud his 2018 State of the Union speech "un-American." This list could be far longer. Gun lovers, conspiracy mongers, and the mushrooming array of camouflage-clad private militias in this country are energized in a way they have not been for decades.

Around the world, not just the present but the past has become a battleground. Those right-wingers were in Charlottesville to protest a plan to remove a statue of the Confederate General Robert E. Lee. In Hungary, a German ally in the Second World War, monuments have been installed and museum exhibits altered to portray Hungarians, not Jews, as victims of the Nazis. In the 1990s, many Russians told me of their hope that a few of the old Soviet labor camps could be preserved or restored as memorials to those who died and reminders that such events must never happen again. Instead, at the only place where a restoration has been completed, near Perm, in the Ural Mountains, the camp has become a site of pilgrimage for enthusiastic followers of Vladimir Putin who want to celebrate the glorious days of Stalin's rule.

We have some tough years ahead of us. The title piece of this collection, about America's early twentieth-century red scare, could just as well be called "Lessons *for* a Dark Time." But when times are dark, we need moral ancestors, and I hope the pieces here will be reminders that others have fought and won battles against injustice in the past, including some against racism, anti-immigrant hysteria, and more. The Trumps and Putins of those eras have gotten the ignominy they deserve.

A few words about what you'll find in these pages:

I've chosen the articles for this book from a much larger number I've published over the past two decades or so. Most have to do with the forces that have prevented us, today or in earlier centuries, from living in a fairer and more humane world. Some are about people who tried to bring that world closer; others deal with writers who explored the injustices of their times. Some of what's here reflects my travels: you won't find Cannes or Tuscany, but you will find a prison in Finland, descendants of slaves gathering in a London park, and a day on the campaign trail with Nelson Mandela. Sadly, many of the men and women whose voices I was privileged to hear are no longer with us: Mandela, of course, plus the environmentally pioneering architect Laurie Baker, the Gulag survivor Nadezhda Joffe, and—dying much too young of a heart attack while weakened by malaria—the brave Congolese crusader against rape, Masika Katsuva.

What has drawn me to such people, I think, has a lot to do with coming of age in the early 1960s, a decade that left its mark on so many of us. In Washington, the president was a young John F. Kennedy, who, despite his flaws, inspired a wave of hope and idealism unlike any this country has seen.

In the South, the civil rights movement was reborn, awakening tens of millions of Americans to the harsh wrongs that should have been ended by the Civil War. As fellow college students of mine returned from "freedom rides" to desegregate Southern bus terminals, I saw that there was a world of ferment outside the campus, and I was hungry to explore it. And then, like all men subject to the draft, I found the Vietnam War looming over me and had to ask whether I was willing to risk my life in a senseless conflict on the other side of the globe. Living through that time gave me a lifelong interest in people who took a stand against despotism, who spoke out against unjust wars, or who saw the evils of institutions like slavery or colonialism when, all around them, others took such things for granted. Those are the kinds of subjects I've always been drawn to write about.

The articles in the first section of this book also have their origins in those years, even though they were written decades later. Many of us working in the movement against the Vietnam War began to suspect that we were being watched. Sometimes, J. Edgar Hoover's FBI *wanted* you to know you were being watched: I remember a little group of four men in trench coats and fedoras glowering at the edge of a demonstration on the Boston Common, grabbing for the press releases I was handing out but not taking notes as reporters would have. Just how thorough the watching was I learned only in the late 1970s when under the Freedom of Information Act, after many delays, I was finally able to get heavily redacted copies of more than a hundred pages of files on myself from the FBI, the CIA, and military intelligence. What I found did not inspire confidence in the expertise of these sleuths. One example: my wife Arlie and I were married soon after having briefly been civil rights workers in Mississippi, and in lieu of wedding presents we asked people to make donations to a group we had worked with, the Student Nonviolent Coordinating Committee. In a report by a CIA informant whose name had been blacked out, this was garbled into "gave his wedding presents to Goodwill."

Such experiences left me with a lifelong interest in government spying on civilians, which led me to the stories here about the FBI, the CIA, the shadowy figure of subversive-hunter Major General Ralph H. Van Deman, and the era of surveillance and vigilante justice that began when the United States entered the First World War. Because so many of the historical figures I've written about were activists, I was always curious about how they were seen by the equivalent, in other times and places, of those men in trench coats on the Boston Common. Reading such records often tells you not just about those watched but about the mind-set and prejudices of the watchers. My research for various books has taken me to Scotland Yard reports on the pacifists of 1914–18, FBI and Justice Department accounts of surveillance of American radicals over several decades, Soviet secret police interrogation transcripts, and a British officer's confidential report to London in 1791 about rebellious slaves in the West Indies.

The subject matter of the next section, Africa, for me is also is connected to the 1960s, when I spent a summer as a college student working for an anti-apartheid newspaper in South Africa. It was a searing, life-changing experience to live in a police state for the first time, to see that battle for justice at close hand, to meet people who had been in prison and knew they were likely to be there again, and to realize, to my dismay, how complicit was the U.S. government with that regime. It led me to go back to that country several times in the 1980s, out of which came a book, *The Mirror at Midnight,* about the most repressive period of apartheid. After that, how could I not return to South Africa to cover the country's first democratic election in 1994? A few months after returning from that trip, I began writing *King Leopold's Ghost,* about the bloodiest single episode of the European colonization of Africa, the seizure of the Congo by Leopold II of Belgium. The articles here about Stanley and Livingstone and about Joseph Conrad's *Heart of Darkness* stem from that interest. Immersion in that period of history made me curious to see the Belgian monarch's former colony today, so when an investigator for Human Rights Watch invited me to come on a trip there, I immediately said yes, and two of the stories here report what I saw. We brought along a carton of my book's French-language edition to distribute to local schools, which are desperately short of teaching materials.

The articles in the section on Europe are also connected to previous books of mine, and so here, as elsewhere, please forgive the occasional patch of self-plagiarism. Without experiencing the ferment of the 1960s, I might not have been drawn to the Spanish Civil War, a time of hope and passion for an earlier generation. I was lucky to get to know several of the surviving American veterans of that conflict. In the course of writing a book about the war, I realized that a memoir that had helped form my picture of it, the American edition of George Orwell's *Homage to Catalonia,* had not been published in the form he wanted. Now at last it has been, and the essay on Orwell here is the foreword to that book's new edition.

In the 1780s, the early British abolitionists invented virtually every organizing tool I had seen used in the movements against segregation, the Vietnam

War, and apartheid: the political poster, a campaign logo, the consumer boy-cott, the very idea of an organization headquartered in a national capital with branches around the country. I was fascinated by these remarkable organizers and wrote a book about them, *Bury the Chains,* which, in turn, made me curious about why their lives were so sanitized in a widely seen film. A long-standing love of Russian literature and history led me to the author Victor Serge, whom you'll meet in these pages, and then to some months spent traveling across Russia, visiting the ruins of old prison camps and talking to their survivors in order to write *The Unquiet Ghost,* about how Russians were coming to terms with the legacy of Stalin. That, in turn, drew me to the subject of another article here, about Americans in the Gulag.

Arlie, on sabbatical from her teaching job, had very tolerantly kept me company for the five months I spent researching the Russia book, beginning when we landed in January in Moscow, where the temperature promptly dropped to -40°. So for her next sabbatical she chose the country, which was what landed us in steaming-hot south India, the subject of several articles in another section. We spent most of our time in Kerala, which, although far from being India's wealthiest state, has long boasted the country's highest rates of literacy and life expectancy. But as you'll see, we found Kerala's story much more complex than it first appears.

Coming back to our own continent, I've begun with Mark Twain (another foreword, this one to a collection of his nonfiction), because in his loathing of racism, his hostility to imperial conquest, and his puncturing of humbug, he is a model for us all. An America today awash in humbug—denial of glo-bal warming, "tax reform" that fills the pockets of billionaires, and much more—needs him more than ever. And surely a president whose three-story New York penthouse is decorated everywhere with 24-karat gold seems almost to spring from the imagination of the writer who brought us the term "Gilded Age." Twain is also an intriguing example of something else I talk about in several pieces in this book: the way our collective memory of people and events gets distorted by those who appropriate the role of its keepers. It took a half-century after his death before all of Twain's anti-imperial writings were published in full, uncensored form.

. . .

The French artist Pierre Bonnard was notorious for wanting to retouch his canvases years after he had first created them. He would try to borrow them back from people who had bought them or would sneak into a gallery at the Musée du Luxembourg with a small box of paints under his coat and have a friend distract a guard while he went to work. Writers often have the same impulse when they look back on what they've published, a feeling normally impossible to act on. But one enjoyable thing about putting together a collection like this is that you get to do some retouching. And so in the pieces that follow I've sometimes added a dab of paint here or smoothed out a wrinkle in the canvas there. I have not, however, updated events or statistics; instead, I've noted at the end of each article the year when it first appeared.

You can read these pieces in any order you wish. Dividing them as I have, mostly by geography, is rather arbitrary, since so many of them deal with the connections between parts of the world. The work of European writers as different as Orwell, Conrad, and Sven Lindqvist, for example, was profoundly shaped by what they saw in the global South. Some roots of trouble in today's Africa go back to the European colonialism that began a century and a half ago. And General Van Deman learned surveillance fighting America's first counterinsurgency war in Asia, in the Philippines, then applied those skills back home against civilians in the United States. We live in a world whose parts are infinitely more connected than many people— including the owner of that penthouse full of gold leaf—are willing to see. I hope this book makes some of those connections clearer.

The Surveillance State

SUPPLEMENT. DATED
18 SEPT 1968

TO: DATED
      13 APRIL 1967

HOCHSCHILD, Adam Marquand

1.

The 28 October 1962 issue of the Boston Globe carried an item
on a demonstration held 27 October 1962 against U.S. invasion of Cuba, in which
Adam HOCHSCHILD was named as one of the leaders.

August 1965 HOCHSCHILD /   in contact with leaders of
the W.E.B. DUBOIS CLUBS of America, who were also Communist Party members, concerning protests against U.S. action in Vietnam. In September 1965, as a
representative of the press, he was in contact with known leaders of the Vietnam
Day Committee of Berkeley who were interested in obtaining publicity for a
planned demonstration.

2.

He traveled to Cuba from Mexico City on 24 June 1968.
HOCHSCHILD has stated that he traveled extensively in Western
Europe, Latin America, and the Soviet Union during the period 1948 to present
(August 1968).

APPROVED FOR RELEASE
Date Feb 19, 1976

FIGURE 2.   Page from the author's CIA file.

ONE

Lessons from a Dark Time

FROM THE MOMENT HE TOOK OFFICE, American newspapers and TV screens have overflowed with President Donald J. Trump's choleric attacks on the media, immigrants, and anyone who criticized him. It makes you wonder: what would it be like if nothing restrained him from his obvious wish to silence such enemies? For a chilling answer, we need only roll back the clock a century, to a time when the United States endured a three-year period of unparalleled surveillance, censorship, mass imprisonment, and anti-immigrant terror. And, strangely, all this happened under a president usually remembered for his internationalist idealism.

When Woodrow Wilson went before Congress on April 2, 1917, and asked it to declare war on Germany, the country was as riven by divisions as it is today. Even though millions of people, from the perennially bellicose Theodore Roosevelt on down, were eager for war, President Wilson was not sure he could count on the backing of some nine million German Americans or of the 4.5 million Irish Americans who might be reluctant to fight as allies of Britain. Hundreds of elected state and local officials belonged to the Socialist Party, which strongly opposed American participation in this or any other war. And tens of thousands of Americans were "Wobblies," members of the militant Industrial Workers of the World, or IWW, and the only battle they wanted to fight was that of labor against capital.

The moment the United States joined the conflict in Europe, a second, less noticed war began at home. Staffed by federal agents, local police, and civilian vigilantes, it had three targets: anyone who might be a German sympathizer, left-wing newspapers and magazines, and labor activists. The war against the last two groups would continue for a year and a half after the First World War ended.

In strikingly Trumpian fashion, Wilson himself helped sow suspicion of dissenters and hidden enemies. He had run for reelection in 1916 on the slogan "he kept us out of war," but he was already quietly feeling out congressional leaders about joining the conflict, and he also knew American public opinion was strongly anti-German. Well before the declaration of war, he had ominously warned that "there are citizens of the United States, I blush to admit, born under other flags . . . who have poured the poison of disloyalty into the very arteries of our national life. . . . Such creatures of passion, disloyalty, and anarchy must be crushed out."

Once the United States entered the war, shortly after Wilson's second term began, the crushing swiftly reached a frenzy. The government started arresting and interning native-born Germans who were not naturalized U.S. citizens—but in a highly selective way, rounding up, for example, all those who were IWW members. Millions rushed to spurn anything German. Families named Schmidt quickly became Smith. German-language textbooks were tossed on bonfires. The German-born conductor of the Boston Symphony Orchestra, Karl Muck, was locked up, even though he was a citizen of Switzerland; notes he had made on a score of J. S. Bach's *St. Matthew's Passion* were suspected of being coded messages to Germany. Berlin, Iowa, changed its name to Lincoln, and East Germantown, Indiana, became Pershing, named after the general leading American soldiers in their broadbrimmed hats to France. Hamburger was now "Salisbury steak" and German measles "Liberty measles." The *New York Herald* published the names and addresses of every German or Austro-Hungarian national living in the city.

The government stepped up its spying on civilians. An army intelligence agent in New York became expert at the new art of tapping telephones and loaned his skills around the country as required. With odd clicks on their calls and strangers taking notes at rallies and meetings, it was not long before dissidents realized they were being watched. When a Socialist Party official addressed a crowd on the Boston Common in June 1917, he began "Mr. Chairman, friends, conscripts, and secret agents . . ."

Soon things went far beyond surveillance. In Collinsville, Illinois, the following year, a crowd seized a coal miner, Robert Prager, who had the bad luck to be German-born. They kicked and punched him, stripped off his clothes, wrapped him in an American flag, forced him to sing "The Star-Spangled Banner," and lynched him from a tree on the outskirts of town. No matter that he had tried to enlist in the U.S. Navy but been turned down because he had a glass eye. After a jury deliberated for only forty-five minutes, eleven members of the mob were acquitted of all charges, while a military band played outside the courthouse.

The next stage of conflict was an assault on the media unmatched in American history before or—so far—since. Its commander was Wilson's postmaster general, Albert Sidney Burleson. A pompous former prosecutor and congressman whose father had fought for the Confederates, Burleson was the first Texan to serve in a U.S. cabinet. On June 16, 1917, he sent sweeping instructions to local postmasters ordering them to "keep a close watch on unsealed matters, newspapers, etc." for anything "calculated to . . . cause insubordination, disloyalty, mutiny. . . . or otherwise embarrass or hamper the Government in conducting the war." What did "embarrass" mean? A new Burleson edict gave examples, from saying "that the Government is controlled by Wall Street or munition manufacturers" to "attacking improperly our allies."

One after another, Burleson went after newspapers and magazines, many of them affiliated with the Socialist Party, including the popular *Appeal to Reason,* which had a circulation of more than half a million. Virtually all Wobbly literature was banned from the mails. Burleson's most famous target was Max Eastman's vigorously antiwar *The Masses,* a literary journal that had published writers from John Reed to Sherwood Anderson to Edna St. Vincent Millay to the young Walter Lippmann. While *The Masses* never actually reached the masses—its circulation averaged a mere 12,000—it was one of the liveliest magazines this country ever produced. Burleson shut it down; one of the items that drew his ire was a cartoon of the Liberty Bell crumbling. "They give you ninety days for quoting the Declaration of Independence," Eastman declared, "six months for quoting the Bible."

With so many recent immigrants, the United States had dozens of foreign-language papers. All were now required to submit English translations of all articles dealing with the government, the war, or American allies to the local postmaster *before* they could be published—a ruinous expense that caused many periodicals to stop printing. Another Burleson technique was to ban a particular issue of a newspaper or magazine and then cancel its second-class mailing permit, claiming that it was no longer publishing regularly. Before the war was over seventy-five different publications would be either censored or completely banned.

Finally, the war gave business and government the perfect excuse to attack the labor movement. The preceding eight years had been ones of great labor strife, with hundreds of thousands of workers going on strike every year, and now employers could brand all who did so as traitors to the war effort. Virtually every IWW office was raided; at the group's Chicago headquarters, police smashed tables and chairs, left papers strewn all over the floor, and took away five tons of material, including even some of the ashes of the popular Wobbly songwriter Joe Hill, recently convicted of murder on shaky evidence and executed. In Seattle, authorities turned Wobbly prisoners over to the local army commander, who then claimed that because they were in military custody, they had no right of habeas corpus. When 101 Wobblies were put through a four-month trial in Chicago, a jury found all of them guilty on all counts after a discussion so brief it averaged less than thirty seconds per defendant. The judge passed out sentences totaling 807 years of prison time.

Others sent to jail for opposing the war included not only well-known radicals like Emma Goldman and Eugene V. Debs but hundreds of conscientious objectors to the draft. The C.O.'s were dispatched to military prisons, where some were shackled to cell bars so they would have to stand on tiptoe nine hours a day. A haunting charcoal drawing of this ordeal was later made by one of the victims, the *Masses* illustrator and cartoonist Maurice Becker. By the time of the Armistice, there would be nearly 6,300 warranted arrests of leftists of all varieties, but thousands more people, the total number unknown, were seized without warrants.

Much repression never showed up in statistics because it was done by vigilantes. In June 1917, for example, copper miners in Bisbee, Arizona, organized by the IWW, went on strike. A few weeks later, the local sheriff formed a posse of more than two thousand mining company officials, hired gunmen, and armed local businessmen. Wearing white armbands to identify themselves and led by a car mounted with a machine gun, they broke down doors and marched nearly 1,200 strikers and their supporters out of town. The men were held several hours under the hot sun in a baseball park, then forced at bayonet point into a train of two dozen cattle and freight cars and hauled, with armed guards atop each car and more armed men escorting the train in automobiles, 180 miles through the desert and across the state line to New Mexico. There, after two days without food, they were placed in a U.S. Army stockade. A few months later, in Tulsa, Oklahoma, a mob wearing hoods seized seventeen Wobblies and whipped, tarred, and feathered them.

People from the highest reaches of society bayed for blood like a lynch mob. Elihu Root, a corporate lawyer and former secretary of war, secretary of state, and senator, was the prototype of the so-called wise men of the twentieth-century foreign policy establishment who moved smoothly back and forth between Wall Street and Washington, DC. "There are men walking about the streets of this city tonight who ought to be taken out at sunrise tomorrow and shot," he told an audience at New York's Union League Club in August 1917. "There are some newspapers published in this city every day the editors of which deserve conviction and execution for treason."

Although Woodrow Wilson fruitlessly tried to persuade the American people to join the League of Nations, so as to peacefully resolve conflicts abroad, his zeal for reforming the international order included no tolerance for dissent at home. His Justice Department, for example, encouraged the formation of vigilante groups with names like the Knights of Liberty and the Sedition Slammers. The largest was the American Protective League, whose ranks filled with employers who hated unions, nativists who hated immigrants, and men too old for the military who still wanted to do battle. APL members carried badges labeled "Auxiliary of the US Department of Justice" and the Post Office gave them the franking privilege of sending mail for free. The organization rapidly mushroomed into an ill-controlled mass of some 250,000 members, who gathered more than a million pages of wildly unreliable surveillance data spying on Americans they claimed might be aiding the German war effort.

The government offered a $50 bounty for every proven draft-evader, which brought untold thousands to the hunt, from underpaid rural sheriffs to big-city unemployed. Throughout the country, the APL carried out "slacker raids," sometimes together with uniformed soldiers and sailors. One September 1918 raid in New York City and its vicinity netted more than 60,000 men. Only 199 actual draft dodgers were found among them, but many of the remainder were held for days while their records were checked. Wilson approvingly told the secretary of the Navy that the raids would "put the fear of God" into draft dodgers.

A surprisingly diverse array of Americans opposed the war. Fifty representatives and six senators voted against it; one of the latter, Robert La Follette, who had listened to Wilson's speech to Congress asking for war with conspicuous defiance, crossing his arms and chewing gum, then began receiving nooses in his office mail. Men who failed to register for the draft, didn't show up when called, or deserted after being drafted totaled well over three million. "A higher percentage of American men successfully resisted conscription during World War I," the historian Michael Kazin writes, "than during the Vietnam War." Several men and women, among them Norman Thomas, A. Philip Randolph, and Jeannette Rankin, lived long enough to vocally oppose both wars.

Although brave and outspoken, such war opponents were only a minority of the population. The Wilson administration's harsh treatment of them, sadly, had considerable popular support. The targeting of so many leftists and labor leaders who were immigrants, Jewish, or both drew on powerful undercurrents of nativism and anti-Semitism. And the United States was inflamed with war fever that left millions of young American men, still ignorant of trench warfare's horrors, eager to fight and hostile to anyone who seemed to stand in their way of doing so.

. . .

By the time the war ended the government had a new excuse for continuing the crackdown: the Russian Revolution. It was blamed for any unrest, such as a wave of large postwar strikes in 1919, which were ruthlessly suppressed. Gary, Indiana, was put under martial law, and army tanks were called out in Cleveland.

That year also saw anarchist bombings make headlines across the country. An alert New York postal worker intercepted suspicious-looking packages addressed to sixteen prominent political and business figures, but a number of other mail bombs reached their destinations. One killed a night watchman guarding a judge's home in New York, and another severely damaged the house of Attorney General A. Mitchell Palmer in Washington, DC. Government officials had evidence that the bombs were all the work of several dozen Italian-American anarchists—one of whom managed to blow himself up while planting the explosives at Palmer's home. But it did not suit them to solve the case by prosecuting such a small group when what they really wanted was to wage a far more sweeping war on communism and organized labor. The director of the Bureau of Investigation, predecessor of the FBI, claimed that the bombers were "connected with Russian bolshevism." With the bombings providing the perfect excuse, the crackdown on radicals intensified. Two hundred and forty-nine foreign-born leftists were placed under heavy guard on a decrepit former troopship and deported to Russia. One of them, Emma Goldman, reportedly thumbed her nose at the rising young Justice Department official J. Edgar Hoover, who was seeing off the ship from a tugboat in New York Harbor.

The tumultuous year 1919 also brought an outburst of protest by black Americans and violence against them. Nearly 400,000 blacks had served in the military and then come home to a country where they were denied good jobs, schooling, and housing. As they competed with millions of returning white soldiers for scarce work, race riots broke out, and in the summer of 1919 more than 120 people were killed. Lynchings—a steady, terrifying feature of black life for many years—reached the highest point in more than a decade; seventy-eight African Americans were lynched that year, more than one per week. But all racial tension was also blamed on the Russians. Woodrow Wilson, himself a Southerner and ardent segregationist, predicted that "the American negro returning from abroad would be our greatest medium in conveying Bolshevism to America."

This three-year period of repression reached a peak in late 1919 and early 1920 with the "Palmer Raids" under the direction of Attorney General Palmer. He had been understandably jarred by the anarchist bombing of his house, but his raids, with the help of Hoover, cast a net that scooped up every imaginable variety of radical or dissenter. On a single day of the raids— January 2, 1920—5,483 people were arrested; one scholar calls it "the largest single-day police roundup in American history." The raiders were notoriously rough, beating people and throwing them down staircases. After one raid, a *New York World* reporter found smashed doors, overturned furniture, wrecked typewriters, and bloodstains on the floor. Eight hundred people were seized in Boston and some of them marched through the city's streets in chains on their way to a temporary prison on an island in the harbor. Another eight hundred were held for six days in a windowless corridor in a federal building in Detroit, with no bedding and the use of just one toilet and sink.

Palmer was startlingly open about the fact that his raids were driven by politics. Attacking "the fanatical doctrinaires of communism in Russia," he vowed "to keep up an unflinching, persistent, aggressive warfare against any movement, no matter how cloaked or dissembled, having for its purpose either the promulgation of these ideas or the excitation of sympathy for those who spread them." Campaigning for the Democratic nomination for president, he hysterically predicted a widespread Bolshevik uprising on May Day, 1920, giving authorities in Chicago the excuse to put 360 radicals into preventive detention for the day. When the date passed and absolutely nothing happened, it became clear that the United States never had been on the verge of revolution; membership in the country's two feuding communist parties, after all, was miniscule. Citizens—most notably a committee of a dozen prominent lawyers, law professors, and law school deans—were finally emboldened to speak out against the repression, and the worst of it came to an end. But it had accomplished its purpose. The IWW was crushed, the Socialist Party reduced to a shadow of its former self, and unions forced into sharp retreat: even the determinedly moderate work-within-the-system American Federation of Labor would lose more than a million members between 1920 and 1923.

. . .

Once the war was over, all the surveillance and repression were carried out in the name of anticommunism. We think of that set of beliefs as a reaction to the Russian Revolution, but Nick Fischer points out in his provocative *Spider Web: The Birth of American Anticommunism* that anticommunism in the United States never has had much to do with Russia. For one thing, it had already been sparked by the Paris Commune, decades before the Revolution. "Today there is not in our language ... a more hateful word than communism," thundered a professor at Union Theological Seminary in 1878. For another thing, after the Revolution, anticommunists knew as little as American communists about what was actually happening in Russia. The starry-eyed communists were convinced it was paradise. The anticommunists found they could shock people if they portrayed the country as ruled by "commissariats of free love," where women had been nationalized along with private property and were passed out to men. Neither group had much incentive to investigate what life in that distant country was actually like.

All along, the real target of American anticommunism was organized labor. Employers were the core of the anticommunist movement and early on began building alliances. One was with the press, whose owners had their own fear of unions: as early as 1874 the *New York Tribune* was talking of how "Communists" had smuggled into New York jewels stolen from Paris churches to finance the purchase of arms. That same year the *New York Times* spoke of a "Communist reign of terror" wreaked by striking carpet weavers in Philadelphia. In 1887, *Bradstreet's* decried the idea of the eight-hour workday as "communist."

The anticommunist alliance was also joined by private detective agencies, which earned millions by infiltrating and suppressing unions. These rose to prominence in the late nineteenth century, and by the time of the Palmer Raids, the three largest employed 135,000 men. Meanwhile, the nation's police forces began developing "red squads," whose officers' jobs and promotions depended on finding communist conspiracies.

Another ally was the military. "Fully half of the National Guard's activity in the latter nineteenth century," Fischer writes, "comprised strikebreaking and industrial policing." Many of the handsome redbrick armories in American cities were built during that period, some with help from industry. Chicago businessmen even purchased a grand home for one general.

By the time the United States had entered the First World War, the Bureau of Investigation and the U.S. Army's new Military Intelligence branch were also part of the mix. An important gathering place for the most influential anticommunists after 1917, incidentally, was New York's Union League Club, where Elihu Root had given his hair-raising speech about executing newspaper editors for treason. And anticommunism seamlessly fitted together with another ideology in the air, restricting immigration. John Bond Trevor, for example, an upper-crust WASP (Franklin and Eleanor Roosevelt attended his wedding) got his start as director of the New York City branch of Military Intelligence in 1919. He moved on the following year to help direct a New York State investigation of subversives, which staged its own sweeping raids, and soon became active in the eugenics movement. He was influential in crafting and lobbying for the Immigration Act of 1924, which sharply restricted arrivals from almost everywhere except northwestern Europe. In a pattern still familiar today, his life combined hostility to dissidents at home and to immigrants from overseas.

· · ·

What lessons can we draw from this era when the United States, despite sharing victory in the European war, truly lost its soul at home?

A modestly encouraging one is that sometimes a decent person with respect for law can throw a wrench in the works. Somewhere between 6,000 and 10,000 aliens were arrested during the Palmer Raids, and Palmer and Hoover were eager to deport them. But deportations were controlled by the Immigration Bureau, which was under the Department of Labor. And there Assistant Secretary of Labor Louis F. Post, a progressive former newspaperman with rimless glasses and a Vandyke beard, was able to stop most deportations.

A true hero of this grim era, Post canceled search warrants, restored habeas corpus rights for those detained, and drastically reduced or eliminated bail for many. This earned him the hatred of Palmer and of Hoover, who assembled a 350-page file on him. Hoover also unsuccessfully orchestrated a campaign by the American Legion for Post's dismissal and an attempt by Congress to impeach him. All told, Post was able to prevent some three thousand people from being deported.

A more somber lesson offered by the events of 1917–20 is that when powerful social tensions roil the country and hysteria fills the air, rights and values we take for granted can easily erode: the freedom to publish and speak, protection from vigilante justice, even confidence that election results will be honored. When, for instance, in 1918 and again in a special election the next year, Wisconsin voters sent a socialist to Congress, and a fairly moderate one at that, the House of Representatives, by a vote of 330 to 6, simply refused to seat him. The same thing happened to five members of the party elected to the New York state legislature.

Furthermore, we can't comfort ourselves by saying of these three years of jingoist thuggery, "if only people had known." People *did* know. All of these shameful events were widely reported in print, sometimes photographed, and in a few cases even caught on film. But the press generally nodded its approval. After the sheriff of Bisbee, Arizona, and his posse packed the local Wobblies off into the desert, the *Los Angeles Times* wrote that they "have written a lesson that the whole of America would do well to copy." Knowing the facts is not enough. The public, the press, and the courts also have to believe that no one is above the law.

The final lesson from this dark time is that when a president has no tolerance for opposition, the greatest godsend he can have is a war. Then dissent becomes not just "fake news" but treason. We should be wary.

2017

TWO

Students as Spies

THANKS TO THE WHISTLE-BLOWER EDWARD SNOWDEN, we've learned that our national security apparatus has for years been secretly gathering the e-mails and telephone records of millions of Americans. It would be reassuring to think that such an arrogant use of power is a rare overreach. But it is not. Intelligence agencies have gone off the rails before, and for one particularly egregious instance some years ago, I had a view from a ringside seat. I'll come back to that in a moment.

Karen Paget lays out the full history of this episode in her book *Patriotic Betrayal: The Inside Story of the CIA's Secret Campaign to Enroll American Students in the Crusade against Communism.* Soviet communism may have vanished, but the events she describes have profound, disturbing relevance for anyone who cares about reining in the surveillance state.

Paget met her future husband when they were both undergraduates at the University of Colorado, where he became student body president. Together they attended the 1964 annual conference of the National Student Association, the country's premier student group. Delegates came from all over the nation, as if for a presidential nominating convention. Having been raised in a small town, Paget found that for her the experience opened up an "astonishing world.... I was riveted by the political speeches. I had never seen or heard anything like it. I had grown up more devoted to cheerleading and baton twirling than political or intellectual pursuits."

For several decades after the Second World War, national student unions were where the politically ambitious first tried out their wings. Figures as varied as Congressman Barney Frank, the assassinated Swedish prime minister Olof Palme, and UN Secretary-General Kofi Annan were all active in student unions. In the United States, the National Student Association represented some four hundred American campuses at its peak, and during the Cold War, both the United States and the Soviet Union used student politics as a proxy battleground for their rivalry.

In 1965, Paget and her husband were invited to a National Student Association (NSA) seminar that was far more exclusive than the previous year's annual conference, with only a dozen other students, most of them college newspaper editors or student body presidents. The group enjoyed sessions with experts on Africa and Latin America and a visit to the State Department. When the seminar ended, the NSA offered Paget's husband a job on its international staff in Washington, DC. He was given a good salary, they were living in the nation's capital, and at the next national NSA conference Paget got to sit on the dais while Vice President Hubert Humphrey gave a speech. "Our new life seemed almost magical," she writes. But then one day she found herself alone with two men, one of whom "told me that my husband was 'doing work of great importance to the United States government,' and handed me a document to sign. . . . My host then revealed that he worked for the Central Intelligence Agency . . . and that he was my husband's case officer." The National Student Association, Paget discovered, was underwritten by the CIA.

Her husband, she found out, had just signed a similar document, something called a national security oath. He had been, she writes, "deeply shaken by the revelation, which turned our time in Washington from a period of elation to one of confusion and, later, fear. . . . We told no one . . . we felt isolated." The couple soon learned that revealing the NSA's CIA ties would be a felony violation of the Espionage Act, punishable by twenty years in prison. Suddenly they were in far over their heads; he was twenty-two, she was twenty, and they had a baby. What they had believed to be a democratically controlled group of student idealists turned out to be something much darker. "We kept asking ourselves: How could this have happened?"

In the many years she spent working to answer that question, the CIA sometimes stone-walled her requests for data. Her attempt to get two reports from 1949, for example, took nine years. The story she tells is an impressive, devastating evening of the score by the woman who felt trapped and violated a half-century ago. It offers a sobering lesson about what can happen when a country loses control of its intelligence services.

. . .

In the 1950s and 1960s, the National Student Association and similar unions from other Western democracies belonged to the International Student Conference (ISC), headquartered in the Netherlands. Student groups from the USSR and its allies were members of a rival federation in Prague. The two international groups competed fiercely for the allegiance of students in nonaligned countries. But the ISC, like the National Student Association, was funded largely by the CIA, and huge amounts of agency money were covertly spent on its annual meetings and in support of its sixty-person secretariat. NSA and ISC staff traveled all over the world on the CIA's dime to lobby student unions in other countries. They also arranged grants to establish student unions to the CIA's liking in countries that didn't have them and to create well-funded new unions to compete with those considered too far to the left. The CIA infiltrated nearly every level of the era's student politics: in 1959, for instance, it recruited a recent Smith College graduate named Gloria Steinem to lead some one hundred Americans in disrupting proceedings and distributing pro-Western literature at a Soviet-sponsored youth festival in Vienna.

The CIA's control of the National Student Association gave it not just a means of influence but a fount of intelligence. NSA staffers made "fact-finding" trips to other countries, where they interviewed student activists at length and wrote reports on them; foreign student leaders also took part in NSA seminars on international issues, as Paget and her husband had done. Over the course of six weeks, a seminar leader would encourage participants to freely voice their opinions, would read what they wrote in essays, and could see who was friendly or unfriendly to American foreign policy. Hundreds of reports about the students taking part flowed back to CIA headquarters in Langley, Virginia. These seminars were such an intelligence gold mine that the CIA organized them throughout the world: thirty-three were staged in Africa alone. One resulting report described a Congolese student as "the conservative, intelligent, French-speaking African people have been looking for." A Cameroonian was rated well because he was "a genuine nationalist, though perhaps of the more revisionist moderate variety."

These reports provided the CIA with information about men and women who would someday be cabinet ministers, ambassadors, and UN officials. More ominously, they also gave the agency data to trade with other intelligence services. That, after all, is something all such agencies do. Many of the governments the United States was friendly with, however, were brutal dictatorships. For example, the National Student Association was deeply involved in Iraq. In the early 1960s, the CIA backed the Baath Party, which it saw as tough on communism. The NSA dutifully passed resolutions in favor of the Baathists, and its international staff supported a new Iraqi student union to counter the existing pro-Soviet one. Once the Baathists took power in a coup, they arrested some ten thousand Iraqis, of whom they executed about half. Then a different Baathist faction seized power in a second coup and arrested students who had worked with the Americans. How many of the student victims in both groups were targeted via NSA reports that had been passed on to Iraq? We will never know.

In Iran, the CIA in the 1950s had helped the Shah to depose a leftist prime minister and establish his notoriously ruthless secret police. But at the same time, NSA staff—some of them genuinely opposed to despotism and unwitting about the CIA connection—were helping an anti-Shah union of Iranian students in the United States, all the while filing the usual reports about the union's members. "My God," a former NSA president burst out at an alumni gathering decades later. "Did we finger people for the Shah?"

For twenty years, the CIA successfully kept its control over the National Student Association secret. Students recruited for the NSA's international staff, or those who were urged to run for its key elective offices, were carefully vetted by veterans of the organization who had the CIA's interests in mind. Once in place, and pleased to have an exciting job with the chance to travel, a new NSA official would be told that he (it was almost always a he) was about to be given some highly confidential information. Who would turn down the chance to hear a secret—and who won't promise, in return, to keep it?

Given the CIA's vast budget, money was never a problem: once an NSA project had been approved by Langley, the financial spigot gushed in response to a mere one- or two-page funding proposal. Over a million dollars in today's money was spent organizing a single conference in Ceylon in 1956. A decade later, using various foundations as conduits, the CIA was spending twenty times that much on student operations each year. In case anyone asked questions about the lavish funding for NSA programs or the association's comfortable double townhouse headquarters near Dupont Circle—were there no strings attached to any of these plentiful foundation grants?—there was a handpicked advisory board that could be counted on to say that all was on the level. But then suddenly everything came unglued.

. . .

In January 1967, I was working as a young staff writer at the San Francisco–based *Ramparts* magazine, which had established itself as a saucy new journal of investigative reporting. One day a frightened, bushy-haired young man named Michael Wood approached us with a story so far-fetched that at first no one believed him. Wood explained that he had been hired as the National Student Association's fund-raiser. Like anyone in such a role, he knew that an organization's most promising source of donations was those who had already given. But he was baffled when he was specifically told not to contact a number of foundations that had been the NSA's most generous supporters, such as the innocuously named Foundation for Youth and Student Affairs. He repeatedly protested to the friend who had hired him, NSA president Philip Sherburne, and eventually Sherburne sat him down for a confidential talk. After having been elected, Sherburne said, he had been horrified to learn that most of the NSA's money was coming from the CIA. He had brought in Wood to try to raise funds from other sources so that this embarrassing connection could be severed.

The CIA, however, was alarmed at the prospect of losing its hold over the student union. To prevent this from happening, it began playing hardball. The shadowy Foundation for Youth and Student Affairs abruptly claimed that the NSA owed it large amounts of money. A number of staff members, including Sherburne himself, had their CIA-arranged draft deferments canceled—with hundreds of thousands of American troops fighting in Vietnam, this was a lethal threat. And when the CIA learned that Sherburne had violated his national security oath by talking to Wood, the agency became nastier still. Fearful of a possible prison term, Sherburne had sought legal advice from Roger Fisher, a distinguished Harvard Law School professor. Soon after, a senior CIA official appeared at Fisher's office and asked him to drop his client. When Fisher refused, the man hinted that there could be unfortunate consequences for Fisher's brother, a foreign aid official stationed in Colombia. Fisher, to his credit, was not swayed.

Meanwhile, having made up his mind to disclose the secret, Michael Wood came to *Ramparts,* which began trying to confirm his extraordinary tale. When a *Ramparts* researcher in Boston began to investigate the foundations that Wood said had funded the National Student Association, he discovered that most were housed in law firms, where attorneys refused to talk about their clients. The researcher then consulted a legal directory and suddenly realized that the law firms all had something striking in common: each had at least one senior partner who, during the Second World War, had served in the Office of Strategic Services, the predecessor of the CIA.

Several of us at *Ramparts* were working on the story. My own part was small: I rewrote one section of it and traveled to interview a former NSA officer, who, unsurprisingly, denied everything. It soon became clear that the CIA knew what we were up to, and the magazine took all sorts of frantic precautions: we made furtive calls from pay phones and hired a bored-looking Pinkerton guard to sit by the front desk. Wood came and went from the office, and one evening when he and I and a few others were working late, we were jarred by a string of loud explosions in the street outside. Was this how it was all going to end? Should we dive for cover? But it turned out there was no CIA assault team. The office was on the edge of Chinatown, and we had forgotten that it was the Chinese New Year.

In mid-February 1967, after pursuing the story for several weeks, we got word that the National Student Association was about to call a press conference, intending to reveal the CIA ties itself and put its own spin on the revelation. The issue of *Ramparts* with the exposé was still being edited, and this was of course decades before the Internet. What could be done? Warren Hinckle, the magazine's editor, had the brilliant idea of placing a full-page advertisement announcing the story in the next morning's *New York Times* and *Washington Post.* The NSA was upstaged, the story and its reverberations were on newspaper front pages for a week, and a group of members of Congress signed a protest letter to the president. This began a long period of public embarrassment for the CIA, climaxing in the 1970s with the disclosure that it had tried to assassinate several foreign leaders.

In the immediate wake of the *Ramparts* story, something happened that none of us at the magazine had anticipated. Reporters began to look at public records to see what else the CIA's conduits, like the mysterious Foundation for Youth and Student Affairs, had funded.

They found hundreds of recipients: the American Society for African Culture, the International Commission of Jurists, the American Friends of the Middle East, programs within the AFL-CIO and the National Council of Churches, journalists' groups, and more. As with the NSA, usually a few key people in the organization knew where the money was coming from, but most others did not. The CIA wanted to foster the impression that, from many walks of life—professional, religious, ethnic, educational—scores of organizations were of their own free will taking a strongly anticommunist stand. If these groups mixed that with liberalism on other issues, so much the better, many in the CIA felt, for it was liberals and leftists abroad whose minds the agency most hoped to sway.

No single group was more important to the CIA, however, than the National Student Association. After the exposé, some CIA defenders argued that it had been a good thing to create a democratically oriented international student federation as an alternative to the communist-dominated one. Paget adds a curious fillip to the argument, which should be a warning to any regime that thinks it can secretly pull the strings of a front group forever. Many of the top officials of the USSR's own puppet international student federation in Prague were Czechs. Surprisingly, the group's three most important leaders all became major figures in the Prague Spring of 1968, the sweeping array of democratic changes that lasted more than six months before it was crushed by Warsaw Pact troops. Prague Spring started less than a year after the *Ramparts* story broke. It's a pleasure to imagine spymasters in Moscow and Langley pounding their desks at almost exactly the same time, in fury at the young people who had escaped their control.

. . .

And pound their desks they certainly did. When President Lyndon B. Johnson heard about the impending *Ramparts* story, he summoned CIA chief Richard Helms back to Washington from a trip to the nuclear lab at Los Alamos. The CIA, in turn, called home some two hundred agents from overseas to discuss damage control. The agency quickly persuaded some friendly members of Congress to declare that they had known and approved of the agency's relationship with the NSA (not true), and twelve former NSA presidents signed a statement that the CIA had never interfered with their activities (also a lie—the CIA had directed much of what they did). Paget dryly notes that three of the statement's signers were CIA career agents at the time; all but one had continued to work for the agency after his term as NSA president expired.

Learning of the close tie between the two organizations left many people feeling not just shocked but personally betrayed. A year or so after the

Ramparts story was published, I met a former South African student leader, a committed anti-apartheid activist. After his student days, he had gone on to try to gather support overseas for an underground resistance movement. In this effort he had found a sympathetic ear in an American with a deep interest in Africa who had been a top official of the NSA and then worked at the pro-Western International Student Conference in Holland. The two became such close friends that one was the best man at the other's wedding. Now, stunned by the *Ramparts* article and the revelation that the American must have been reporting to the CIA all along, the South African was agonized, wondering how much of what he had confided had made its way back to the apartheid regime in Pretoria.

He was right to wonder, for we know now that despite Washington's routine public denunciations of white rule, the U.S. intelligence establishment shared a huge amount of data with Pretoria for decades. This included satellite intercepts of African National Congress radio communications as well as the information, passed on by a CIA officer in Durban, that allowed the South African police to put their roadblock at the right place to seize Nelson Mandela in 1962, the arrest that began his twenty-seven years behind bars.

The CIA clearly knew that revealing its control of the NSA could have reverberations around the world and might unravel its whole web of covertly funded organizations. When it discovered that we were putting together the story, it established a "*Ramparts* Task Force" at Langley and gathered information on many of us who worked at the magazine. A decade after the exposé, under the Freedom of Information Act, I was finally able to get some of these CIA files and found myself described as "a needle to the Agency," even though I was a very low man on the *Ramparts* totem pole. It was chilling to discover how closely the agency was watching the magazine and its editors and writers.

Do democratic governments have the right to collect intelligence and to gather it secretly? Of course: we live in a world full of malicious regimes and movements. But intelligence gathering can all too easily expand into realms that have nothing to do with thwarting possible attacks. This can mean passing on information about student leaders to repressive regimes, or, as we learned more recently, eavesdropping on the cell phone of German Chancellor Angela Merkel, or vacuuming up the e-mails and text messages of millions of people at home and abroad—and all of this while the highest intelligence officials deny to Congress that any such thing is happening.

The more clandestine intelligence operations are, the more we need rigorous vigilance to ensure that the ends do not corrupt the means. Otherwise we start to look like our enemies: to combat a Soviet front organization, we create a front organization of our own; to build allegiances against communist secret-police regimes, we finger people for the Shah's secret police; to fight the brutality of Al Qaeda, we torture prisoners at secret sites. The power that the CIA wielded over the NSA was financial; the power whose abuse Edward Snowden alerted us to was electronic. In neither case were there checks or balances. Both scandals warn us of what can happen when great power is exercised without oversight or conscience.

2015

THREE

Hoover's Secret Empire

ANTICOMMUNISM HAS ALWAYS BEEN FAR LOUDER and more potent
in the United States than communism. Unlike sister parties in France, Italy,
India, and elsewhere, the Communist Party in this country has never controlled a state or major city, or even elected a single member to the national
legislature. American anticommunism, by contrast, built and destroyed
thousands of careers; witch-hunted dissidents in Hollywood, universities,
and government; and was a force that politicians like Joseph McCarthy and
Richard Nixon rode to great heights. This was not the first time that heresy
hunters have overshadowed the actual heretics: consider the Inquisition,
which began before Martin Luther, the greatest heretic, was even born, or
how Stalin shot or imprisoned so-called Trotskyists by the millions—numbers many times those of Trotsky's beleaguered, faction-ridden followers.

No one hunted heretics more fiercely than J. Edgar Hoover in his decades-
long reign as director of the FBI. More than forty years after his death, we
know a great deal about this manipulative, power-hungry man, but the
California investigative journalist Seth Rosenfeld adds significantly more in
Subversives: The FBI's War on Student Radicals, and Reagan's Rise to Power.
It is based on some three hundred thousand pages of documents pried out of
the resistant FBI over more than two decades in a series of lawsuits. These
papers document FBI surveillance, disinformation, and other monkey business during the student revolts that roiled the University of California at
Berkeley in the 1960s.

At that time, these upheavals made Berkeley surely the only college campus in the world with four full-time daily newspaper correspondents stationed on it, and as a greenhorn reporter for the *San Francisco Chronicle,* I
was one of them. I spent close to a year sharing a ramshackle office with writ-

ers for rival papers, within earshot of the campus's wide, sun-drenched central plaza, where speeches and demonstrations took place. We would call in photographers if a major press conference or clash with the police seemed in the offing. I spent considerable time covering such events in Berkeley before and after that year as well, watching firsthand, for instance, the mass arrest of 773 Free Speech Movement sit-in demonstrators in December 1964 for demanding an end to restrictions on political speaking and organizing on campus. That day the university's stately buildings looked like an armed camp as police and sheriff's deputies dragged protestors down the staircase of the administration building to be bussed off to the county jail. I covered some of the later massive marches and teach-ins against the Vietnam War and witnessed the astonishing sight of a California National Guard helicopter swooping low across the campus in 1969 indiscriminately spraying a dense white cloud of tear gas.

I thought in those years that I could clearly see every aspect of this political battleground. But it turns out there was much that none of us knew. For example, I and dozens of other journalists were on hand to cover one large protest march against the Vietnam War where demonstrators tangled with the Oakland police. But none of us had the slightest idea that the march's monitors, who were trying to keep things peaceful, were having their walkie-talkies secretly jammed by the FBI. Nor did we have any idea of the extent of the bureau's decade-long vendetta against Clark Kerr, who was first chancellor at Berkeley and then president of the entire University of California system.

Everyone knew that the FBI had no love for student leftists, but Hoover's intense hatred for Kerr is the major revelation of Rosenfeld's book—and it was evidently a revelation to Kerr as well when the author shared some of this material with him shortly before Kerr died in 2003. "I know Kerr is no good," Hoover scrawled in the margin of one bureau document.

Although Kerr was largely reviled by the activists of the Free Speech Movement, who were—quite rightly—protesting the university's banning of political advocacy on campus, he was far more than the soft-spoken, colorless bureaucrat he appeared to be. For one thing, he had a wry sense of humor, quipping that the real purpose of a university was to provide sex for the students, sports for the alumni, and parking for the faculty. More important, he was a man of principle. From 1949 to 1951, for example, the university was riven by a fierce controversy over a loyalty oath required of all employees. More than sixty professors refused to sign, and thirty-one of them, as well as many other staff, were fired. Though a staunch anticommunist, Kerr spoke out strongly against the firings and the witch-hunt atmosphere surrounding them. His stand won him the enmity of right-wingers, and he was soon on Hoover's radar.

· · ·

The heresy that Hoover feared most was not communism; it was threats to the power of the FBI. What pushed him over the line from hostility to absolute rage at Kerr was an exam question. High school students applying to the University of California had to take an English aptitude test, which included a choice of one of twelve topics for a 500-word essay. In 1959, one topic was: "What are the dangers to a democracy of a national police organization, like the FBI, which operates secretly and is unresponsive to criticism?"

When he heard about this, a furious Hoover issued a blizzard of orders: one FBI official drafted a letter of protest for the national commander of the American Legion to sign; other agents mobilized statements of outrage from the Hearst newspapers, the Catholic Archdiocese of Los Angeles, and the International Association of Chiefs of Police. An FBI man went to see California Governor Edmund G. Brown and stood by while Brown dictated a letter ordering an inquiry into who had written the essay question.

Hoover himself wrote to members of the university's board of regents, who swiftly apologized. But his ire did not subside; he ordered an FBI investigation of the university as a whole, assigning an astounding thirty employees to the task. The result was a sixty-page report, covering professorial transgressions that ranged from giving birth out of wedlock to writing a play that "defamed Chiang Kai-shek." The report also noted that seventy-two university faculty, students, and employees were on the bureau's "Security Index," a list Hoover kept of people who in a national emergency were to be arrested and thrown into preventive detention.

This new trove of documents reveals that when the FBI didn't have another weapon handy, it sent poison-pen letters. The man initially suspected of writing the offending essay question, for instance, was a quiet UCLA English professor and Antioch College graduate, Everett L. Jones. When intensive sleuthing couldn't find anything to tie Jones to the Communist Party—the usual FBI means of tarring an enemy—someone in the bureau wrote an anonymous letter on plain stationery to UCLA's chancellor, signed merely "Antioch—Class of '38," saying that the writer had known Jones and his wife in college, where "they expressed views which shocked many of their friends" and later became "fanatical adherents to communism."

Hoover's anger at Clark Kerr was reignited in 1960, when thirty-one Berkeley students were among those arrested in a demonstration against a House Un-American Activities Committee hearing in San Francisco's City Hall—an early landmark in what would be a tumultuous decade of American student protest. Hoover was outraged when Kerr refused to discipline the students taking part. Reasonably enough, Kerr said that any student demonstrators were acting as private individuals and "were not in any way representing the university."

The upheavals of the Free Speech Movement, which had Berkeley in turmoil during the 1964–65 school year, and of the protests against the Vietnam War that began shaking the campus soon after, brought renewed scrutiny by the FBI. As always, Hoover's anticommunism had little to do with the USSR: although the FBI's responsibilities include counterespionage, only twenty-five agents in Northern California were assigned to this, while forty-three were at work monitoring "subversives," which meant people like Berkeley students—and, it turns out, even people the student activists thought were their enemies, like the university's regents.

Gathering information about several liberal pro-Kerr regents, Hoover funneled it and other ammunition to a major enemy of Kerr, regent Edwin Pauley, a wealthy Los Angeles oilman. An FBI official then reported back to Hoover that an appreciative Pauley might be a useful informant and could "use his influence to curtail, harass and . . . eliminate communists and ultraliberal members on the faculty."

California's governor and several other state officials were ex officio regents, and the political balance on the board changed when Ronald Reagan was elected governor in 1966. At Reagan's first meeting, Kerr was fired. Even though Hoover can't be blamed for costing Kerr his job, he had already made sure that there was another one the educator didn't get. Some months earlier, President Lyndon B. Johnson had decided he wanted Kerr to be his next secretary of health, education, and welfare. "I've looked from the Pacific to the Atlantic and from Mexico to Canada," LBJ told Kerr in his famous arm-twisting mode, "and you're the man I want." Kerr said he would think it over. Meanwhile, Johnson ordered the usual FBI background check. Hoover sent the president a twelve-page report that included allegations from a California state legislative red-hunter who claimed that someone named Louis Hicks had worked with Kerr in the 1940s and declared that Kerr was "pro-Communist."

"Hoover's report failed to note, however," Rosenfeld writes, "that when FBI agents interviewed Hicks he denied making the charge." The report made a string of similar misrepresentations, among them another such charge—with no mention of the FBI investigation that found it untrue. Before Kerr could tell LBJ that he had decided to turn down the post, the president withdrew the offer.

. . .

Hoover's FBI did its best not only to wreck the careers of its enemies but to promote those of its friends, like Reagan. It is jarring to see how much help he got from an agency that is supposed to have nothing to do with partisan politics. Reagan had been trading information with the FBI about alleged radicals ever since his days as president of the Screen Actors Guild in the 1940s, and he continued to feed the bureau Hollywood political gossip long afterward. The FBI did work for him in return, for example, investigating whether a live-in boyfriend of his estranged daughter Maureen was already married (he was).

Another FBI favor for Reagan also concerned a wayward child: his son Michael. In 1965, after Hoover had at last, reluctantly and under much pressure, finally begun investigating organized crime, an agent reported that "the son of Ronald Reagan was associating with" the son of Mafia clan chief Joseph "Joe Bananas" Bonanno. Both sons enjoyed pursuing girls and driving fast cars, and the young Bonanno already had a police record at eighteen. The logical procedure would have been for FBI agents to interview Michael Reagan for any information about the Bonannos he might have learned, but Hoover ordered instead that the agents should simply suggest to his father that he tell Michael to find another companion. Reagan, just then gearing up for his first run for governor, was most grateful.

The FBI did him many other courtesies over the years: a personal briefing from Hoover, data for his speeches, and quiet investigations of people the University of California was thinking about hiring—even though screening applicants for jobs outside the federal government was not in the bureau's jurisdiction. But Hoover's biggest favor of all for Reagan was something he didn't do. In 1960, an informer thought "reliable" reported that Reagan secretly belonged to the John Birch Society—an organization even the FBI thought so extreme (it considered President Eisenhower a communist) that it was kept under surveillance. Rosenfeld says that he could not tell from the available records whether this claim was true. But, he notes, "it was precisely the kind of uncorroborated information" that the bureau had quietly slipped to dozens of politicians or journalists over the years when it wanted to damage somebody's reputation. This report, which could easily have wrecked Reagan's future political career, Hoover kept quiet.

. . .

One appeal of hunting heretics is that it is easy. By contrast, good police work—such as building a solid legal case against the Bonanno family or a sophisticated white-collar criminal—is extremely hard. Small wonder that Hoover preferred the first to the second. But what happens to a professional anticommunist when, on the home front anyway, there are almost no more communists left? After 1956, when Khrushchev's admission of Stalin's crimes and the Soviet invasion of Hungary drove thousands out of the Party, there were only about five thousand Party members left in the United States, some 30 percent of whom were FBI informants. The FBI then rather clumsily began looking for new targets. In a curious echo of the hostility of the USSR and its satellite regimes toward the antiauthoritarian overtones of rock music, Hoover grew alarmed about the counterculture. Ken Kesey and his Merry Pranksters came into his sights, as did organizations like Berkeley's Sexual Freedom League.

But the world was shifting under the FBI's feet. In the good old days, if you couldn't wreck someone's career by tying him or her to a known communist, you could still do so by exposing a sexual misdeed. Or you could simply hint that you had such information—something Hoover did for decades to blackmail potential congressional critics into silence. The bureau dispatched a poison-pen letter in 1965 revealing that a prominent Berkeley antiwar activist had fathered an illegitimate child, but the FBI's Northern California chief wrote Hoover bemoaning the fact that such leaks were no longer effective. These student radicals, he explained, "do not have the same moral standards as a Bureau employee." In such treacherously changing times, what was a poor blackmailer to do?

Rosenfeld's many years of digging have produced other notable revelations. The most controversial concerns Richard Aoki, a military veteran and particularly confrontational student leader in the later stages of Berkeley 1960s activism; he urged his comrades, for instance, to steal weapons from National Guard armories. Aoki also provided guns to Black Panther Party members and gave them weapons training. When his book was first published, Rosenfeld startled just about everyone by showing that Aoki was an FBI agent provocateur. This accusation generated a furious fusillade in Aoki's defense in the pages of the *Chronicle of Higher Education* and other publications. But in my reading of both sides, the charge seems well documented and convincing; moreover, when Rosenfeld asked him directly if he was an informer, Aoki gave a vague and ambiguous answer.

Aoki's defenders do not believe that so charismatic a leader could have been anything other than the passionate fighter for justice he appeared to be. Yet in the murky world of surveillance and double agents, some people can serve two masters. Perhaps the most famous such figure was Yevno Azev (1869–1918), for a decade and a half the key informer for the tsarist secret police, for whom he infiltrated the Russian revolutionary movement and betrayed hundreds of his comrades. But while leaking the details of some assassination plots to the authorities, he nonetheless zestfully helped plan others, including the murders of a provincial governor, the Grand Duke Sergei (the tsar's uncle), and the minister of the interior. Neither Azev nor his alarmed police handlers, it appears, ever figured out which side he was really on. Was that true for Richard Aoki? We will never know: ill with kidney disease, he committed suicide several years before Rosenfeld published his findings.

Aoki's record raises other questions: Were more undercover agents whom we don't yet even know about responsible for the move toward violent confrontation in the late 1960s by other groups, such as the Weather Underground? Was the Black Panther Party's long descent into criminal violence mainly the work of FBI agents provocateurs? I think the answer is no—even though we know now that both groups were heavily infiltrated. There was already plenty of madness in the air by end of the 1960s. The trail of Black Panther extortion, beatings, murders, and other crimes—especially in Northern California—is so long as to be beyond the FBI's ability to create it. And by 1970, there were also too many white leftists who romanticized third-world revolutionaries, talked tough, wore military fatigues, and spoke a different language than the nonviolent one of Berkeley's 1964–65 Free Speech Movement.

The leaders of that movement knew their fight was a universal one. They cared about civil liberties from Mississippi (where FSM leader Mario Savio had been a civil rights worker) to Moscow (FSM veterans held a Berkeley campus rally for two imprisoned Soviet dissidents). The outstanding FSM figure was Savio, whom I came to know toward the end of his too-short life—he died of heart problems at fifty-three in 1996—a gentle, eloquent, deeply intelligent man whose passion for civil liberties and social justice had the strength of a religion. Even though Savio's lifelong battle with depression and keen belief that the movement could not thrive if it were centered on him personally led him to stay in the background after 1965, it did not prevent the FBI from following his every move, monitoring his bank account, and aggressively questioning his neighbors, employers, friends, and landlords.

Even at its worst, the FBI was far less draconian than dozens of secret police forces active around the world, then and now. Poison-pen letters are one thing; torture and summary execution another. But changes in technology have made surveillance temptingly easy. In the 1950s, in order to eavesdrop on a meeting in the author Jessica Mitford's house in Oakland, two bumbling FBI agents hid in a crawl space beneath it; their mission almost came to grief when one fell asleep and started snoring. But today those agents—and, of course, powerful corporations—would have access to vastly more: not just Mitford's phone calls, which they were already tapping, but her credit card statements, her Google searches, her air travel itineraries, her bookstore purchases, her e-mails, her text messages, her minute-by-minute locations as signaled by the GPS in her mobile phone. A $2 billion National Security Agency center in Bluffdale, Utah, which holds longtime records of this sort on whomever the NSA chooses to monitor, is the largest intelligence data storage facility on earth—five times the size of the Capitol building in Washington, DC. Naturally, it's all in the name of stopping terrorism, but the combination of electronic data collection, a vague and nebulous foreign threat, and tens of billions of dollars pouring into "homeland security" each year makes a heady mix for new demagogues. That essay question on the 1959 University of California entrance exam is one we must never stop asking.

2013

FOUR

The Father of American Surveillance

MANILA, 1901. THE CITY IS A STEAMY mix of grand Spanish colonial buildings mildewed from tropical humidity, the ramshackle dwellings of hundreds of thousands of Filipinos, and horse-drawn wagons rumbling through squares and gates with names like Plaza de Cervantes and Puerta de Isabel II. Hastily erected hotels, houses of prostitution, and gambling dens cater to a flood of newly arrived Americans: bureaucrats, missionaries, merchants, speculators—and soldiers. Despite its swift victory in the Spanish-American War three years earlier, the United States is now in the middle of its first protracted war in Asia. Filipino nationalists, delighted to be free at last from several centuries of Spanish rule, have discovered that the U.S. troops, with leggings tucked into their high boots, whom they first hoped were liberators, are in fact here to establish an American colony. The brutal conflict now under way will eventually leave more than two hundred thousand Filipinos dead.

Although he may have watched the Army-vs.-Marines baseball games when off duty, Captain Ralph H. Van Deman was almost certainly too abstemious to loiter in the city's bars and brothels or place bets at the Manila Jockey Club, but for an ambitious U.S. Army officer, wartime Manila was nevertheless the place to be. Van Deman was far from the usual picture of a dashing young warrior: tall, gray-eyed, and almost cadaverously thin, he had a long, hawklike face and ears that seemed to jut out from his head at right angles. His route to the military had been an unusual one, for after attending college first in Ohio and then at Harvard, he had studied law for a year, then completed medical school. An early experience that may have influenced him more than these many classrooms, however, had been serving, during his student years, in the Ohio National Guard when it suppressed a violent coal miners' strike. By 1901, Van Deman had been on active duty for ten years.

When he took up a new post in Manila in February that year, the lanky 35-year-old polymath at last discovered his métier, an endeavor that would remain an obsession for the rest of his life. The conflict in the Philippines, now largely forgotten, was a counter-insurgency war, and for that the U.S. military needed not battleships and fortresses but intelligence information. In an old Spanish military building in a walled quarter of the city, Van Deman was placed in charge of the Bureau of Insurgent Records—a post that would turn him into the founding father of American surveillance. His assiduous spying in war and peace would span half a century and three continents and presage a vengeful nastiness eerily familiar to us today: racial stereotyping, the smearing of political enemies with fact-free rumor, and charges that those who opposed U.S. government policy were unpatriotic or treasonous. Van Deman's career would culminate in helping a particularly unscrupulous future president on his path toward the White House.

In Manila, the American occupation authorities were deeply alarmed that so many Filipinos wanted independence. Van Deman put the Army's intelligence operation into high gear, ordering 450 officers throughout the archipelago to provide data "from every possible source" on all mayors, priests, and "active civilian sympathizers." As a sign of his operation's growing importance, it was moved to U.S. Army headquarters on the bank of the Pasig River, one floor down from the commanding general. To compile his storehouse of data on suspect Filipinos, Van Deman used the most sophisticated information management system of his day: file cards. Each had printed at the top DESCRIPTIVE CARD OF INHABITANTS, with spaces beneath for an American officer to fill in such details as a person's appearance, age, occupation, "blood connections," and "relative importance in the community."

The prisoner Santiago Nepomuceno, for example, suspected of killing an American, was "very ignorant and depraved." Escolastico Salandanan was "very thick with former leading insurgent officers." Under the "Attitude toward U.S." section of the cards, comments range from "doubtful" and "presumably treacherous" to "ostensibly very friendly, but in his heart I believe him strongly antagonistic to Americanism."

For the data on his cards, Van Deman drew not only on U.S. Army officers but on the territorial and Manila police, both under American control. In the capital alone, his office had two hundred undercover agents on the payroll. Tips also flowed in from the tax and customs authorities. Alfred W. McCoy, a University of Wisconsin history professor who has closely studied Van Deman's career, concludes that, combined, these forces amounted to "a modern surveillance state." Surveillance, of course, is always about control—in this case suppressing the independence movement. It soon withered, not only because of American military might but because nationalists suspected, correctly, that their organizations were infiltrated.

On the thousands of Van Deman's dusty file cards that survive today, one fact goes eerily unmentioned: much of the information about these Filipino patriots was obtained by torture. The U.S. Army's routine method of interrogation on the islands was a precursor to modern-day waterboarding. "Now, this is the way we give them the water cure," an infantryman named A. F. Miller wrote to his family in Nebraska in 1900. "Lay them on their backs, a man standing on each hand and each foot, then put a round stick in the mouth and pour a pail of water in the mouth and nose, and if they don't give up pour in another pail. They swell up like toads." Photographs show Filipinos enduring this.

Why did these "insurgents" want independence? According to Van Deman, it was "owing principally, I am sorry to say, to advice from anti-imperialist and anti-administration citizens in the United States." Like so many white men of his era, he felt anyone who resisted colonialism must be a dupe of outside agitators.

The security apparatus Van Deman helped build would last through several decades of American colonial rule. By the 1920s, Manila's police force would have some two hundred thousand alphabetized file cards, covering fully 70 percent of the population, a surveillance-lover's dream. As in so many countries since then, ruthless police and military forces built or heavily aided by the United States have continued to burden the Philippines ever since the country finally became independent in 1946.

Van Deman was not the only white man of his era who saw colonialism as natural. Rudyard Kipling, after all, had urged America to "take up the white man's burden" by annexing the islands. Caucasians, millions believed, had a God-given right to rule everywhere over their black and brown inferiors. Among those who disagreed, however, were some of the 6,000 black U.S. Army soldiers who took part in the Philippine War. Horrified generals withdrew some "colored regiments" ahead of schedule after twenty or more black soldiers deserted, most joining the other side. Van Deman would have heard much talk of such doings over the Australian beef and French wines at

Manila's Army and Navy Club, and his belief that black Americans were not to be trusted would be a cornerstone of the next stage of his work in surveillance.

. . .

After returning home in 1903, Van Deman married a woman fifteen years younger than he. Like so many women of her time, Sadie Van Deman left little trace in the written record, with one startling exception: she was the first woman in the Americas to fly. She was a friend of Wilbur and Orville Wright's sister Katherine, and she asked if she could join Wilbur on a four-minute flight in 1909. On several later trips, he allowed her to take the controls. After some years, however, the couple divorced. Van Deman continued to rise up the military promotion ladder and was selected for the first class to attend the new Army War College. In early 1917, he married again, and that union would last.

At this time, the United States was bitterly torn over whether to enter the vast, bloody war raging in Europe. Many Americans resisted the push to war, particularly radicals who believed that workers should be fighting the ruling class, not each other. But public outrage was rapidly growing over the sinking of American ships by German submarines and the notorious "Zimmerman Telegram" from the German foreign minister urging Mexico to ally itself with Germany and regain its "lost territory in Texas, New Mexico, and Arizona." The day that President Woodrow Wilson went to Congress to call for war, an angry mob broke into the headquarters of the Emergency Peace Federation across the street from the White House, smashing chairs and desks and spattering the office with yellow paint. When the New York Yankees played their season opener the following week, they marched onto the diamond in military formation, resting bats on their shoulders like rifles.

America's declaration of war on April 6, 1917, found the gaunt figure of Van Deman stuck in a staff position at the War Department, frustrated that the Army did not have an intelligence agency. He put this proposal to Army chief of staff General Hugh Scott, who turned him down. Then he made an adroit but risky leap over Scott's head and used two go-betweens to place the idea before Secretary of War Newton Baker. His lobbying was successful, and Baker ordered him to set up a new Army intelligence branch. Soon promoted to colonel, Van Deman pursued the task with zeal, his staff swelling to 282 officers, 29 sergeants, and more than 1,000 civilians, most of them volunteers.

The war Van Deman was intent on waging was not in the trenches of France but at home. To his mind, Germany and its allies were far from the only enemy. The year 1917 also saw the Russian Revolution, and the triumph of the Bolsheviks greatly inflamed American political tensions between powerful captains of industry and a militant labor movement; between the long-dominant Protestants of northern European descent and waves of later immigrants, mostly Catholic and Jewish, who were often sympathetic to socialism and anarchism; and between the propertied classes of small towns—like Van Deman's native Delaware, Ohio—and the rapidly growing big cities, which seemed filled with threatening foreigners and radicals.

Van Deman could amass his huge staff because his worldview so embodied that of the American establishment of his time. Deeply distrusting immigrants, people of color, and any political activism they engaged in, he saw himself as defending the traditional social order against rebels at home and revolutionary ideologies from abroad. He warned the Justice Department, for instance, of weekly meetings at the home of the principal of the Colored High School in Baltimore, "presided over by a white man" of "loose habits" who had allowed talk that "the atrocities committed by Germany are no worse than the lynchings and burnings which have taken place in the South."

"In the fall of 1917," he later wrote, "it became evident that agents of the Central Powers were circulating among the Negro people of the United States." This was nonsense, for it did not take any German or Austro-Hungarian spies to make black Americans angry that they were forced into underfunded schools and low-paid jobs and that in the first two decades of the twentieth century alone more than 1,400 black men were lynched.

Nothing was beyond suspicion. One report to his office related "several incidents of where colored men had attempted to make appointments with white women." Van Deman was ready to believe the wildest of rumors, asking an agent to investigate word that "fortune tellers, supposed to be gypsies ... [are] entering the kitchens of well-to-do residents and telling the fortunes of the servants. These fortunes ... all point out that unless Germany wins the war the colored race will be made slaves again." He gave credence to another claim that Germans stirring up blacks were going door to door posing as sewing-machine salesmen. From an agent in New York came a report that "German money in large sums is being used in the Harlem district among the negro population" to purchase $600,000 worth of property.

Just as in the Philippines, surveillance was about control. When a Howard University dean wrote a pamphlet against lynching, Van Deman sent an agent to have a stern talk with him. Black newspapers were monitored closely—and threatened. The most influential, the *Chicago Defender*, was visited by one of his agents, who reported that the editor had "been told that he would be held strictly responsible and accountable for any article appearing in his paper in the future that would give rise to any apprehension. . . . I have . . . informed him that the eye of the government is centered upon his paper." Van Deman urged the YMCA to keep the NAACP's *The Crisis* out of its reading rooms, where it might be seen by black soldiers.

One object of his intelligence unit's suspicions in 1917 was the Reverend A. D. Williams, the pastor of Ebenezer Baptist Church in Atlanta. A forceful organizer, Williams helped put together an Equal Rights League to protest discrimination in voting, and he helped set up a branch of the NAACP that would register black voters. "It behooves us," said one telegram, "to find out all we possibly can about this colored preacher." A report in Williams's file termed him a "radical Negro agitator" because of his campaign to create a black high school. A grandson of "this colored preacher" would eventually become a pastor of the same church and in turn the subject of a later generation of government surveillance: Dr. Martin Luther King Jr.

. . .

Labor organizers were another group Van Deman went after. As with anti-lynching campaigners, he was convinced that such homegrown organizations as the Industrial Workers of the World, the "Wobblies"—founded in Chicago well before the war—must be connected to the enemy. He asked for a federal investigation of deposits made in Wobbly bank accounts in Arizona and referred to "the many rumors that the recent I.W.W. activities are supported by funds from German sources."

Also under suspicion was the Conference of Christian Pacifists in California, a group he judged "watery and neutral as far as its war loyalty is concerned." In a letter to the Secretary of War's office, he boasted of his threats against the organization: "ample warning . . . has been given to all concerned in these activities. Public opinion finally was aroused at various points on the Pacific Coast regarding their pernicious public gatherings." To the warden of the federal penitentiary in Atlanta, where the anarchist Emma Goldman was locked up, Van Deman sent word that Goldman was still wielding influence from behind bars and suggested "that it might be well to place greater restrictions upon her."

Always alert to possible rivals, Van Deman artfully blocked an attempt by the Army's Signal Corps to start its own domestic counterespionage operation. And, however unreliable it was, the stock of intelligence gathered by his huge staff allowed him to deal with officials who far outranked a mere colonel. He corresponded, for example, with former President Theodore Roosevelt and with the governor of Montana, whom he warned about a possible mining strike. At military intelligence headquarters, cabinet members and newspaper correspondents were regular guests at a weekly luncheon he hosted, known as the General Hindquarters.

But then, testifying before the Senate Military Affairs Committee in April 1918, he fatally overreached himself. The country needed military tribunals to take "quick and summary action" against Americans who opposed the war, he told the senators, because the existing courts were "tied up with forms and red tape and law." Note the last word.

Despite the administration's draconian crackdown on anti-war dissent, President Wilson immediately declared himself "wholly and unalterably opposed" to such tribunals. By this point, senior military and Justice Department officials were feeling their power threatened by Van Deman's burgeoning surveillance empire and saw to it that he was dispatched, with only the vaguest of assignments, to Europe.

For a skilled navigator of the military hierarchy, however, this merely offered new opportunities, particularly since the American commander at the front, General John J. Pershing, was an Army War College classmate. When the fighting ended, Van Deman managed to get himself placed in charge of all security arrangements for the months-long peace conference at Versailles, with a staff of fifty-six.

Paris in the spring of 1919 was a social climber's dream: There was a whirl of military band concerts and embassy dinners and balls, as Allied diplomats and generals exultantly redrew the maps of Europe, Africa, and the Middle East with little thought of where the smoldering resentment of a defeated Germany might lead. Van Deman's letters home to his wife, Irene, known as Cherry, are a curious mixture of passion ("Cherry dearest . . . to think of holding you tight in my arms again!"), dire political warnings ("There is a widespread attempt to start a world revolution along Bolshevic [sic] lines"), and bureaucratic triumphs ("Gen. Pershing had personally told the Adjutant General . . . to issue an order saying definitely that I was to perform my duties in connection with the Peace Commission in addition to my other duties and that I was not to be detached from G-2, G.H.Q.A.E.F.").

After Versailles, Van Deman resumed his rise in the Army, although jealous rivals kept him away from anything to do with intelligence. When he retired in 1929, it was as a major general.

. . .

With its balmy climate and dense array of Army, Navy, and Marine bases, San Diego had long been a favorite spot for those leaving the armed forces, and that was where the Van Demans settled. His friends included many other retired military men, and he found this conservative part of the country congenial. Even local labor leaders had a right-wing bent, and San Diego—with only a small Latino population at that point—was dominated by a Protestant, Anglo oligarchy, a far cry from the East Coast cities filled with recent immigrants and subversive ideas.

Within a few years of moving to San Diego, Van Deman embarked on yet a new phase of his passion for surveillance. The operation to which he would devote the remaining two decades of his life did not even have a name. With volunteer help from his wife and a retired officer friend, plus two clerks paid for by the Army, he quietly created a private intelligence bureau. Its records came to almost fill an apartment adjoining his own. "I'm sure I am not exaggerating," he told his Harvard classmates in a volume of autobiographical reports, "when I say that since 1932 I have devoted at least twelve hours a day to this work." His efforts, he hinted, were aided by funds contributed by wealthy sympathizers. As in the Philippines thirty years earlier, to record details about people he was watching, Van Deman used file cards. Eventually 85,000 of the cards would index and summarize the contents of a dozen filing cabinets containing more than ninety linear feet of agents' reports, photographs, letters, and other documents. "It was a rare Red," the San *Diego Union* would write years later, "whose appearance in this area was not noticed."

"Essentially Van Deman was a vigilante," says Athan Theoharis, a professor emeritus of history at Marquette University and the author of a number of books about the FBI and surveillance. "A self-appointed one. Talk about a true believer! This was his life's work. He saw himself as a savior of the nation. He had this mission, which was amazing in terms of the amount of information he collected and turned over to people who could act on it."

Among those who did were district attorneys eager to prosecute subversives and employers' groups who wanted to know who was trying to organize their workers. Always an adroit networker, Van Deman traded information with them as well as with police and sheriffs' departments and old friends in military intelligence who were spying on civilians. One Army unit in San Francisco made copies of so much material for him that it made a rubber stamp, "VanD." Writing to "My dear General," an official in the San Diego post office happily supplied the return addresses of packages and letters sent to an unnamed "person in regard to whom we have had recent conversation."

For hunters of subversives, the 1930s were busy years. The devastating toll of the Great Depression spurred the growth of radical and socialist groups. Police red squads cracked heads at picket lines, while organizations from the American Legion to the U.S. Chamber of Commerce set up departments to hunt communists. Nowhere were tensions higher than in California, where existing hunger and joblessness were exacerbated by desperate migrants fleeing into the state from the Dust Bowl.

Van Deman's undercover agents monitored the Communist Party so thoroughly that one account reports on a meeting that drew only four people. Nonetheless, the general accumulated reports on everything from a Young Marxian Pioneer Troop to "Airplane Pilots with Red Tendencies." For him, surveillance was a labor of love—or, as he would say, patriotism—not profit. He apparently charged no one for the information he shared, even though detective agencies were making the same kind of espionage a multimillion-dollar business.

Communists were indeed working with, among others, the state's miserably paid farmworkers, many of them Mexican or Mexican-American. Growers' organizations like the Associated Farmers of California became grateful consumers of Van Deman's information. From friends in Navy intelligence in 1933, the general heard that a communist named James Dixon would be organizing a strike of celery pickers near San Diego, word he relayed to others in his network. He exchanged information about a lettuce harvesters' strike with the district attorney of Imperial County, a place where labor protestors were repeatedly beaten up by vigilantes deputized by local sheriffs and police. When San Francisco saw a massive waterfront strike in 1934, Van Deman obtained a list of suspected agitators and was soon discussing the situation with the city's Industrial Association.

Although much in his files came from police departments or other agencies, thousands of pages are from his own undercover operatives. Some of the correspondence is written in invisible ink, with agents identified only by letters and numbers. B-11, for example, was a particularly active fellow who posed as a communist recruiting seamen and then farmworkers and who reported on a meeting of the American Civil Liberties Union—a frequent target of the general's scrutiny. Another agent posed as a delegate to a convention of the Cannery and Agricultural Workers Industrial Union. The general's crew was not above the occasional burglary: Agent C-14 provided a list of distributors and subscribers of the communist newspaper *People's World*— "found in trunk of Celia Shermis' car."

By now, Van Deman had also grown obsessed with the film industry. A report on the movie star James Cagney notes darkly that "he wrote a piece for the Screen Actors Guild, which . . . is the employes *[sic]* rebellion against the producers." In *Here Comes the Navy*, Cagney's character "is antagonistic to and creates hatred for his superior officers." Even more sinister, Cagney had reportedly contributed to a relief fund for striking cotton pickers.

Schools and colleges were another arena for vigilance. An ally on the San Diego Board of Education used the Van Deman files to vet anyone who applied to host an event on school property. A long list of "Radical Professors and Teachers" ranged from Columbia University to Milwaukee State Teachers College. A list of suspicious professors at UCLA and the University of Southern California noted that one was "an admirer of [the socialist novelist] Upton Sinclair" and another was "questionable . . . is married to a Polish Jewess."

Jews, indeed, were often among Van Deman's targets. In a letter to an Army colleague, he declared himself "convinced that there may be more than a modicum of truth" in the connection between "Bolshevism and Semitism." The general trafficked in conspiracies, and one document in his files reports on a veritable trifecta of villains by citing a "Yiddist *[sic]* pamphlet" that "urges the Masonic Fraternity to come to the support of the Soviet Union." Duly filed as well is a chart someone sent in claiming that both Franklin and Eleanor Roosevelt had Jewish ancestry.

Among other sources feeding Van Deman's anti-Semitism was agent B-31, one of the few operatives whose name we know; historian McCoy has identified her as a California advice and gossip columnist, Mary Oyama Mittwer. During a 1946 trip to the East Coast, she reported that "organized Jewry is out to control organized labor." Furthermore, "the Jewish people are slowly but surely securing a stranglehold on the poultry and egg business." And worse lay ahead: Jewish refugees "are coming in here by the shiploads, they have Hotels in NY City where they are re-outfitted, their jewelry is turned into cash; and then . . . homes are purchased for them." A shadowy plot was behind it all: "Felix Frankfurter and possibly Henry Morgenthau manage to pull a lot of strings in the background. . . . The motion picture and stage industry . . . is practically controlled by the Jewish race."

The general was deeply suspicious of President Roosevelt and the people around him. One report notes that Frances Perkins—longtime secretary of labor and the first woman in an American cabinet—"admitted her married name is Mrs. Paul Wilson." A follow-up investigation Van Deman ordered to this apparently incriminating piece of information produced a copy of a 1910 Massachusetts marriage certificate showing a Paul Wilson marrying someone else—possible evidence of further skullduggery. (The general had both the date and place wrong: Perkins had quite publicly married another Paul Wilson in New York in 1913.)

During these California years, Van Deman found what every zealot yearns for: a disciple. This was a younger man named Richard Ellis Combs. For the nearly two decades that their professional lives overlapped, Combs considered the general his mentor, living for a time with him and his wife in San Diego. "Van Deman taught me that to master the field of subversion," he said years later in a rare interview, "you must read with notebook in hand, summarize everything, then type your own file card. . . . You must do this yourself. You can't divide the job and let a secretary help. You do it and it becomes your knowledge, your resource. After a while, you will command everything in the field."

In 1941, the tall, red-haired Combs began an influential thirty-year tenure as chief counsel and lead investigator for the California Un-American Activities Committee, or CUAC. This was the most powerful and choleric of the state legislative groups that echoed witch-hunters at the national level like the House Un-American Activities Committee (HUAC) and later Senator Joseph McCarthy. Over the years, bolstered by intelligence passed on by Van Deman, CUAC held hearings, fiercely grilled witnesses, and built up its own gargantuan files, which eventually came to cover 125,000 individuals and organizations. Even public school sex education programs in the town of Chico came under the committee's scrutiny as possibly communist-inspired.

We don't know everything Van Deman and Combs did together, because the general was always discreet. "There are a lot of things that I want to talk over with you when you come down," he once wrote to Combs, "which are just as well not put on paper." But we do know that the two strategized how to use the mysterious death of a UCLA student after attending a political meeting in 1948 to fan the flames of anticommunism. Their efforts helped feed a frenzy that soon resulted, among other things, in the University of California requiring all employees to sign a loyalty oath. The subsequent firings of those who refused to sign sent a chill through the state's entire educational system.

. . .

In his zeal for surveillance, his sweeping hostility to African American activism, and his approval of black-bag jobs by his agents, Van Deman foreshadowed no one so much as a figure thirty years his junior, J. Edgar Hoover. Indeed, the two men knew each other. Van Deman always had an eye for those on the rise, and in 1922 he had pulled strings to get an Army Reserve commission for Hoover, then a 27-year-old Justice Department official. In the next decade, the general resumed contact with Hoover. His letters to the FBI chief were almost fawning; in 1938, he apologized for having made "an attempt to break in on the privacy of a very busy man trying to get a little well earned rest." Van Deman's courting of Hoover was successful, however, because he was included in a crucial meeting Hoover hosted in the run-up to American participation in the Second World War. On May 31, 1940, Hoover assembled high officials from the Army, Navy and State Department in his office to divide up intelligence-gathering territory. "This was like the Pope dividing the unexplored world [between Spain and Portugal] in 1493," McCoy says. "The FBI got counter-intelligence at home—and operations in Latin America. Military intelligence, out of which the OSS and then the CIA evolved, got the rest of the world."

Van Deman's presence at the meeting is testimony to his ability to ingratiate himself with the powerful, for at this point he had been retired from the military for eleven years and had no government job. Hoover soon asked a San Diego FBI agent to "devote himself exclusively to the task of reviewing General Van Deman's files and extracting all information of value to the Bureau."

The FBI came to rely on Van Deman's archive so much that the general developed a library card system showing when the bureau had borrowed and returned a file. The FBI's San Diego office informed Hoover that agents were in touch with the general "almost daily." After he turned eighty in 1945, Van Deman began suffering various illnesses and an FBI man in San Diego kept

Hoover apprised, sometimes giving the address of a hospital so that "the Director" could send a get-well-soon letter or telegram.

As Van Deman aged, he fretted about the fate of his treasured files. The FBI, however, began to develop a few doubts about the reliability of his data, and it also discovered a major bureaucratic obstacle to merging his files with its own: The general's 85,000 file cards were on four-by-six-inch cards, while the FBI used three-by-five-inch cards. Nonetheless, a few months before Van Deman died at the age of 86 in 1952, the FBI chief in San Diego recommended to Hoover that the bureau take custody of the files when the time came, because "if the General were to become aware of the fact that neither the Army nor the Bureau had any interest ... this thought would most certainly leave him heart-broken, disillusioned and possibly hasten his death."

· · ·

In the end, the files continued to be used by various government agencies for well over a decade, and were largely divided between the Army and a secret library maintained by friends of Van Deman's in a California National Guard armory. About half of the general's documents have disappeared; the remainder eventually came to rest in the National Archives, where you can examine ninety-seven boxes of them, containing more than forty-two linear feet of paper. But before the files landed there, the general's allies stripped out a great deal of material, including the identities of the various undercover agents and of the donors who financed the private intelligence network. Nonetheless, the files contain much of interest, including a few hints of the support Van Deman provided to a cunning and unscrupulous politician who would reach the most powerful position in the land.

In 1946, a popular, liberal, five-term congressman from Southern California, Jerry Voorhis, was running for reelection against a political unknown—a 33-year-old former Navy logistics officer named Richard Milhous Nixon. Voorhis had explicitly rejected the backing of any group that didn't disavow communism. But Nixon, onstage in a debate in South Pasadena, thunderously brandished at him a piece of paper that supposedly contained an endorsement by a communist-infiltrated organization. Nixon followed this up with a well-financed advertising campaign darkly hinting at more of the same. He pulled off a stunning upset on election day and quickly gained a seat on the House Un-American Activities Committee.

When Nixon went on to run for a U.S. Senate in California in 1950, against Congresswoman Helen Gahagan Douglas, it was again on a wave of flamboyant red-baiting. Workers from Nixon's phone banks called hundreds of thousands of registered voters, asked if they knew that Douglas was a communist and then hung up. White voters received postcards from a nonexistent Communist League of Negro Women saying, "Vote for Helen for Senator."

Under warm sunny skies at a Douglas campaign rally of five thousand people in Long Beach's Bixby Park, with Eleanor Roosevelt speaking, Douglas supporters noticed people passing out leaflets on pink paper that accused their candidate of sinister communist ties. Nixon claimed that his opponent—who, he noted, was married to the Jewish actor Melvyn Douglas—was "pink right down to her underwear." The "pink sheets" helped defeat Douglas, and two years later Senator Nixon was elected vice president.

What remains in Van Deman's well-expurgated files shows few traces of his aiding candidates for elective office—something which would have been illegal for a man whose clerical help was provided by the U.S. Army. Nonetheless, several clues in the 97 boxes suggest that the general played a role in Nixon's rise to power. The ambitious young politician had been no stranger to Van Deman. He had ties to the general's protégé, Combs, and had been a featured speaker at a conference of state legislature red-hunters from around the country that Combs and Van Deman had helped organize in 1948. Van Deman's files hold hints of the help he provided Nixon. One is a photograph of a Nixon campaign event where a demonstrator opposing the candidate is identified by one of Van Deman's trademark code numbers. Another is an agent's report with a revealingly hostile reference to Nixon's adversary: "A few more Helen Gahagan Douglas's and the left-wing congressmen will be prying open the most secret records of the federal security agencies." Finally, Van Deman's spies had long been collecting damaging information on Douglas's actor husband: Agent B-11 listed him, for example, as a supporter of efforts to send bandages and clothing to victims of the Spanish Civil War, and another report identified him as supporting striking lettuce pickers.

California Democrats later charged that some of the scurrilous material in the Nixon campaign's "pink sheets" against Douglas had come from Van Deman. When these accusations were renewed after Nixon became president, unnamed White House officials queried by the *New York Times* did not deny the charge. They said only that it was no longer "pertinent." But for Van Deman to help Nixon at this ruthless stage of his ascent toward the nation's highest office was highly pertinent. Ironically, the blueprint for the Watergate scandal that finally forced the 37th president to resign could have been taken from Van Deman's own life's work: a black-bag job, a secret search for information about political enemies, a mania for surveillance.

Today, all of us leave behind so many electronic traces that spying is both easier and more complex than it was Van Deman's agents stole papers out of car trunks. But there is still a dark thread that stretches back across generations. The general, happily, never reached the White House. But someone who recently did was helped by the release of information pilfered from the opposing political party and then built a presidency on a way of thinking very similar to Van Deman's, from hostility to immigrants to conspiracy theories to treating wild rumors as fact. Donald Trump has probably never heard of Ralph Van Deman, but one person knew them both: Richard Nixon, a man who, according to Trump, "always wanted me to run for office." Nixon and Van Deman might both now be smiling.

2018

FIVE

_____

Prison Madness

SOME TIME AGO, I WAS TAKING PART in a book festival in Finland. When there was a free day coming up, the publisher who had invited me asked if there were any local sights I would care to see. Medieval churches, perhaps? I said I'd like to visit some prisons. Finland locks people up at well under 10 percent the rate we do in the United States, a gap far more dramatic than any differences between the people of the two countries can explain. I was curious to learn more. Happily, my publisher's neighbor was a criminologist, and they arranged a tour for me the next day.

Kerava Prison, the first of two that I saw, was in the countryside half an hour's drive north of Helsinki. Its governor—by design, the title has a civilian sound—was a warm, vivacious, gray-haired woman named Kirsti Nieminen, a former prosecutor. On this wintry morning, she had about 150 prisoners in her charge, all men. Her office wall was lined with portraits of former governors, the first a heavily bearded one from the 1890s. Next to these was a framed drawing by a convict—Snoopy typing a letter, which she translated for me: "Dear Governor, please give me a leave!"

The equivalent of an American medium-security prison, Kerava had barbed-wire fences, bars on some windows, and plenty of locked doors. Some inmates worked in greenhouses outside the walls, but only if they were trusties or under guard. Most resemblance to American prisons ended there. In the greenhouses the inmates raised flowers, which were sold to the public, as were the organic vegetables they grew. As we walked around the prison grounds, Nieminen pointed out a stream where prisoners could fish, a soccer field, a basketball court, a grain mill, and something she was particularly proud of, a barn full of rabbits and lambs. "The responsibility to take care of a creature—it's very therapeutic," she said. "They are always kind to you. It's easier to talk to them."

For an hour or so, I had coffee with half a dozen prisoners. The heavily tattooed Marko, 36, wore a visor and said he was here for a "violent crime" he did not specify. Jarkko, a burly 26-year-old, was doing three years and ten months for a drug offense; Reima, 36, blond and tough-looking, was in for robbery. Kalla, at 48 the eldest, had committed fraud; Fernando (his father was from Spain) was 26, convicted of armed robbery and selling heroin; Harre, 27, was doing five years for selling Ecstasy. Also sitting with us, and translating, were Nieminen, a young woman from the national prisons service who came here with me, and two of Kerava's teachers, also both women. No armed guards were in sight, and both officials and convicts wore their own clothes, not uniforms.

This was still a prison, however, and at 7:30 each evening the inmates are locked into their two-man cells. These are not large but somewhat more spacious than those I've seen in American prisons, each with a toilet and sink in a cubicle whose door closes. Prisoners are allowed TVs, stereos, and radios. Down the corridor from the cells are a shower room and sauna—something no Finn could imagine being without.

Prisoners are assigned jobs, but most spend much of their day in classes, on subjects including auto repair, computers, welding, and first aid. A library holds several thousand books—more than you would find in many American high schools—and inmates can use the national interlibrary loan system to order others. I sat in on a cooking class and then shared a tasty lunch its students had prepared: Karelian stew, which included beef, pork, potatoes, and cranberries.

. . .

All this is obviously another world from the overcrowded prisons of the United States, where gardens are scarce and classes, if they happen at all, are often an afterthought. When the former Missouri state senator Jeff Smith was sentenced to a federal prison in Kentucky, he hoped that as a Ph.D. who had taught at Washington University in St. Louis, he would be put to work teaching. Instead, as he writes in his *Mr. Smith Goes to Prison: What My Year Behind Bars Taught Me About America's Prison Crisis,* he was assigned to a warehouse loading dock, where he observed and took part in the pilfering of food by both inmates and guards. A month from the end of his stay he was finally transferred to the education unit—and assigned to sweeping out class-rooms. A computer skills class consisted of the chance to sit at a computer for thirty minutes, with no instruction whatsoever; at a nutrition class, a guard "handed out a brochure with information about the caloric content of food at McDonald's, Bojangles, and Wendy's and released us after five minutes."

Particularly at the college level, an effective prison education program, like the well-known one run by Bard College, can cut the recidivism rate—in the United States, 67.8 percent after three years—down to the single digits. The Bard program offers classes taught by professors from its campus and others and is attended by nearly three hundred inmates in six New York State pris-ons. A debating team drawn from these students won national attention recently when it beat a team from Harvard. Reducing recidivism through such efforts not only is humane but also saves money: it costs New York State more each year to house and guard a single prisoner than the total tuition, room, and board for an undergraduate on that Harvard debating team. You would think that budget-conscious legislators would act accordingly, but reason has never played much of a part in the American prison system.

Some of what Smith writes recalls many other American prison memoirs: he describes de facto racial segregation, rapes, etiquette (never sit on someone else's bunk), and the underground economy. Prices for pornography, cell phones, and other contraband rose sharply, for example, when snow on the ground made footprints visible or when a notoriously vigilant guard was on duty. And contrary to the film *The Shawshank Redemption,* in which the character played by Morgan Freeman wryly observes, "Everyone in here is innocent," Smith says that few prisoners make that claim. Instead, they blame their fate on the "snitch" who turned them in. (Curiously, he does somewhat the same thing himself when he writes about the friend who got him in trouble for breaking a campaign-spending law.)

The most moving part of Smith's story is his picture of what prison does to families. He points to research showing that before they were imprisoned, "half of all incarcerated fathers lived with their children, a quarter served as primary caregivers, and over half provided primary financial support." When a man goes to jail, his family shatters:

> While I was waiting to use a phone, it was hard to avoid hearing their anguished phone conversations with ex-girlfriends who controlled access to their children, with rebellious teenagers who—lacking a male authority figure at home—were in some cases following in their fathers' footsteps, and with dying parents far away.

One of Smith's workmates, known as Big E, had been an ace basketball player and was serving seventeen years for possession of crack cocaine. One Saturday in the television room there was none of the usual haggling about which sports game would be watched. Big E's son, a college freshman, was playing, "and Big E, the best shooter on the compound, had never seen his son play." He had been in prison since the age of nineteen.

. . .

How did we get to the point where a nineteen-year-old who has done nothing violent can be put away for almost as long as he has lived, where prisons break up millions of families, and where we have a larger proportion of our people incarcerated than almost any other country in the world, even Putin's Russia? And at a time when crime rates have been in a long-term decline? With a twentieth of the world's population, the United States has a quarter of its prisoners. The number is so high that the American unemployment rate for men would be 2 percent higher (8 percent higher for black men) if they were all suddenly let out. If all Americans behind bars constituted a state, its population would be greater than that of fifteen other states, big enough to be entitled to three seats in the House of Representatives. Our jails are so packed that the website www.jailbedspace.com allows wardens and sheriffs to look for space in other facilities if their own is full.

The two most conspicuous causes of this tragedy are the unwinnable war on drugs and Republican tough-on-crime politicking, which reached a nadir* with the notorious Willie Horton ad in George H. W. Bush's successful 1988 presidential campaign, which attacked the Democratic nominee, Michael Dukakis, for backing a weekend furlough program that gave Horton, a convicted murderer, the chance to commit additional violent crimes. But Democrats were deeply involved in building the prison system as well. Starting in the 1940s, looking for ways to stop the lynching of blacks and their abuse by police in the South and fearing a recurrence of the Second World War–era race riots in the North, liberals pushed for more professional training for law enforcement officers.

However, the southern Democrats who then controlled Congress transformed these efforts into block grants to states. As a result, police depart-

* Since this article was written, of course, Donald Trump has carried this kind of demagoguery to new depths.

ments received more money and more advanced weaponry with which to do business as usual. Liberals also pushed for standardized sentences that would curb the discretionary powers of racist judges. But these mandatory minimums inched upward and became cruelly high, and the definition of crimes, with no mention of race, ended up with vastly greater penalties for possession of crack cocaine (used mostly by blacks) than for possession of powdered cocaine (used mostly by whites). Although data show that Americans of different races use drugs in similar proportions, if you're black you're more than five times as likely to end up jailed for doing so than if you're white.

The 1960s brought immense social turbulence and a sharp rise in almost all types of crime. New York Governor Nelson Rockefeller sponsored drug laws that put several generations of men, most of them black, away for decades. Quick to moralize against disorder and drawing on the deep American reservoir of racism, politicians at every level promised a ruthless response. This could take effect so easily because the United States chooses a sizable proportion of its judges and almost all of its district attorneys and county sheriffs by popular election, something that would be thought bizarre almost anywhere else in the world. Prosecutors have enormous power as to what to charge someone with—which can determine whether those mandatory sentences apply or not—and whether to charge a person at all. And judges, in turn, often have great discretion in sentencing. Both prosecutors and judges keep a close eye on the voters who elect them. One recent study of Washington State judges found that the sentences they passed out lengthened by an average of 10 percent when reelection day approached.

By the time Bill Clinton entered the White House in 1993, he and congressional Democrats were determined to show that they were even tougher on crime than Republicans. The following year Congress passed the brutally severe Violent Crime Control and Law Enforcement Act and the Federal Death Penalty Act, which, among other things, added some sixty offenses to the list of capital crimes. With their communities ravaged by crack, most black politicians supported such measures. The number of prosecutors soared during the 1990s, too, and with them the number of prisoners.

The prison boom has also provided a chance to make money. One private company alone, the Corrections Corporation of America, today runs the country's fifth-largest prison system, after those of the federal government and three states. The less money such companies spend on staff training, food, education, medical care, and rehabilitation, the greater their profits. Recidivism produces what every business wants, returning customers, so it's no wonder these companies push hard for three-strikes laws and similar measures. In 2011, the two biggest private prison firms donated nearly $3 million to political candidates and hired 242 lobbyists around the country.

The vast majority of prisoners, however, are in public prisons, whose staffs would shrink dramatically if the number of inmates dropped, providing another group with a strong motive for locking people up. Many state prisons are in poor or rural areas, like upstate New York, with few other sources of jobs. Jeff Smith points out that food wholesalers, who know that this market of 2.2 million people is powerless to protest if much of what they have to eat is well past its sell-by date, also have a vested interest in keeping prisons full.

. . .

The prison-industrial complex is now as deeply rooted as its military counterpart. With both corporate profits and government salaries at stake, it will be equally difficult to shrink or transform. Everyone from the ACLU to the Koch brothers seems to agree, however, that our prisons are too full, and politicians from both Left and Right have floated cautious proposals for reform. In her superb, comprehensive book *Caught: The Prison State and the Lockdown of American Politics,* the University of Pennsylvania political scientist Marie Gottschalk shows why few of the proposed solutions, either singly or together, are going to reduce the proportion of Americans in prison to anywhere near what it was fifty years ago.

Repeal absurdly punitive drug laws? Fine. But "if all drug cases were eliminated, the U.S. imprisonment rate would still have quadrupled over the past thirty-five years." Reduce the appalling disparities in how different races are treated by the law? Fine. But even the rate at which *white* Americans are locked up is more than four times that of all prisoners in multiethnic France. Far more lenient penalties for nonviolent offenses? Fine. But nearly half of those behind bars in America are there for violent crimes. Get rid of private prisons? Fine. But they contain less than 10 percent of Americans behind bars.

Few officeholders, Gottschalk explains, are willing to take two uncomfortable steps, each of which means reversing decades of political rhetoric. One is to admit that as punishment for a wide variety of crimes, prison sentences accomplish little. They do not undo a crime or make it certain that the same person won't commit the same crime again. Communities ranging from Brooklyn, New York, to Oakland, California, have made encouraging experiments in "restorative justice," in which convicted criminals are sentenced to apologize to those they hurt, repay people they robbed, and do community service in the neighborhoods they have harmed. But, for most prosecutors, promoting such programs is not a promising path to election.

The other urgent task, according to Gottschalk, is to ensure that when we do send people to prison, they have much shorter sentences. It used to be that a life sentence meant that a well-behaved American inmate was likely to be released after ten to fifteen years—a recognition that merely growing older has far more influence than length of time served on the likelihood that someone might commit another crime. But U.S. prisons are now full of people serving several consecutive life sentences or life without parole—a punishment that virtually did not exist half a century ago and is almost unknown in the rest of the world.

"The total life-sentenced population in the United States is approximately 160,000," she writes, "or roughly twice the size of the *entire* incarcerated population in Japan." And some so-called reforms are meaningless: "The governor of Iowa commuted all the mandatory life sentences of his state's juvenile offenders but declared that they would be eligible for parole only after serving sixty years." This reminds me of a similar act of clemency under King George IV of Britain in 1820, when five members of the revolutionary Cato Street Conspiracy were sentenced to be hanged, drawn, and quartered, and the last two parts of the sentence were remitted to mere beheading.

Breaking the pattern that has so many men, women, and teenagers wasting their lives in custody also demands bettering their opportunities for education, jobs, and much more on the outside. It is telling that the Nordic countries, with some of the world's lowest imprisonment rates, are highly developed welfare states far more egalitarian than the United States. Programs that promise inmates "a second chance" on release, Gottschalk declares, mean little when "many of the people cycling in and out of prison and jail were never really given a first chance."

This is all too true. But much as I prefer Nordic social democracy to our own wildly unequal distribution of wealth and opportunity, that change is not likely to arrive any time soon. We cannot wait until then to drastically reduce the number of people we have in prison. Even counting white prisoners alone, the United States has well over twice as many people, per capita, locked up as Spain, where 20 percent of the population is out of work and the welfare state is weaker than in Scandinavia. And we have more people per capita of any single race in prison than South Africa, where the unemployment rate for the black majority is catastrophic and the welfare state is fragile at best.

. . .

Was there ever a country that was once as enthusiastic about imprisoning people as we are but changed its ways dramatically? There was—and it was Finland.

In 1950, with a prison system and criminal code that had changed little from their origins under the Russia of the tsars, Finland had a higher incarceration rate than we then had in the United States. In Finland, 187 people out of every 100,000 were behind bars, as against only 175 here. A long series of reforms—not without their hard-line opponents—brought the Finnish rate of incarceration far down, just as our own soared. Today, we have 710 people per 100,000 in prison in the United States, compared to 58 in Finland. "One important idea that emerged," write two scholars of Finland's changes, "was that prison cures nobody. As a result policies were enacted that prison sentences should rarely be used in smaller crimes and other penalty systems should be developed instead."

Although the prisons I saw in Finland certainly isolated inmates from the outside world, much that happened inside them was directed toward making sure that released prisoners could return to society. If you had half your sentence completed and had permission, you could leave Kerava Prison on weekends. Everything possible was done to ease that transition. The diploma you get on completing one of the classes I saw, for instance, is certified by an outside organization; it doesn't say you received your training in prison.

A host of offerings within the walls addressed the problems that landed men in trouble in the first place. There were programs for anger management and drug rehabilitation, as well as both individual and group psychotherapy. Prisoners could also take part in a twelve-step program similar to that of Alcoholics Anonymous and a class in life skills that met three times a week. And, in an idea copied from Sweden, the prison hosted a series of speakers: former convicts who shared their experiences of readjusting to the world.

A released prisoner in the United States is frequently barred from voting, public housing, pensions, and disability benefits, and is lucky if he receives anything more than bus fare and, according to Jeff Smith, a routine farewell from a guard: "You'll be back, shitbird." At Kerava prison in Finland, before an inmate is released, a social worker travels to his hometown to make sure that he will have a job and a safe place to live.

2016

Africa

FIGURE 3. Gold miners in eastern Congo.

SIX

_____

The Listening House

AS IF THE DEMOCRATIC REPUBLIC of Congo had not already suffered enough, in 2002, nature dealt it a stunning blow. Mount Nyiragongo, the volcano whose blue-green bulk looms above the dusty, lakeside city of Goma in the country's east, erupted, sending a smoking river of lava several hundred yards wide through the center of town and sizzling into the waters of Lake Kivu. More than 10,000 homes were engulfed. Parts of the city, packed with people displaced by the country's civil war, are still covered by a layer of purplish rock up to twelve feet thick. In the two- or three-story buildings that survived, the second floor has become the first.

Far greater destruction has come from more than a decade of bewilderingly complex civil war. No one knows the full death toll, but it may well be in the millions, if you count those who died because fleeing their homes to disease-ridden refugee camps cut them off from adequate food and medical care. This has not been a conflict driven by ideology but rather a multisided free-for-all seeking plunder. No fewer than two dozen armed groups signed the most recent of several shaky peace deals. Among the warring parties have been the ineffectual national government, an array of feuding local ethnic warlords, and nearby African countries hungering for a share of Congo's great natural wealth. First, neighboring Uganda and Rwanda supported a rebel force that overthrew the longtime dictator Mobutu Sese Seko in 1997. Soon afterward, the new government fell out with its backers, and later Uganda and Rwanda fell out with each other. Before long, they and five other nearby nations had troops on Congo's soil, in alliance either with the national government in the capital, Kinshasa, or with a mushrooming number of rival warlords, particularly here in the mineral-rich east. Those foreign soldiers are almost all gone now, but fighting between the government and remaining rebel groups continues. For several weeks, I had the chance to observe the war's effects with the best possible traveling companion, Anneke Van Woudenberg, a senior researcher for Human Rights Watch, whose reports have been an authoritative source of information on the country for years.

No one has been harder hit by the fighting than Congo's women, for almost all the warring factions have used rape as a method of sowing terror. An hour and a half southwest of Goma, on a bone-jolting road up a valley, stand several low buildings of planks and adobe; small goats wander about bleating, and a cooking fire burns on one dirt floor. Above us loom steep-sided hills where maize, beans, and cassava grow in a patchwork of fields of brown and dazzling green. There is no electricity. A sign reads *Maison d'Écoute*, Listening House. The office of the 42-year-old director, Rebecca Masika Katsuva, known to all as Mama Masika, extends from the side of one of the buildings; its other three walls are thin green tarpaulin, through which daylight filters. The floor is gravel. Masika pulls out a hand-written ledger to show to Anneke, her colleague Ida Sawyer, and me. Ruled columns spread across the page: date, name, age of the victim, and details. Almost all are gang rapes, by three to five armed men. Since the Maison d'Écoute started, it has registered 5,973 cases of rape in the surrounding district. The ages of the victims just in the past six months range from two to sixty-five. On the ledger's most recent page, the perpetrators listed include three different armed rebel groups, plus the Congolese national army.

"What pushed me into this work," says Masika, speaking softly in a mixture of Swahili and hesitant French, "is that I am also one who was raped." This first happened a decade ago; the rapists were from the militia of a local warlord backed by Uganda. "Their main purpose was to kill my husband. They took everything. They cut up his body like you would cut up meat, with knives. He was alive. They began cutting off his fingers. Then they cut off his sex. They opened his stomach and took out his intestines. When they stabbed his heart, he died. They were holding a gun to my head." She fought her captors, and shows a scar across the left side of her face that was the result. "They ordered me to collect all his body parts and to lie on top of them and there they raped me—twelve soldiers. I lost consciousness. Then I heard someone cry out in the next room, and I realized they were raping my daughters."

The daughters, the two oldest of four girls, were twelve and fifteen. Masika spent months in the hospital and temporarily lost her short-term memory. "When I got out I found these two daughters were pregnant. I fainted. After this, the family [of her husband] chased me away. They sold my house and land, because I had had no male children." From time to time Masika stops, her worn face crinkles into a sob, and she dabs her eyes with a corner of her apron.

"Both girls tried to kill their children. I had to stop them. I had more difficulties. I was raped three more times when I went into the hills to look for other raped women." Part of her work is to go to villages and talk to husbands and families, because rape survivors are so often shunned. In one recent case, for instance, a woman was kidnapped and held ten months as a sex slave by the FDLR (Forces démocratiques de Libération du Rwanda), the Hutu perpetrators of the Rwandan genocide and their followers, long the most intransigent rebel group here. After she returned to her village with a newborn baby, her husband agreed to take her back, but only if the baby were killed. Masika intervened and took in the child at the Listening House. Living here now are six women and seventeen children—some of whom keep scampering up to an opening in the tarpaulin to giggle and look in at us.

At one point Masika has to break off talking with us because a new victim walks in off the road, a 47-year-old woman who says she was raped just three days ago by three Congolese army soldiers who barged into her house after she came home from church. For twenty minutes, Masika takes down her story and then quickly sends her to a nearby clinic: if anti-retroviral drug treatment is begun within seventy-two hours of a rape, it can usually prevent HIV/AIDS.

The last time Masika herself was raped was only five months ago. The attackers, members of rebel group that has since been integrated into the Congolese army in a new peace deal, were four soldiers who targeted her because they knew the work she was doing. "After having raped me, they spat in my sex, then shoved a shoe up my vagina. When I arrived home I cried a lot and was at the point of killing myself."

Shocking as ordeals like Masika's are, they are all too similar to what Congolese endured more than a century ago. Rape was then also considered the right of armies, and, as now, it was how brutalized and exploited soldiers took out their fury on people of even lower status: women. From 1885 to 1908, when this territory was the personally owned colony of King Leopold II of Belgium, he pioneered a forced labor system that was quickly copied in French, German, and Portuguese colonies nearby. His private army of black conscript soldiers under white officers would hold women hostage in order to force their husbands and sons to go into the rainforest for weeks at a time to harvest lucrative wild rubber. "The women taken during the last raid . . . are causing me no end of trouble," a Belgian officer named Georges Bricusse wrote in his diary on November 22, 1895. "All the soldiers want one. The sentries who are supposed to watch them unchain the prettiest ones and rape them."

Like rape, forced labor also continues today. The various armed groups routinely conscript villagers to carry their ammunition, collect water and firewood, and, on occasion, dig for gold. A 2007 survey of more than 2,600 people in eastern Congo found over 50 percent saying that they had been made to carry loads or do other work against their will in the previous decade and a half. A few miles down the road from the Maison d'Écoute, I meet one such person in a camp for people who have fled the fighting; several thousand of them are living here in makeshift shelters of grass thatch, the lucky ones with a tarpaulin over the top. The man is twenty-nine, in T-shirt and sandals, and doesn't want his real name used. He arrived at the camp two days ago from Remeka, a village a few days' walk from here that has changed hands several times in recent fighting between the FDLR and the national army. A bandage covers his left eye.

Congolese army soldiers corralled him last week as a porter. The troops then came under fire, and "I took advantage of that to flee. I spent a night in the bush, and when I came back to the village I found the army had pillaged it, and everyone had fled. Other soldiers told me again to carry supplies. When I refused they took a bayonet and jabbed me in the eye." He can see a little out of the eye, but not clearly. Doctors don't know if its sight will fully return. His wife and two children, aged two and eight, fled the village, and he thinks they are still in the bush.

. . .

Where does such cruelty come from? Four problems, above all, drive Congo's unrelenting bloodshed. One is long-standing antagonism between certain ethnic groups, particularly here in the troubled east. A second is the 1994 Rwandan genocide and the two million or so people who flowed across Congo's border in its aftermath: Hutu killers, innocent Hutu who feared retribution, and a mainly Tutsi army in pursuit, bent on vengeance. A third is that this is the largest nation on earth that has virtually no functioning national government—over sixty-five million people in an area roughly as big as the United States east of the Mississippi. The corrupt and disorganized regime of Joseph Kabila provides few services, especially in the more distant parts of the country, such as Goma, which is more than a thousand miles east of the capital. And, finally, perhaps above all, there is the vast wealth in natural resources—from tungsten to diamonds to copper, and more—that gives ethnic warlords and their backers, especially Rwanda and Uganda, such an incentive to fight.

Evidence of the nation's natural riches is everywhere. Aging Soviet-era Antonov cargo planes continually descend into Goma airport, filled with tin ore from a big mine in the interior now controlled by Congolese army officers. On a country road, a truck stacked high with timber passes by, heading out of the rainforest toward the Ugandan border. And then one day in Goma, while I am walking with Anneke, Ida, and another foreigner, a man approaches and asks: Would we like to buy some uranium?

He is perhaps forty, with expensive-looking walking shoes. He claims to have had clients from South Africa, Europe, and Saudi Arabia. This uranium, he tells us, the Belgians left behind when they had to pull out of the territory in a hurry in 1960. (Possible: a major mine, which had supplied most of the material for the Hiroshima and Nagasaki bombs, was hastily shut down at that time.) The uranium has been tested with Geiger counters, and it's *de bonne qualité!* And safely packed: two kilos inside each seventeen-kilo radiation-proof container. The price? $1.5 million per container. But this is negotiable . . .

Also on all sides is evidence of the lack of an operating national government. One half-finished housing development is composed of empty new cinder-block homes with no doors and no glass in the windows. Kabila promised to build them during his 2006 election campaign, but the funds drained away into various officials' pockets. Millions of children are not in school; working schools are likely to be those run by aid agencies or churches. Once-paved streets have long since reverted to Africa's red dirt, and trucks kick up huge clouds of it as they pass.

The absence of a government that works does not mean that there are no government officials; on the contrary, they are everywhere—and are self-supporting. On rural roads where fewer than a dozen vehicles pass in an hour are clusters of yellow-shirted traffic police waving them down; we see three large trucks stopped at one, their drivers negotiating. Even when we fly from one city to another inside the country, we still have to go through customs on arrival; the passport control officer asks me if I have a present for him. On a road into one town, where people are wheeling bicycles piled high with charcoal, bananas, and other goods to a weekly market, blue-uniformed police are stopping them to collect a "tax."

There are even dilapidated court buildings in cities large and small, but, a lawyer tells us over dinner, with great feeling, "I've never, *ever,* seen a judge who wasn't corrupt." This is so routine, he and a colleague explain, that in civil lawsuits, the judge gets a percentage of the monetary value that a bribe-payer receives. The judge, in turn, is then expected to send some of his take back up the line to whomever appointed him; this is called *renvoyer l'ascenseur*—sending back the elevator. Being a judge in an area full of mining rights disputes is particularly profitable. Other civil servants also earn extra: Goma is on the border with Rwanda, and one of the lawyers explains that the very hotel where we're having dinner was built by a customs official. They point along the street to two more hotels owned by customs men.

Government as a system of organized theft goes back to King Leopold II, who made a fortune here equal to well over $1.1 billion in today's money, chiefly in rubber and ivory. Then for fifty-two years this was a Belgian colony, run less rapaciously, but still mainly for the purpose—as with colonies almost everywhere—of extracting wealth for the mother country and its corporations. The grand theft was continued when, with strong American encouragement, an army officer named Joseph Mobutu seized power in a military coup in 1965. For thirty-two years he maintained a repressive, disastrous dictatorship, changing his name to Mobutu Sese Seko. Delighted to have an anticommunist ally who was friendly to American investors and helpful in covert military operations, the United States provided him with more than $1 billion in aid over the decades. President George H. W. Bush welcomed Mobutu to the White House as "one of our most valued friends." Before he was deposed and then died in 1997, Mobutu pocketed an estimated $4 billion, buying grand villas all over Europe (one, on the Riviera, was almost within sight of one of Leopold's).

The dictator built palatial homes throughout Congo as well, one of them here in Goma. It is now the provincial governor's office, and President Kabila stays there when he's in town: a sprawling red-brick mansion, whose green lawn, dotted with palms and other trees, rolls down to Lake Kivu. A staff member is happy to show us around. The floors are white marble, and a curving marble staircase leads up to Mobutu's circular office, where there is a huge kitschy chandelier of hundreds of little glass balls; the frames of the windows looking out on the lake are tinted gold. The initials M and B, for Mobutu and his second wife, Bobi Ladawa (his first, appropriately enough, was named Marie-Antoinette), are intertwined in gold, with many curlicues, on top of an inlaid wooden desk and elsewhere throughout the house. Two walk-in closets, each some ten feet long, once held her clothes. Of the his-and-hers bathrooms, hers, in pink marble, is the more spectacular, with two sinks in the shape of shells and a large Jacuzzi.

Police protect official buildings like this, but little else, and that means boom times for private security firms, whose jump-suited guards are everywhere. Hotels, restaurants, and larger businesses tend to be in guarded compounds behind high walls, often with coils of razor wire running around the top. Such a wall even surrounds a Catholic mission station we stay at in one town. You honk or knock at a sheet-metal gate, and a guard comes out, takes a look, and then lets you in. Such businesses have their own generators as well, since municipal electricity often shuts down. But for the vast majority of people who can afford none of this, security, electricity, and much else is scarce.

. . .

Into the void of the world's largest failed state, a wide array of organizations have stepped, wanting to help. In Goma, it sometimes seems as if every other vehicle on the deeply rutted streets is an SUV with a logo on the door: Oxfam, Action contre la faim, World Vision, Norwegian Refugee Council, HopeInAction.eu, and dozens more. Many also sport a window sticker: a red slash mark across a submachine gun and the legend NO ARMS/PAS D'ARMES. But the biggest foreign presence consists of people who do have arms: more than seventeen thousand United Nations troops and military observers, assisted by several thousand civilians. They are quickly visible in blue helmets, blue berets, blue baseball caps, or the blue turbans worn by Sikh soldiers from India. Almost all are from poor countries, where UN peacekeeping is a big moneymaker for their armies. The wealthy nations, although they contribute a few higher-ranking officers and civilian specialists, have been generally loath to risk their soldiers' lives in someone else's civil war. However, they pay most of the cost. A plan that we have to join one Bangladeshi unit on patrol is scrubbed at the last minute because it receives word that the ambassador of Japan—a major source of funds—is to visit the base the next day, and all hands are needed to prepare.

The UN presence is a mixed story. Far better equipped and disciplined than the Congolese army, these troops have kept a bad situation from getting worse. Yet it is hopeless to expect so few soldiers to keep peace throughout such a vast country. "How many troops would it really take to stop all the fighting here?" I ask one UN official, out of his office. "Oh, about 250,000," he replies.

On the record, however, officers are brisk, upbeat, and, in the way of soldiers everywhere, bristling with acronyms. In the UN military headquarters in Bunia, several hundred miles north of Goma, a cheerful Pakistani paratrooper colonel holds forth in a room filled with wall maps showing the AORs (areas of responsibility) of battalions from Nepal, Bangladesh, Pakistan, and Morocco—Nepbat, Banbat, Pakbat, Morbat. Other troops in the area, he says, include Indonesians (who repair roads), Uruguayans (boat patrols on lakes and rivers), Guatemalans (special forces), South Africans (military police), and Indians (helicopters). Tunisians and Egyptians are on the way. "Last week we carried out a heli-recce," the colonel says, of one trouble spot; when aid groups have trouble going somewhere, the UN provides a "heli-insertion."

One of the UN's jobs here is to train the Congolese army—more discipline, less theft—and this, too, he assures us, is on track. Next on that particular agenda, he says, is training forward air controllers (puzzling, since Congo has virtually no air force). And how will they do this, given that few UN officers speak either French—the official language of government—or any local tongue? Simple, they will find English-speaking Congolese officers (although veteran aid workers here say they've rarely seen any). And what if forward air controlling is not their specialty? "We're training the trainers!"

When speaking not for attribution, UN officials are far more somber. I talk to four more, military and civilian, African and European. All agree that the biggest single problem is the chaotic Congolese army itself, which numbers some 120,000 ill-trained men. The United States and the western European nations, working through the UN, have basically decided that backing the nominal national government and its military is the least-bad alternative here. But the army is a mess. Top-heavy with colonels to begin with, it has swollen mightily in recent years, since the price of a series of half-effective peace accords has been the absorption into the army of a number of predatory warlords and their followers.

One result is a great mismatch between soldiers and equipment. On a country road leading to a combat zone where one army unit is relieving another, we see hundreds of soldiers in green fatigues, but not once a truck carrying them. Bearing rifles or grenade launchers, the men are hitching rides with passing cargo trucks and motorcycles. They wave at us, bringing hands to their mouths to beg for cigarettes. Beneath a piece of canvas strung between trees, a solitary sentry manning one checkpoint is sound asleep.

What can be done? The outside world has some influence over the Congolese army, because it's partly paying for it. The national government depends on aid money to make ends meet, depends on the UN force to retain control of the east, and sometimes needs UN planes to transport its soldiers, for there is no drivable road from one side of the country to the other. But getting a disparate group of nations to put pressure on Congo to purge its army of thugs is by no means easy.

In one realm, aid donors are applying limited pressure. Soldiers often don't get paid, one reason for the army's habit of looting. "The money comes from Kinshasa," a UN official explains to me, "then goes to Kisangani"—a city three-quarters of the way to the eastern border—"and by the time it gets down to company level there's not much left." To deal with this problem, the European Union has sent a fifty-five-man military mission here.

One member is a sergeant major in the Dutch army, Bob Arnst, a short, wiry soldier with a crew cut. He spells his last name for me as I make notes: "Alpha, Romeo, November, Sierra, Tango." He is stationed in Bunia, where the blackened shells of burned-out buildings are a reminder of recent fighting, and he talks about his work one evening in the UN's simple café and recreation center, where a security guard at the gate has the job of keeping out local prostitutes.

"Everything is in cash. They bring the money in big packages, 120 by 80 by 20 centimeters. In great bricks. We're expecting a convoy now. When the money arrives, they count it again, bill by bill." Arnst and two French soldiers watch the count at the local army headquarters, after which paymasters from half a dozen battalions arrive in SUVs to collect the funds for their units. "Most of them [the paymasters] have very nice clothing. Once a colonel showed up with his bodyguard and I asked, 'What are you doing here?' And he said, 'I've come to see where my money is.' And I said, 'It's not your money.'"

In the days following the distribution of cash to the paymasters, Arnst and his French colleagues visit Congolese battalions in the field, usually dropping in by surprise in a UN helicopter. "We ask soldiers, 'Did you get your payment?'"

And if they didn't? On three occasions in the last few months, entire units were not paid. Arnst reported each case to his EU superiors in Kinshasa, and a Dutch colonel applied pressure at the Ministry of Defense. Each time, the commander was forced to turn over the money to his troops—but was not arrested or disciplined.

The situation is worse in some outlying areas; Arnst cites one remote town in the north, where some troops, he believes, may not have been paid for four months. Food destined for soldiers sometimes disappears as well. "If they don't have any money, they have a weapon, so ... " his voice trails off. Furthermore, commanders often pocket pay for "ghost soldiers" who've deserted. And the pay is woeful to begin with: only about $40 per month, and another $8 for living expenses. "And if a soldier does get his money, he's got no way to bring it to his family." Hence families tend to follow military units around the country, "living in tents with holes in them." The officers are little better off. "Last week a captain came to me and said, 'Can you give me twenty dollars? Ten dollars?'"

. . .

From the dozen years of intermittent war, almost everyone has searing memories. Fabien Kakani, thirty-eight, is a nurse at a Protestant mission hospital whose low brick and cinderblock buildings spread across a patch of lush, green savannah in the town of Nyankunde. One day in 2002, militia from the Ngiti ethnic group and an allied force overran the hospital, burned the mission library of more than ten thousand books, and began killing an estimated three thousand people of other ethnicities—hospital staff, patients, and residents of the nearby town. "I was working in the ICU that day. I had just made the rounds with the doctor and we heard shots from the hill behind the hospital." He points out the window. "We brought more patients in and locked ourselves in. Then they went to the maternity ward and the pediatric ward, and I heard screams as they massacred people there. Throughout the night, we heard shots. I was a Bira [a different ethnic group], and I knew they would be looking for me."

The raiders then broke into the ICU, and Kakani and some seventy other people were tied up and marched to a room he now shows us in another hospital building, which we pace out as being about ten by twenty-one feet. "We spent three days here. No food, no drink, we had to defecate and urinate on the floor. Children died because there was no milk in their mothers' breasts. We were passing their dead bodies out the windows."

So many people were killed at Nyankunde hospital alone that there was no time to dig graves; the bodies had to be thrown into pit latrines. And the leader of the Ngiti troops who carried out the massacre? He was Kakani's brother-in-law. He wanted to kill members of several rival groups, including the Bira, even though he was married to a Bira, Kakani's sister. The commander of an allied militia force involved in the attack was not on the scene, but in close communication by radio, well aware of what his troops were doing. Following one of the incorporate-the-warlords peace agreements, he became Congo's foreign minister. He is still in the cabinet today, in another position.

. . .

After two weeks my notebooks overflow with such stories. But looking at people I meet, even groups of ex-combatants, do I see those who look capable of killing hospital patients in their beds, gang-raping a woman like Mama Masika, jabbing a young man's eye with a bayonet? I do not. Men and women are warm, friendly, their faces overflow with smiles; seeing a foreigner, everyone wants to stop, say *"Bonjour!"* and shake hands, whether on a small town's main street or on a forest path. I've never seen more enthusiastic hand-shakers. At night, when the electricity works, the warm air echoes with some of Africa's best music. There is no shortage of ordinary acts of human kindness. When our car's left front wheel goes sailing off to the side of a rough mountain road, leaving one end of the axle to gouge a long furrow in the dirt, the driver of a passing truck immediately stops and crawls under the car, using his jack in tandem with ours to solve the problem and get us on our way.

What turns such people into rapists, sadists, killers? Greed, fear, demagogic leaders who claim that violence is necessary for self-defense, seeing everyone around you doing the same thing—and the fact that the rest of the world pays tragically little attention to one of the great humanitarian catastrophes of our time. But even the worst brutality can also draw out the good in people, as in the way Masika has devoted her life to other raped women. In Goma, I saw people with pickaxes laboriously hewing the purple lava that had flooded their city into football-sized chunks with flattened sides, then using these, with mortar, to build the walls of new homes. Can this devastated country as a whole use the very experience of its suffering to build something new and durable? I hope so, but I fear it will be a long time in coming.

2009

SEVEN

All That Glitters

"A STREAM OF MANUFACTURED GOODS, rubbishy cottons, beads and brass-wire" flowed into the interior, Joseph Conrad writes in *Heart of Darkness,* describing the colonial economy he saw when traveling up the Congo River in 1890, "and in return came a precious trickle of ivory . . . The word 'ivory' rang in the air, was whispered, was sighed. You would think they were praying to it."

The trickle of ivory that Conrad described was highly visible: elephant tusks carried on the shoulders of exhausted porters from the African hinterland to the coast, where they could be shipped off to Europe. More than a hundred years later, far more wealth flows out of this same territory, now the Democratic Republic of Congo. But these days much of the wealth you can't see. If, for example, you stand beside the washboard dirt road that winds out of the hot scrubland of the Ituri district of Congo's northeast, you will see a few vehicles, not more than five or ten an hour: a dusty SUV, an army jeep, two men on a motorbike, an ancient truck with a precariously high load of fruits and vegetables and a layer of people hitching a ride on top. But you won't see the treasure they are carrying, for it is too small. It will be in little plastic bags in someone's pocket, or perhaps, better to be concealed from thieves and greedy policemen, sewn into a shirt seam or slipped under a shoe's insole. In this part of the country, the main wealth is gold. More than $1 billion worth is mined in Congo each year, and a good portion of it comes down this road.

Gold is only one of a half-dozen or more lucrative minerals to be found here, and together they constitute perhaps the worst case on Earth of the resource curse. As inevitably as oil drew the United States into Iraq, it is the temptations of this wealth that have turned Congo into the horrific battleground it has been in recent years. A country with a lavish array of natural riches and a dysfunctional government is like a child heiress without a guardian: Everyone schemes for a piece of what she's got.

As far back as the territory's history is recorded, the wealth from this vast natural treasure house has flowed almost entirely overseas, leaving some of the planet's best-endowed land with some of its poorest people. I have often heard Congolese friends say, "We wouldn't have so much trouble if we weren't so rich."

Of all the minerals to be found here, none has for so long lit up the eyes of foreigners as the yellow metal that has shaped the course of conquest on almost every continent. And today, with worldwide economic troubles and ever-rising demand from electronics manufacturing sending its price to unimagined heights, a new gold rush is in the making here. Some of the richest goldfields in East Africa lie up this dirt road, which begins some 350 miles east of the turnaround point of Conrad's nightmare steamboat trip. My journey up the road, I hope, will be a way of seeing some of this country's tragic—there is no other word for it—wealth at its point of origin, before it vanishes into jewelry stores and bank vaults and electronics plants in Europe and China, New York, and California.

The road begins in war-battered Bunia, capital of the Ituri district, a West Virginia–sized region that has some of the country's most lucrative mineral deposits. Climbing out from under a mosquito net on the morning our trip begins, I hear the bells of a Catholic church summoning the faithful, the dawn call to prayer from a nearby mosque, roosters crowing, and a bugler at the barracks of the United Nations peacekeeping force stationed here. On the city's rutted dirt streets, women with babies on their backs balance laundry bundles or buckets on their heads; men wheel bicycles piled with precarious loads of cabbages, charcoal, grass for thatching roofs, or yellow jerricans of kerosene. One man carries cargo in a wheelbarrow that, except for its iron wheel, is made entirely of interwoven tree branches. Local merchants buy old clothing from overseas by the bale, and so some people wear American football jerseys or T-shirts promoting an ice rink or ski resort.

Driving up the road to the west, through the East African savanna toward the rainforest of the interior, is like a journey in time. Each bend takes you past reminders of the region's long, unhappy history and of the successive waves of people who have sought wealth here, most recently in more than a dozen years of sporadic, bloody fighting.

In 1903, two Australian prospectors hired by the colonial authorities examined a riverbed near a village called Krilo and confirmed that it was a potentially rich source of gold. Whites promptly mangled the name into Kilo, and a few years later the first leg of this road was built for bringing in mining equipment by oxcart. The gold diggers put to work here by King Leopold II of Belgium, who then owned the territory, were different from those mining gold at the same time in the Klondike, for they arrived in chains. Leopold's entire colonial economy was based on forced labor, and the system continued after the king, in 1908, sold his private colony to the Belgian government and it became the Belgian Congo.

By the following year, there were 1,400 African forced laborers at Kilo; within six years, as nearby mining sites proliferated, the number of people conscripted to dig gold reached 7,500, and it would expand far more. The arrival of miners was an unexpected boon for white ivory traders: they now had a market for the rest of the elephant, selling dried meat to the mines for their workers. The Belgians requisitioned laborers from local chiefs and supplied the chains and metal collars or yokes in which they were taken off to the mines. Chiefs were punished if they failed to provide their quota of men and were required to supply food and building materials from their villages as well. The mining industry was hungry for labor, not just to dig for gold but to be porters carrying supplies, firewood, and equipment to the mine sites. Of the women I see now in long, brightly colored dresses eking out a living selling bananas spread on pieces of cloth at the dusty roadside, how many, I wonder, are the great-granddaughters of those who were marched to the mines in chains? One eyewitness account from 1914 describes mothers nursing babies as they carried loads of up to thirty kilos, or sixty-six pounds.

Some Kilo miners were compelled to work for a decade or more and released only when they supplied sons to take their places. Repeated uprisings against the forced labor regime were brutally suppressed, and thousands of deserters were recaptured and put to work again. The mines paid bonuses to overseers based on the amount of gold dug by the Africans under their control, whose workday rose to twelve hours during the First World War. Discipline was enforced by armed mine police and by the *chicotte,* a whip of sun-dried hippopotamus hide with razor-sharp edges, whose blows were meticulously tabulated. Records from one group of northeastern Congo gold camps register 26,579 lashes applied to miners during the first half of 1920 alone. Forced labor remained part of the economy here, as it did almost everywhere in colonial Africa, until the 1940s. The whip lasted even longer.

Despite having no political rights, the Congolese, ironically, enjoyed their highest standard of living in the decade or so before the colony won independence in 1960. Belgians invested heavily in the gold mines, and although profits continued to flow back to Europe, colonizers came to understand that this industry and others would produce more if workers were well fed, healthy, and literate. Not too literate, mind you: the colony had one of the best elementary education systems on the continent, but virtually no Africans were trained for management positions. Under Belgian rule, schools for whites and blacks were segregated, of course, and no black schools in the gold-mining towns went beyond 8th grade. As we drive farther along the road, past trees with high green bunches of papayas, we can see aging brick health clinics and primary schools built during the late colonial era.

Other buildings, abandoned, tell the next phase of the story. Sucking his country's economy dry during his thirty-two years in power, the dictator Mobutu Sese Seko spent much of the national treasury on assorted palaces, a huge yacht, an airport near his Congo birthplace, and renting Concordes to pick him up there for trips to Europe. Plum executive positions like those at the Ituri mines Mobutu passed out to members of his clan and to political allies, who knew little about mining, pocketed profits, and let machinery wear out. By the end of Mobutu's reign, most industrial gold mining had come to a halt. One town we pass, formerly a depot for mining vehicles, is filled with empty workshops, garages, and jumbles of rusted old machinery. We spot the gray concrete bottom of what was once an Olympic-sized swimming pool. The ladder into the pool and the iron framework of two high-dive platforms are still there. Some old men sitting in the shade tell us that this was a club for European skilled workers and company officials. The whites all left soon after independence, they say; the pool closed later.

As we continue driving up the road, buildings scarred or demolished by artillery or mortar shells are signs of the long period of civil war that followed the end of Mobutu's rule. Here in the Ituri district alone, at least sixty thousand people were killed outright, and many more died as refugees. Most of the combat in this region has been between two shifting coalitions of militias, each of them intermittently supported by neighboring Rwanda or Uganda. Both countries have eagerly eyed Congo's gold—and its wealth of other metals, including tin ore, coltan, and tungsten, necessary to make everything from computers to cell phones.

Today, with some help from UN peacekeepers, the Ituri goldfields are back under the Congolese national government's control, but the evidence of fighting is everywhere you look. We pass the town of Bambu, once the administrative center for the network of Belgian mines in the region. A guidebook from some sixty years ago recommends the company-run hotel—now long defunct—to the white visitor. Palm trees shade the dirt streets; the firs that line one were obviously imported from Europe. A spacious white plaster and brick villa on a hilltop above town was once the home of the mines' Belgian manager. When rival warlords and their Ugandan and Rwandan backers battled for control of the area, each side occupied it in succession. "They always liked these buildings high on a hill, especially if the Belgians once had them," my traveling companion, Anneke Van Woudenberg, explains. In her work for Human Rights Watch she has written a report on exploitation by the mining industry in this region, *The Curse of Gold*, well known here in its French translation.

Today, the Congolese army has taken over the villa as its local headquarters, and several dark green military trucks are parked outside. Like the rebel warlords before them, many army officers have profited from gold. Officers seek posts according to which mining areas the position controls. In half a dozen larger Congolese cities, you can find luxurious houses, surrounded by high walls and security guards, owned by generals whose nominal pay is less than $100 a month.

Along the side of the dirt road walk men in gum boots and sweaty T-shirts, balancing heavy sacks of rocks on their heads. They will put the rocks in a metal bucket and pound them into dust with an iron bar. Then they will combine the dust with water and mercury—which attracts the specks of gold—and, trying not to breathe the toxic fumes, will heat the gold-mercury mix in a pot over an open wood fire to evaporate the mercury.

We drive up to a checkpoint where two armed sentries wave our car to a stop. "*Du thé! Un sucré!*" (some tea, something sweet—slang for bribes) they say through the car window, each rubbing thumb and forefinger together. Van Woudenberg, undaunted, gets out to deal with them and with their commanding officer, who wears a brimmed military cap and red braid and emerges sternly from a little guardhouse. Anywhere you travel in Congo, uniformed men demand money; soldiers and police are paid little to begin with, and much of that vanishes into the pockets of higher-ups before it reaches them. But this time a curious thing happens. When the chief of this little extortion post takes Van Woudenberg's passport, he at first frowns, then looks up and says in French, "You're the woman who wrote *The Curse of Gold!* I've read it three times!" He sends us on our way with a smile. There is something moving about this: a petty thief applauding someone who has exposed grand theft.

. . .

Half a day up the bumpy road we reach Mongbwalu, which sits next to a gold deposit so coveted that the town changed hands five times in battling between rival ethnic militias in one decade, leaving some two thousand people dead. Warlords wanted the gold to buy weapons—often from the corrupt national army that supposedly was trying to suppress them. The old gold refinery here is now a rusted skeleton, destroyed by fighting in 2002. Some eerie video footage taken here that year provides a microcosm of the entire war. Civilians are seen fleeing, carrying rolled-up mattresses on their heads. Meanwhile, officers in berets, boots, and camouflage fatigues from the militia group Union des Patriotes congolais, which had taken the town a few days before, are carefully examining still-intact refining machinery, a crushing mill, and football-size chunks of gold ore. A Ugandan TV correspondent, doubtless at the request of the militiamen who've invited him along, goes on camera to urge "foreign investors" to help get the mines working again. The militia assumed that multinational corporations would have few scruples about dealing with warlords if the stakes were high enough, and they were right.

We spend the night under mosquito nets at the town's Catholic mission, and I'm awakened in the morning by the sound of hymns. The colonial-era guidebook describes Mongbwalu as having "hospitals for Europeans and natives," but today the surviving relic of those times is a spacious cathedral, built by the Belgians in the 1930s, with arched windows and a dark-stained wood ceiling above which priests hid during the last round of massacres. From the cathedral's front steps is a lovely view of green hills that are the western edge of the great equatorial rainforest.

Above the altar hangs a huge, mural-like painting that offers an extraordinary glimpse into the colonial past. Madonna and child float on a golden cloud; on the ground below, offering flowers in adoration, are nine or ten African adults and children, several carrying a flag emblazoned with the name of the old Belgian mining company. In a bottom corner, a frightened-looking witch doctor, with feather headdress and necklace of shells, is fleeing the scene, vanquished by the combination of corporate power and the Virgin Mary.

Although large-scale mining has reaped billions from Ituri over the decades, during the civil war it was largely on hold. Multinational corporations prefer a government weak enough not to tax and regulate heavily but strong enough to guarantee order. Today the fighting in the goldfields area has subsided, the price of gold is soaring, and the conveniently weak Congolese government is back in control. Industrial mining appears about to begin again.

Just as Australian prospectors set off the first scramble for Ituri gold a century ago, an Australian is chief prospector in Mongbwalu today. The geologist Adrian Woolford, who is thirty, he says, "and getting older by the minute," is exploration manager for a subsidiary of South Africa–based AngloGold Ashanti, the world's third-largest gold mining company. Tall, thin, bearded, in khaki shorts and khaki shirt with the sleeves rolled up, Woolford draws the good pay necessary to lure highly trained specialists to this bleak spot. He gets two weeks off for every six he works. On his last break, he vacationed in Cambodia; on the next, he will go to Brazil. Several hundred yards away people are living in dirt-floored huts lit by candles or kerosene lanterns, but in the mining company's hilltop compound, we are in a little Western island of modern offices, flush toilets, and working electricity.

On his computer monitor, Woolford shows us a three-dimensional image, which he can rotate so we can see it from any side or from above or below, of what's underground at Mongbwalu. Bodies of gold ore in brilliant red and yellow are separated by thin green lines of other rock. The image also shows many of the more than five hundred sampling holes that have been sunk in the ground with diamond-bit drills, some of them extending nearly two thousand feet down. Outside the building we're in, dozens of cylindrically shaped samples of ore from these holes are piled up, like a collection of large gray plumbing pipes, awaiting testing.

The drilling has confirmed a treasure trove. Beneath less than a half a square mile of ground, next to the hill we're on, Woolford says, are more than 2.5 million ounces of gold, worth about $3 billion at current prices. And it is found at the rate of about three grams per ton of rock—an extraordinarily high batting average for a deposit this big—all of it within an easy eight hundred feet of the surface.

The company has about 250 employees on this site. For now, they mostly work inside the compound, tightly protected by private security guards who include Nepalese Gurkha veterans of the British army. The compound's gates, floodlights, and high razor-wire fence prompt Joel Bisubu, a Congolese human rights activist traveling with us, to call it "Guantanamo."

AngloGold Ashanti recently finalized a series of agreements with the government under which it can begin mining here and at another site not far away. At Mongbwalu, it will have an 86 percent share of the operation; the near-bankrupt former state mining company, now being privatized, will have the remainder. Four other multinationals—based in England, Canada, and South Africa—have concluded other closed-door agreements over mining rights. No one will ever know what Congolese government officials reaped from these deals in the way of quietly promised jobs, favors, or money under the table, in a country where such rewards are routine. Representatives of villages in the area, meanwhile, find it hard to get a seat at the negotiating table. Seldom, in fact, do local communities gain much from such agreements; that is part of the resource curse.

This pattern is all the stronger in a place where the national government has as fragmentary a hold as it does here. A failed state fails its people in many ways, and one of them, in a world of powerful corporate players, is that a weak and corrupt government has no bargaining power. For industrial mining that could create new skilled jobs, Congo desperately needs the expertise and investment capital that, for better or worse, only a multinational can offer. But a company like AngloGold Ashanti, with more than sixty thousand employees at work on four continents, can easily invest elsewhere if the terms in Congo are not to its liking.

The company would not score high in any social responsibility ratings. During the war years, lucrative mining concessions changed hands many times between corporations eager for future profits and warlords happy to sign contracts. Despite a United Nations embargo on dealings with rebel groups, when a rebel warlord controlled Mongbwalu some time back, AngloGold Ashanti made payments to him, also providing him and his entourage with rides in company planes and vehicles and a house on its concession. While spending millions of dollars prospecting, it has made only small contributions to a local hospital, schools, a soccer tournament, and the like, keeping at arm's length a coalition of local groups and churches lobbying for this desperately poor community.

"Of everything we've put in our list of demands and grievances," says Richard Magabusini, an elected chief and member of the coalition, "nothing has been done. They keep saying, 'We're just prospecting. We'll look at all this later.'" AngloGold Ashanti prefers to deal instead with a collection of more pliable community representatives it has assembled, rather like a company union.

Another point of tension with people here is whether the company will dig a large open-pit mine or sink shafts to tunnel underground. For gold deposits nearer the surface, it almost certainly will do the former, which is far cheaper; people who live here want it to do the latter, for open-pit mining strips away fertile topsoil, leaves a huge gouge in the landscape, and can pollute rivers and streams. Here, it would also require moving an entire village. "We have our ancestral secrets in our communities that must not be disturbed," says Chief Magabusini. "We are categorically demanding that they not move people." But he has no power to prevent this from happening.

As the company takes its slice of Africa's riches, only a tiny percentage of the proceeds from those 2.5 million ounces of gold is likely to stay in Congo— and even then, much of what does will leak into high officials' private bank accounts. AngloGold Ashanti mined more than $1.5 billion worth of gold in neighboring Tanzania between 2000 and 2007, but only 9 percent of that money remained in the country as taxes or royalties. Where do the profits go instead? A good chunk comes to the United States; the company's largest single shareholder, the hedge fund billionaire John Paulson, lives on New York's Upper East Side and summers in the Hamptons.

. . .

The big money in gold comes to those who can afford to dig massive mines and build refineries to process the ore. But those who cannot, an estimated seventy to one hundred thousand people in Congo's northeast—including some ten thousand children—dig for gold literally by hand, much the way men did in California's Gold Rush of 1849.

Even at 8:30 on a Sunday night, the streets of Mongbwalu, bordered by open sewage ditches with small plank bridges across them, are filled with rubber-booted miners and lined with people and businesses wanting a share of whatever pittance they have earned: gaudily dressed prostitutes, cafés, a bar with a picture of Jesus on the wall, and dozens of shops that buy gold and sell miners what they need. A raindrop-sized silvery globule of mercury in a plastic baggie goes for the equivalent of 75 cents.

We enter one shop, La Grâce à Dieu—Chez Johnny. A big man in his late thirties chewing a toothpick, Johnny sits behind the dimly lit counter. On a handheld scale, he weighs gold flakes, the occasional tiny nugget, and *amalgame,* the gold dust separated by mercury from crushed rocks, which is 80 to 90 percent pure. From here the gold will quietly find its way across Congo's porous border with Uganda, on to refining in Dubai, and then into the voracious world market. An estimated 97 percent of Congo's gold leaves the country without ever being taxed.

The weights Johnny uses to measure gold are *kitcheles*—penny-size coins that date from forty or fifty years ago, when Congo still used coins. Now, after decades of headlong inflation, there are only bills. Each seller is paid with a big brick of them, since even the largest denomination is worth less than $1. The person whom Johnny is buying from when we come in, a stocky, silent man of perhaps forty, who doesn't want to say where his gold came from and looks too old to have mined the metal himself, Van Woudenberg and Bisubu think; he's probably a middleman who spent the day buying from miners. He walks off with a wad of bills about three inches thick, worth some $60.

Most of the men who sell gold to Johnny spend some of their earnings in his store, buying soft drinks, rice, biscuits, toilet paper, sardines, flour, or lanterns, all arrayed on shelves behind him. He also sells mining supplies, of which the most important, for the equivalent of $5 apiece, are shovel blades; one of these lasts two months, less if you're digging in rocky soil. But, as always seems to be the case in Congo, the shop's profits are going elsewhere, for this is not Johnny's own business, he explains; its *patron,* or owner, is in Butembo, many hours away. He calls Johnny every morning on his cell phone—there are no landlines here—to tell him the price to pay for gold that day.

. . .

The next morning we jounce and bump a half-hour farther into the hills, past the village of round huts that will vanish if AngloGold Ashanti digs its open-pit mine, to the small town of Pili-Pili. From its one sweltering, sunbaked dirt street we descend another half-hour on foot, on a path that goes steeply downward into a valley, past flame trees with red blossoms, butterflies flitting about blue flowers, and grass that reaches higher than our heads.

On a patch of land most of the way down is a camp where hundreds of miners live. These are people mining by hand, many of whom may be thrown out of work as industrial mining starts up again. The miners are divided into teams of up to fifteen men, who live here in huts whose walls are reddish mud packed around interwoven sticks. The overhanging roofs are grass thatch; sometimes a blue plastic sheet with a UNICEF emblem—from aid supplies to refugee camps—is thrown on top for additional rain-proofing. All food, drinking water, and mining tools are carried in. On the walls of the camp chief's dirt-floored hut are two large Inauguration Day posters of Barack Obama.

It's only about 10 a.m., but the tropical sun is already broiling. We keep on descending, and farther down the trail we stop to talk to a young miner with a gentle smile and intelligent eyes, walking back uphill to Pili-Pili. His name is Alex, and he is twenty-two. He says he had to drop out of high school two years ago for lack of money and has been mining ever since. "There is no work in Congo. We suffer a lot." He and the friend who is with him, he explains, are *cascadeurs*—a word that most commonly means movie stuntmen but here refers to someone working in a pair or on his own, who does not belong to one of the fifteen-man teams. Alex shows us a small plastic bag of sand with tiny flecks of gold in it, which, he estimates, the two of them can sell in Pili-Pili for the equivalent of $1. That's their usual take for an entire day, and they are delighted to have found this much so early. They bid us a warm goodbye and continue up the trail.

The bottom of the valley is dotted with clusters of men in their teens and twenties. Miners usually have to buy their places on these fifteen-man teams, often going into debt to do so. We talk to men in one group, who say they started work by lantern light at 3 a.m. to get as much as possible done before the midday heat. Shovels are their only visible hand tools, and with them they have gouged out of the side of the hill an indentation perhaps twenty feet wide and twenty deep. At the bottom of it, they've also dug a tunnel about three feet high, with just enough room to enter on your hands and knees. It extends twelve to fifteen feet into the earth, as far as you can go without danger of the tunnel collapsing. They believe the dirt farther back has a higher concentration of gold.

A man-high mound of red earth from all their digging is piled up next to the stream that runs along the valley floor, and now two of the men turn to another task: one tossing shovel-loads of dirt and the other pouring pans of water into a homemade chute of boards. Mud flows down the chute, across a patch of woolen blanket crossed by leafy twigs, which slow down the flow and give the heavier gold a chance to sink to the blanket, where the shiny specks stick and can be carefully removed. A majority of these men, they tell us with smiles and laughter as we ask each in turn, are former fighters from rival militias. But now this past seems forgotten as they all focus on finding enough gold to survive.

On an average day the team finds $30 to $50 worth of gold to divide fifteen ways. Off the top, however, 30 percent (after a hefty initial fee before the team could even start working here) has to be given to the *patron* who has the mining rights to this site. Gold miners then face a variety of other fees, the largest of which is about $3 per week per miner in payoffs to the army or police, as protection against harassment. What's left, for the average Ituri miner and his family, is roughly $40 to $60 a month.

Finally, we head up the trail again, wanting to climb back to Pili-Pili before the sun reaches its zenith. A miner coming down who passes us wears a T-shirt from one of those imported bales of cheap second-hand clothing; across the chest is printed in English "staytruedreamtrue." Passing back through the miners' camp, we stop to chat for a moment about how hard the work looks and how meager the rewards. One man says simply, "We're on automatic."

Back on Pili-Pili's main street, we run into Alex and his friend, the *cascadeurs*. They've sold their dollar's worth of gold from this morning, he says, and with it bought themselves a breakfast of green beans. Now they're about to head back down to the valley again to try to find enough gold to buy dinner.

2010

EIGHT

A Showman in the Rainforest

FEW HISTORICAL FIGURES SEE THEIR STOCK RISE and fall as dramatically as do explorers. Poor Columbus, formerly revered for discovering the New World, now has Native American protests on the holiday named after him. Robert Falcon Scott, once widely admired for reaching the South Pole, these days is seen as a bumbler who started off too late in the season, brought too little food, and, refusing to use dogs to haul his sleds the final half of his journey, led himself and four exhausted colleagues to a frozen end. His famous last letters about dying for king and country now seem an eerie preview of the senseless deaths of the First World War.

The nineteenth century's most celebrated explorers were Dr. David Livingstone and Sir Henry Morton Stanley. Livingstone, the elder of the two, a physician and missionary, was the first European to cross Africa, where he named a great cataract Victoria Falls after his country's queen, and survived dozens of bouts with tropical diseases and one mauling by a lion. He also crusaded against the slave trade between the east coast of Africa and the Islamic world, which continued after the Atlantic slave trade ended. Physically brave, morally righteous, man of God and man of science, Livingstone was the perfect hero for Britons who wanted to believe that their increasing interest in Africa was a wholly altruistic one.

In 1866, Livingstone set off on a new expedition, one of the aims of which was to find the source of the Nile, an age-old European obsession. When he hadn't been heard from for many months, the enterprising publisher of the *New York Herald,* James Gordon Bennett Jr., sent the young Stanley, his star reporter, in pursuit. After a long and harrowing journey, Stanley was finally able to utter—if we are to believe him—his famous "Dr. Livingstone, I presume?" The two men hit it off and began to explore together; they traveled by boat around the northern end of Lake Tanganyika hoping to find the Nile flowing out but, to their disappointment, found another river flowing in. Nearby, they came upon and christened the New York Herald Islands. Stanley then returned home with the journalistic scoop of the century.

Stanley became a promoter of colonialism and the most successful travel writer of modern times. Several more African expeditions lay ahead of him, most notably a thousand-day trek across the continent, from 1874 to 1877, which for the first time determined the course of the Congo River and led to the colonization of its enormous watershed. He was the right hero for the Scramble for Africa, when Europeans wanted to be told that they were doing a good thing in civilizing the African barbarians, by force if necessary. It is no accident that so many of Stanley's books have "dark" in the title: *In Darkest Africa, Through the Dark Continent, My Dark Companions and Their Strange Stories.*

Livingstone died in Africa in 1873, after braving more illness, plodding farther, and sometimes finding himself neck-deep in swampy water that was not, alas, the Nile. When his body was brought back to England, it was greeted at Southampton by a 21-gun salute and a special train to convey it to London. At his funeral in Westminster Abbey, the Prince of Wales and Prime Minister Benjamin Disraeli were among the mourners. Stanley was equally lionized. When he married some two decades later, it was also in the Abbey, and his coach needed a mounted police escort to get through the wildly cheering crowds. Queen Victoria sent the bride a locket with thirty-eight diamonds. Presidents, kings, and generals were eager to meet him, and as he made a lucrative lecture tour of the United States and Canada, it was in a private railway car named the Henry M. Stanley.

There are more than a hundred biographies of Livingstone alone, and a bibliography from some years ago of works having to do with the two explorers lists 1,766 titles, including *Stanley und Livingstone, Stanley et Livingstone,* and *Stanley y Livingstone.* An international Victoria Falls of words and images still pours forth: TV documentaries, museum exhibits, a Swedish novel in the voice of one of Stanley's followers. Christie's recently sold a collection of Stanley memorabilia, including his Winchester rifle and a water-stained map, for more than a million dollars. Despite the continuing public fascination with the two men, however, the way people look at them has changed sharply. The 1960s, a time of major cultural upheavals and the end of colonial rule in most of Africa, were the Continental Divide of revisionism. Few heroes survived intact, particularly if they were white men in sun helmets trekking through the bush and staking out colonies.

Stanley has fared especially badly. He was driven to his extraordinary feats of exploration by intense shame about his origins, as an out-of-wedlock child named John Rowlands who grew up mostly in a Welsh poorhouse. For a long time, he passed himself off as American-born: Mark Twain even sent congratulations to his "fellow Missourian" on finding Livingstone. Then, as the secret of his early years leaked out, he spun further fictions about his life. About his first two great expeditions to Africa there was no one to contradict him because, most conveniently, the few other white men involved all died along the way. In Stanley's telling, they were cared for by their benevolent leader to the end. "I sprang to him—only in time, however, to see him take his last gasp," he says of one. No journalists bothered to interview these expeditions' surviving African porters, and so Stanley got to shape his own heroic story unhindered. In the past few decades, however, critical biographers, principally Richard Hall, John Bierman, and Frank McLynn, have begun to pull it apart.

Among much else, these writers examined various claims that Stanley made about his youth. According to his *Autobiography,* the teen-age immigrant to America was given a job, then taken in and adopted by a kindly New Orleans cotton merchant named Henry Stanley and his wife. In 1859, Mrs. Stanley died tragically, of yellow fever, but not before saying, "Be a good boy. God bless you!" Soon afterward, her widower embraced his adopted son and told him that "in future *you are to bear my name.*" The two became constant companions, reading aloud to each other, discussing the Bible, traveling on Mississippi riverboats. Then, sadly, in 1861, this generous adoptive father followed his wife to Heaven. Records show, however, that the elder Stanleys lived until 1878 and that their adopted children were both girls. The future explorer stayed not in their home but, according to city directories, in various boarding houses. And at one point the merchant Stanley had a furious quarrel with his young employee, sent him off to work at someone else's plantation in Arkansas, and apparently never saw him again. Much of the *Autobiography* turns out to be a similar tissue of wishful thinking.

Today, it is also hard to look at Stanley without noticing his brutality. Even in his own books, beneath the adventuring and the details about towering jungle trees and exotic wild animals, there is a steady drumbeat of recalcitrant porters being flogged and insolent natives being taught a lesson with bullets. When Hiram Maxim gave Stanley the latest model of his machine gun to take along on an expedition, Stanley said that the invention would be "of valuable service in helping civilisation to overcome barbarism."

David Livingstone has had a more ambiguous revisiting by modern writers, beginning with a judicious 1973 biography by Tim Jeal. As with Stanley, Livingstone's biographers have exposed embarrassing personal details that Victorian mythmakers ignored. The explorer got on well with Africans but was haughty and cruelly insensitive to white fellow-travelers, to the point of having a fistfight with his own brother. He dragged his pregnant wife and children along on one expedition across the Kalahari Desert, which left the children horrendously sick, Mrs. Livingstone partially paralyzed for a few months, and a new baby dead. Afterward, he sent his family to England with no money to live on. His wife became an alcoholic; he saw little of his children, and his estranged oldest son changed his last name.

Stanley himself had been an early burnisher of Livingstone's image, thereby indirectly adding luster to his own. In his newspaper dispatches and in *How I Found Livingstone,* he portrayed a saintly man, confiding only to his private journal his "suspicions . . . that he was not of such an angelic temper as I believed him to be." The editors of Livingstone's posthumously published *Last Journals* further polished the picture. They changed wording, removed ill-spirited jabs at Prince Albert and many others, and censored Livingstone's observations on African sexuality. ("Testicles" became "tenderest parts.") The fact that Livingstone was supposedly found dead in a kneeling position meant, of course, that the good doctor had risen from his deathbed to pray to God "to break down the oppression and woe of the land."

Another facet of Livingstone revisionism, however, makes him a deeper and braver man than his legend. He first went to the continent before African exploration became irrevocably linked to Europe's seizure of African land, and despite his Victorian faith in the magic of free trade and his paternalism toward Africans, he took their side—in a manner that his contemporary admirers ignored—in the struggle with white settlers over that land. In an article that a British magazine refused to publish, he wrote, "No nation ever secured its liberty without fighting for it," and said that the battle for freedom by the Xhosa people of what is today South Africa was morally similar to the 1848 uprising of the Hungarians against Habsburg rule: "England . . . has been struggling to crush a nation fighting as bravely for nationality as ever Magyar did." Kenneth Kaunda, former president of Zambia, calls him "the first freedom fighter," and a major Zambian town is still known as Livingstone. Stanleyville, in the Congo, was long ago renamed.

Movies about the two explorers reflect their changing reputations as well. In a 1939 film, *Stanley and Livingstone,* Stanley is given a comic Wild West sidekick. When their caravan gets attacked by Africans with bows and arrows, he tells Stanley, "Don't stand there in the open! This is Injun fightin'!" A compassionate Livingstone, played by Cedric Hardwicke, says nothing against colonialism or in favor of African land rights and, instead, cures sick children and leads the grateful natives in singing a rousing "Onward Christian Soldiers." Spencer Tracy, as Stanley, has only enough flaws so that he can be transformed by his contact with the gentle doctor. When Stanley finds an African named Bongo trying to steal a pocket mirror from his baggage, he knocks him down. Livingstone reproaches him, saying, "You should never strike one of these simple people." As Stanley leaves, some weeks later, he gives Livingstone the mirror for Bongo.

By contrast, a 1997 TV film, *Forbidden Territory*, tells the story in harsher tones. "If I succeed, it will prove I am somebody," Stanley says at the beginning. Once on the march, he is shown as a brute who screams at the white members of his caravan, whips the black ones, and, at one point, punches an African woman. His transformation differs from the earlier film as well, and Livingstone undergoes one too. Deep in the bush, the two men practice mutual psychotherapy. In modern, confessional style, Livingstone reveals his self-doubt and admits that he wasn't a good father. Stanley tells him, "My whole life has been a lie," and, when they part, tearfully says, "You have been like the father I never knew."

. . .

The changing images of the two explorers over the years offer as rich a terrain for a writer as do the two men themselves. But anyone who expects to see this promising territory investigated in Martin Dugard's *Into Africa: The Epic Adventures of Stanley and Livingstone* will be disappointed. His pedestrian rehash of the story reads almost like one of the Victorian hagiographies. Even its form, with alternating sections about the two men on their separate travels until Stanley utters his " . . . I presume" and their journeys become one, has been used before.

Dugard's prose, not unlike Stanley's, has an over-the-top ring: "Character is built through trials and turmoil"; "What would happen in the next few minutes would alter the future of exploration, Africa, and the world"; "The call to adventure is genetic in a handful of men and women"; Stanley's travels took him to "the entrance to Africa's beating heart"; "He would learn for certain whether the explorer was dead or alive. . . . He could not stomach the maudlin limbo of doubt." Maudlin limbo?

More nettlesome yet, the book is sprinkled with factual errors. Sir Bartle Frere is governor of Bombay on page 5 and governor of India on page 122. It was not King Leopold IV of Belgium for whom Stanley staked out a Congo colony but Leopold II; and it was not the Belgian Congo that first came into being as a result but the État independant du Congo, or Congo Free State. Tanganyika became independent in 1961, not 1964. Britain's population in the eighteen-fifties was not four million but, counting Ireland, more than twenty-seven million.

When a writer stumbles this carelessly over small, obvious details, it's a warning that there may be a broader, more revealing pattern of unreliability at work, and with Dugard there is. Almost always, he accepts Stanley's account of an event at face value. But Stanley, one of the great self-promoters of all time, must always be treated with caution. Should we believe him when, for example, he tells how he quelled a mutiny of his porters, first facing down one armed man who rushed toward him, then whirling around just in time, like a hero beating off multiple villains in a kung-fu movie, to defy another, who was about to fire on him from the other side? Dugard does.

Or take another episode. In the introduction to *How I Found Livingstone,* the first of his many boastful bestsellers, Stanley writes, "A journalist in my position . . . like a gladiator in the arena . . . must be prepared for the combat. Any flinching, any cowardice, and he is lost. The gladiator meets the sword that is sharpened for his bosom—the flying journalist or roving correspondent meets the command that may send him to his doom." He tells a dramatic tale of how he was summoned to Paris by his employer, *Herald* publisher James Gordon Bennett Jr. He found Bennett in his hotel room at night:

"What!" said I, "do you really think I can find Dr. Livingstone? Do you mean me to go to Central Africa?"

"Yes; I mean that you shall go, and find him wherever you may hear that he is. . . . The old man may be in want:—take enough with you to help him should he require it. Of course you will act according to your own plans, and do what you think best—BUT FIND LIVINGSTONE!"

Only slightly altering the punctuation, Dugard reproduces this dialogue and takes it as fact. But, according to Stanley's most careful biographers, Bierman and McLynn, it is doubtful that anything resembling this conversation took place. Records show that Stanley arrived in Paris some ten days later than he said he did. Eight days' worth of pages from his diary around this time have been torn out. The idea of pursuing Livingstone seems to have come from another official at the New York *Herald*. The first correspondent tapped for this assignment apparently couldn't be reached. Stanley, though, had every reason to inflate his own role as a "gladiator" and Bennett's as a bold editorial genius, because when he published his book, which is dedicated to Bennett, he was still on the *Herald*'s payroll and wanted the paper to finance his next expedition to Africa.

That journey became Stanley's greatest feat of exploration, providing the first European look at most of the Congo River and its vast navigable web of tributaries. Subsequently, he spent five years traveling up and down the river network, building way stations and roads, and basically staking out this enormous territory for King Leopold II. This laid the foundation for the king's brutal, privately owned Congo Free State. During Leopold's forced-labor regime and its immediate aftermath, some demographers estimate, the territory's population was cut in half.

Stanley returned to central Africa one last time, between 1887 and 1890. Curiously, like the famous journey that began his exploring career, this final trip was a quest for a missing white physician. In this case, it was an eccentric German Jew who followed Islamic customs, became known as Emin Pasha, and was appointed governor of the southern province of the Anglo-Egyptian Sudan. He was also putting together a collection of stuffed birds for the British Museum. Emin Pasha had sent word that he was under siege from extremist Islamist rebels and needed help. Stanley jumped at the chance to respond.

Embarrassingly, however, it turned out that, by the time the explorer and his bedraggled vanguard finally reached Emin Pasha, he was no longer eager to be rescued. "For him everything depends on whether he is able to take me along, for only then . . . would his expedition be regarded as totally successful," the governor groused in his diary. Stanley wrote another best-seller about the trip, but this time most of his white subordinates survived, and books and journals by them also appeared. They painted a grim picture: of Stanley exploding in temper tantrums, having a deserter hanged, working porters to death, ordering floggings left and right, and administering some himself. When he felt that the expedition might be attacked, one officer wrote, "Stanley gave the order to burn all the villages [a]round." At the height of the imperial age, however, the revelations about Stanley's brutality did little to tarnish his fame.

Why is a book like Dugard's appearing today? Like everything else, books reflect the spirit in the air. And, after taking some searching and long-overdue looks at race and colonialism in the 1960s and 1970s, we are now living at a time when those in power in Washington see the world as a clash of civilizations and are convinced that their civilization has every right to use force to prevail, in Iraq, Afghanistan, or anywhere else, just as Stanley was convinced that he had every right to burn down African villages that impeded his progress. At this imperial moment, it is not surprising that someone like him is viewed in such a friendly light.

2003

NINE

Heart of Darkness

FICTION OR REPORTAGE?

AT THE BEGINNING OF AUGUST 1890, the steamboat *Roi des Belges*—
King of the Belgians—a 65-foot, boxy, wood-burning stern-wheeler with a
funnel, awning, and pilothouse on its upper deck, began a four-week journey
up the Congo River. At the captain's side was a 32-year-old ship's officer in
training, stocky and black bearded, whose eyes, in some photographs, look as
if they were perpetually narrowed against the tropical sun. The Polish-born
Józef Teodor Konrad Korzeniowski had arrived in the Congo some weeks
earlier, his nautical experience almost entirely limited to the sea. This was his
first trip on Africa's largest river, and his logbook from the voyage is filled
with detailed, businesslike notes about such matters as shoals, sandbars, and
refueling points not shown on the primitive navigational chart: "Lulonga
Passage. . . . NbyE to NNE. On the Port Side: Snags. Soundings in fathoms:
2,2,2,1,1,2,2,2,2. . . ."
   It would be almost a decade before he finally committed to paper a great
many other features of the Congo not shown on the map, and by that time
the world would know him as Joseph Conrad:

> Going up that river was like travelling back to the earliest beginnings of
> the world, when vegetation rioted on the earth and the big trees were kings.
> An empty stream, a great silence, an impenetrable forest. The air was warm,
> thick, heavy, sluggish. There was no joy in the brilliance of sunshine. The long
> stretches of the waterway ran on, deserted, into the gloom of overshadowed
> distances. On silvery sandbanks hippos and alligators sunned themselves side
> by side. The broadening waters flowed through a mob of wooded islands; you
> lost your way on that river as you would in a desert, and butted all day long
> against shoals, trying to find the channel, till you thought yourself bewitched
> and cut off for ever from everything you had known.

The European colonization of the African continent, or the Scramble for Africa, was the greatest land grab in history, and one of the swiftest. In 1870, some 80 percent of Africa south of the Sahara was still under the control of indigenous kings, chiefs, or other rulers. Within thirty-five years, virtually the entire continent, only a few patches excepted, was composed of European colonies or protectorates. Great Britain, France, Germany, Portugal, Spain, and Italy had all seized pieces of what King Leopold II of Belgium—who kept an enormous slice for himself—called "this magnificent African cake." The Scramble for Africa redrew the map, enriched Europe, and left tens of millions of Africans dead. But this history is glaringly absent from the work of first-rank European novelists of the day. It would be as if no major nineteenth-century American writer dealt with slavery or no major twentieth-century German wrote about the Holocaust. Joseph Conrad is a rare and brave exception.

The multilayered richness of *Heart of Darkness* has made it probably the most widely read short novel in English, and certainly the most written about. If the pages of monograph chapters, scholarly articles, conference papers, dissertations, and entire books about *Heart of Darkness* were laid end to end, they would stretch, it seems, the full length of the Congo River and back again.

Several curious tensions run through the book. One is between the way the story is painfully rooted in the six grueling months that Conrad spent in the Congo in 1890, nearly dying from dysentery and malaria, and the manner in which the novel is written, where no place—indeed, almost no person—is even named. Not only the colony of the Congo but even the very continent of Africa is never mentioned. If you look at a map, the shape of the "great river" up which Conrad's alter ego Marlow begins steaming suggests the Congo River—"resembling an immense snake uncoiled, with its head in the sea, its body at rest curving afar over a vast country, and its tail lost in the depths of the land"—but it, too, is never named. The key settings (the Central Station, the Inner Station) and most of the people Marlow meets (the manager, the Accountant, the brickmaker, the helmsman) are similarly without proper names.

This technique, used by other writers since Conrad, is certainly one source of the book's haunting power. We feel that we are reading a parable, a fable, something freighted with mythic overtones. After all, what do the snake and "traveling back to the earliest beginnings of the world" conjure up if not the Garden of Eden? For this is a book about the end of innocence and the discovery of evil. Written on the very eve of the twentieth century, the novel portrays a façade of benevolence and glory underlain by hideous violence and mass death, something that seems to look forward in an uncanny way to the era of Auschwitz and the Gulag.

The brutality of those places was foreshadowed by events in colonial Africa. Hitler's top deputy, Hermann Göring, sentenced to death at Nuremberg for his role in the murder of Europe's Jews, was the son of the colonial governor of German South-West Africa (today's Namibia), where the authorities carried out a deliberate genocide when the Herero people rebelled against German rule. The father of Rudolf Höss, commandant of Auschwitz, served as an army officer in German East Africa (today's Tanzania), scene of another notorious colonial-era massacre. And even as late as the 1950s, the British imprisoned tens of thousands of Kenyans in harsh concentration camps for years in the course of ruthlessly suppressing an anti-colonial revolt. The complete list is far longer.

For many decades, critics and readers in the West usually preferred to look at *Heart of Darkness* only for what it says about the eternal human condition, rather than to consider it also as a portrait of a particular time and place. In several of its transformations into film, it has been moved completely out of Africa. In *El Corazón del Bosque* (The Heart of the Forest), the director Manuel Gutiérrez Aragón transplanted it to Spain after the Spanish Civil War. Francis Ford Coppola moved the story to Vietnam in his *Apocalypse Now*. In part these geographical leaps are testimony to the novel's power and universality. But would we not think it strangely evasive if a director filmed Alexander Solzhenitsyn's *One Day in the Life of Ivan Denisovich* but didn't set it in the Soviet Union, or brought Elie Wiesel's *Night* to the screen but moved the story out of Auschwitz?

· · ·

What, then, was going on in the Congo at the time Conrad went there that Europeans and Americans for so many years afterward preferred not to confront?

The colony in which the unsuspecting and still unpublished writer arrived in 1890 was in the early stages of what would be the bloodiest single chapter of the Scramble for Africa. Orchestrating it was Leopold II, the man whose formal title was the name of Conrad's steamboat, King of the Belgians. Brilliant and charming, ruthless and avaricious, a public relations genius who cloaked his greed in the rhetoric of Christian philanthropy, Leopold was openly frustrated with being king of such a small country. *"Petit pays, petit gens,"* he once said: small country, small-minded people. Moreover, he reigned at a time when most European monarchs were rapidly losing power to the electorate. And so he wanted a colony where he could rule supreme. The Belgian cabinet was not interested, but that suited Leopold perfectly: he set off to acquire his own.

To begin with, the king hired the famous explorer Henry Morton Stanley to navigate and reconnoiter the Congo River and its wide web of tributaries for him. Next, he successfully lobbied first the United States and then all the major nations of Europe into recognizing the Congo—a territory more than seventy times the size of Belgium—as belonging to him personally. He proclaimed himself its "King-Sovereign" in 1885. It was the world's only privately owned colony.

In the early years of the Congo Free State, as Leopold misleadingly christened his new domain, the main commodity he coveted was ivory. Elephant tusks were highly prized because they could be easily carved into a wide variety of shapes: piano keys, statuettes, jewelry, false teeth, and more. The king ordered a network of ivory-gathering posts set up along the colony's riverbanks, and men who wanted to make their fortunes flocked to the Congo. These adventurers were often eager not just for riches but for combat. Much of the ivory was seized at gunpoint, and as poorly armed Congolese fought back against the foreigners, there were countless rebellions to put down. For many a young European or American, going to the Congo combined the thrills of joining both a gold rush and the French Foreign Legion.

Like much of the colonization of Africa, the entire ivory-gathering system was based on forced labor. It was forced laborers who carried the white men's supplies into the interior on their backs; bargeloads of forced laborers, pulled behind steamboats, chopped the wood that fueled their boilers; and Congolese conscripts were dragooned into the ranks of the king's private army. Conrad recognized Leopold's forced labor system for what it was. Soon after Marlow, the narrator of *Heart of Darkness,* arrives in the territory, he sees six workers on a railroad construction crew; they "all were connected together with a chain whose bights swung between them, rhythmically clinking." Other workers, exhausted by their labor, have crawled into a grove of trees to die.

Although ivory remained valuable, wild rubber would soon supplant it as the colony's most lucrative treasure. In the years after Conrad's visit, the death toll of this forced labor system would swell to unimaginable proportions. But Conrad saw the beginning of this enormous human catastrophe, and he saw it with piercing clarity.

. . .

The writer's African odyssey began weeks before he was able to board the *Roi des Belges*. He first set foot in the territory on June 12, 1890, when, following the long voyage from Europe, he disembarked just inland from where the "great river" pours its enormous torrent of water—in volume second only to that of the Amazon—into the Atlantic. Soon afterward, he set off, accompanied by one other white man and a caravan of thirty-one porters, on the arduous 230-mile trek around the succession of rapids that the Congo River thunders down on the last part of its journey from the central African plateau to the ocean. It was over this same dirt road, several years previously, that the *Roi des Belges* itself, broken down into more than 250 pieces, had been carried around the rapids on the backs of exhausted porters, or, in the case of heavier pieces of machinery, placed on carriages that each required several hundred men to pull it uphill.

On this caravan route Conrad first recorded signs of the immense violence that underlay the colony's operations. In his diary on July 3, he noted, "Met an off[ic]er of the State inspecting; a few minutes afterwards saw at a camp[in] g place the dead body of a Backongo. Shot? Horrid smell." The following day: "Saw another dead body lying by the path." And on July 29: "On the road today passed a skeleton tied up to a post."

After more than a month of walking, in shaky health, he arrived at the small trading post of Kinshasa; inland from here, it was clear sailing for steamboats for a thousand miles upstream. A day later Conrad was aboard the fifteen-ton *Roi des Belges*. It passed only a half dozen other such vessels during its month of traveling upstream. All day long the boat steamed, the smoke from its boiler leaving a trail in the air, its paddles beating the water of a river that, much of the time, was several miles wide. Typically these boats would travel by daylight and then tie up for the night, either at one of the militarized ivory-gathering posts, where firewood for the boiler could be loaded, or just at a spot on the riverbank where the crew of Congolese woodcutters could go into the rainforest and chop trees for the next day's fuel.

Finally, the steamer reached Stanley Falls, today the sprawling, decrepit city of Kisangani but then a small settlement of ivory warehouses, a jail, military barracks, a powder magazine, and offices for the colonial officials who controlled the eastern part of the colony. A week later, Conrad and the *Roi des Belges* headed back downstream—with the current the voyage would only take some two weeks—carrying cargo and a 27-year-old Frenchman, Georges Antoine Klein, a company agent who was gravely ill. Klein died on board a few days before the steamer's journey ended, a detail echoed in *Heart of Darkness*.

Once he was back in Kinshasa, some bitter disappointments punctured Conrad's Congo dreams. He had hit it off badly with a key official and found that he was not slated to take part, as he had been hoping, in an exploring expedition up one of the Congo River's major tributaries, the Kasai. The venality and greed of the ivory hunters horrified him. And the malaria and dysentery he had been fighting for weeks grew worse, landing him in a primitive hospital at a Protestant mission station where he apparently had to endure some proselytizing. "He is a gentlemanly fellow," the American Presbyterian missionary Samuel Lapsley wrote in his diary. "An English [New] Testament on his table furnishes a handle I hope to use on him." Europeans still had few effective medicines for most tropical diseases, and roughly a third of the white men who came to the Congo in this era died there. Such statistics were kept concealed by King Leopold II, but Conrad saw Klein die and surely heard of many other such deaths. Finally, in October 1890, he canceled his three-year contract and abandoned his African venture. On the long return trip around the lower river's rapids, his illness was at its worst, and he had to be carried by porters. He arrived back in Europe early the next year, his health permanently weakened and his view of humanity forever darkened.

. . .

How much of what he portrayed in *Heart of Darkness* was based on Conrad's actual experience? For most of the century after the book was written, the implicit answer from critics was: not much, except for the superficial details of the steamboat journey up- and downriver. They analyzed the novel in terms of Freud, Jung, and Nietzsche, of patriarchy and Gnosticism, of postmodernism and poststructuralism. Monographs and Ph.D. theses poured forth with titles like "The Eye and the Gaze in 'Heart of Darkness': A Symptomological Reading." By contrast, Conrad himself wrote, "'Heart of Darkness' is experience . . . pushed a little (and only very little) beyond the actual facts of the case."

He is right, and we miss much if we look at the novel only as a work of imaginative literature. "The actual facts of the case" he portrays show the Scramble for Africa at its most naked. Consider the figure at the book's center, Mr. Kurtz. Kurtz is sketched with only few bold strokes, but he has become our time's most famous literary villain: the lone white man with his dreams of culture and grandeur, his great hoard of ivory, and his barbarous fiefdom carved out of the jungle.

No doubt Conrad drew part of Kurtz from deep within himself; that is what gives the reader a tinge of uneasy empathy with Kurtz's boundless ambition and his vision of himself as the apostle of "the cause of progress" among awestruck savages. But Conrad clearly also took aspects of Kurtz from various men whom he encountered or heard about in the Congo.

Look, for instance, at the searing scene in which Marlow gazes from the steamboat at what he first thinks are ornamental knobs atop the fence posts near Mr. Kurtz's house. But through his binoculars he then sees that each is a human head, "black, dried, sunken, with closed eyelids." Biographers long talked of Kurtz's collection of severed heads as a brilliant example of Conrad's phantasmagoric imagination; one, Norman Sherry, even described it as possibly a "macabre transference" by Conrad of a well-known episode when an aggressive white ivory-seeker in the Congo was beheaded by African rivals.

But no macabre transference was necessary: a number of white men in the colony at this time collected African heads and openly bragged about it. One, Guillaume Van Kerckhoven, a dashing, mustachioed Belgian and an officer of Leopold's African army, told a fellow steamboat passenger in 1887 that he paid his black soldiers the equivalent of two and halfpence in British money for every rebel head they brought him after a battle in order to "stimulate their prowess in the face of the enemy." Conrad knew the man to whom Van Kerckhoven made this boast.

Another notorious Belgian head collector was an officer named Leon Fiévez. To a white government agent who visited his post in 1894, Fiévez explained that when local Africans failed to supply his troops with food, "I made war against them. One example was enough: a hundred heads cut off, and there have been plenty of supplies at the station ever since. My goal is ultimately humanitarian. I killed a hundred people, but that allowed five hundred others to live."

We do not know if Fiévez had started these " humanitarian" practices in 1890, but Conrad may have met him that year, for Fiévez had just taken command of the strategic, heavily fortified post of Basoko, a likely refueling and overnight stop for the *Roi des Belges* on its way up and down the river. Nor was it only Belgians who collected heads. One British explorer-adventurer in the Congo, part of an expedition that received a huge amount of press coverage, in 1887 packed an African's head in a box of salt and sent it to his Piccadilly taxidermist to be stuffed and mounted.

The most striking head-collector of all, with an eerie resemblance to Mr. Kurtz on several other counts as well, was a brusque-looking Congo state official named Léon Rom, whose combat exploits earned him various medals and write-ups in Belgian colonial-heroic literature of the day. When commander of the Stanley Falls station a few years after Conrad was there, Rom kept a gallows permanently erected in front of his headquarters. A British journalist who passed through in 1895 described, in the widely read *Century Magazine,* a punitive expedition Rom had mounted against African rebels: "Many women and children were taken, and twenty-one heads were brought to the falls, and have been used by Captain Rom as a decoration round a flowerbed in front of his house!"

In addition, both the real-life Rom and the fictional Kurtz carried out their looting amid pretensions to high culture. In the novel, Mr. Kurtz is an intellectual, "an emissary of . . . science and progress." Rom also had scientific ambitions: he brought many butterfly specimens back to Europe and was elected a member of the Royal Belgian Entomological Society. Furthermore, Mr. Kurtz is an artist—the painter of "a small sketch in oils" of a woman carrying a torch, which hangs on the wall of the Central Station. Léon Rom, when he was not collecting butterflies or human heads, painted in oils as well. The five examples of his work which can be found today in the vaults of a Belgian museum include a portrait, rendered with some skill, of a bare-chested young African woman, arching her back seductively as one strand of a necklace falls between her breasts. One cannot help thinking of the "barbarous and superb woman" of the novel, Mr. Kurtz's mistress.

Mr. Kurtz is also an author. Among other things, he writes a seventeen-page report—"vibrating with eloquence. . . . a beautiful piece of writing"—to the International Society for the Suppression of Savage Customs. Although Conrad was probably unaware of it, in 1899, the same year that *Heart of Darkness* first appeared as a magazine serial, Léon Rom, too, published a report on savage customs. It was a jaunty, arrogant, and sweepingly superficial little book called *Le Négre du Congo.* There are short chapters on "Le

Négre en Général," the black woman, food, pets, native medicine, and many pages about a particular enthusiasm of Rom's—hunting. Of "the black race," Rom says, "its feelings are coarse, its passions rough, its instincts brutish, and, in addition, it is proud and vain. . . . The black man has no idea of time, and, questioned on that subject by a European, he generally responds with something stupid."

One final parallel: Mr. Kurtz succeeds in "getting himself adored" by the Africans of the Inner Station. Chiefs crawl on the ground before him, the blacks obey him with slavish devotion, and from them he has chosen the "barbarous and superb woman" as his bedmate. In 1895, a disapproving Belgian lieutenant confided to his diary a similar portrait of a fellow officer:

> He makes his agents starve while he gives provisions in abundance to the black women of his harem. . . . He got into his dress uniform at his house, brought together his women, picked up some piece of paper and pretended to read to them that the king had named him the big chief and that the other whites of the station were only small fry. . . . He gave 50 lashes to a poor little negress because she wouldn't be his mistress, then he *gave* her to a soldier.

Significantly, the diarist introduces his account by saying, This man wants to play the role of a second Rom.

On August 2, 1890, Conrad and Rom may have met. About five miles before reaching the small riverside post of Kinshasa, where the *Roi des Belges* was waiting, Conrad and his caravan of porters passed through the neighboring post of Leopoldville. All told, only about twenty white men were living in these two places, each of which—long before they were both absorbed into the giant metropolis today called Kinshasa—was just a scattering of thatch-roofed buildings. Léon Rom was then station chief at Leopoldville. His diary, which in a neat, almost calligraphic hand records any raid or campaign that could win him another medal, shows no expedition away from the post that day. If he was on hand, he certainly would have greeted any caravan with white newcomers, for these arrived only a few times a month. Conrad spoke near-perfect French, so they would have had a language in common.

Did Conrad meet Rom—or Fiévez or Van Kerckhoven? Did Rom tell him about his scientific, artistic, and literary ambitions, or did Conrad hear of these from others? Did Conrad see one of Rom's paintings on the wall, as Marlow does one of Kurtz's? We will never know. But whether specific memories provided building blocks for the character of Mr. Kurtz or whether

Conrad simply worked on intuition, the novel captures its place and time with uncanny accuracy.

. . .

Heart of Darkness is not always an easy book to read. At times the voice of Marlow seems too extravagant, and too vague. Marlow's portrayal of Kurtz's appalling brutality seems at odds with his repeated professions of loyalty to the man. Parades of ponderous adjectives—inexorable, unspeakable, unfathomable—rumble past relentlessly. "Sentence after sentence," wrote the novelist E. M. Forster, "discharges its smoke screen into our abashed eyes." The poet John Masefield found the novel to have "too much cobweb."

What accounts for this? When he wrote the book, Conrad was clearly wrestling painfully with something deep within himself. Before his six months in Africa, he once told his friend the critic Edward Garnett, he had had "not a thought in his head." But what he found in the Congo—dead bodies strewn about; the skeleton tied up to a post; workers in chains; an entire economy founded on the whip, the gun, and forced labor—was, he wrote in an essay published only a few months before he died, "the vilest scramble for loot that ever disfigured the history of human conscience." Some of his angst may have stemmed from embarrassment and guilt about his own youthful naïveté. He had hoped for a glamorous job skippering a steamboat on an exploring voyage. But, as his novel says of Kurtz, his time in the Congo may have "whispered to him things about himself which he did not know."

But the whispering was complicated, for there was a political struggle going on in Conrad's soul, although he never articulated it and never would have used that word to describe it. On one hand, he was writing the most scathing portrait of colonialism in all of European literature. No one who reads *Heart of Darkness* can ever again imagine the colonizers of central Africa as benevolent. "To tear treasure out of the bowels of the land was their desire," Marlow says, "with no more moral purpose at the back of it than there is in burglars breaking into a safe." Nor does Conrad imply that there is anything uniquely Belgian about this burglary. Fortune-seekers in the Congo came from throughout the Western world: "All Europe contributed to the making of Kurtz."

What gave Conrad, almost alone among the novelists of his time, the ability to see the arrogance and theft at the heart of imperialism? And to see that Leopold's much-promoted civilizing mission was founded on forced labor? Much of it surely had to do with the fact that he himself knew what it was like to live in conquered territory. He had been born Polish, but throughout the nineteenth century the land that is Poland today was divided among three neighboring empires, Austria-Hungary, Prussia, and Russia. The latter, where most of the writer's family lived, was the most repressive; when Conrad was three, Cossacks charged into churches to break up memorial services for a Polish nationalist hero. Furthermore, for the first few years of his life, tens of millions of peasants in the Russian Empire were the equivalent of slave laborers: serfs.

Conrad's poet father, Apollo Korzeniowski, was a Polish nationalist and, somewhat hazily, an opponent of serfdom, although both he and his wife came from the class of country gentry that had sometimes owned serfs. For his nationalist activities, Apollo was thrown into a harsh Warsaw prison and then exiled to northern Russia. His wife and four-year-old boy went with him, and their time in the frigid climate exacerbated the tuberculosis that would kill her when Conrad was only seven. Apollo died a few years later, and his funeral procession, in Austrian-occupied Kraków, turned into a huge demonstration of Polish nationalism. Although nothing in Conrad's writing makes any comparison between Poland and Africa, should we be surprised that this boy who grew up among prison veterans in exile, talk of serfdom, and the news of relatives killed in uprisings, was ready to distrust imperial conquerors who claimed they had the right to rule or enslave other peoples?

Paradoxically, in everything else about his politics, Conrad was deeply conservative. He hated labor unions. He had no use for the socialist idealism in which so many British intellectuals—including several close friends—had great faith. And above all, he was profoundly loyal to his adoptive country, Britain, which, of course, was the greatest colonial power of them all. Early on in the novel, when Marlow sees a map of Africa dominated by the British Empire's red and feels the color is "good to see at any time, because one knows that some real work is done" he is speaking for his creator. Indeed, Conrad once declared in a letter that "liberty . . . can only be found under the English flag all over the world."

Similarly, despite his searing portrayal of white greed, Conrad was very much a man of his own imperial time when it came to race. The Africans in this novel barely ever even speak. Instead they grunt, they chant, they produce a "drone of weird incantations" and a "wild and passionate uproar," they spout "strings of amazing words that resembled no sounds of human language ... like the responses of some satanic litany." *Heart of Darkness* has come in for some attacks in recent years for its racism, most notably from the distinguished Nigerian novelist Chinua Achebe. Yet there is even a contradiction within this contradiction, because at the same time as Conrad's narrator flaunts these racial stereotypes, calling the Africans of his crew "cannibals," he says, "They were men one could work with, and I am grateful to them." And he speaks of the "subtle bond," a "distant kinship" he felt with his black helmsman.

One final paradox: It was nearly a decade between Conrad's trip up the Congo River, when he saw so clearly the lust for quick riches of his fellow white men, and the time when he finally got that experience onto paper in this novel. In the interim, the novelist made a disastrous try at gaining quick riches himself. Although the details remain shadowy, he apparently invested and lost almost all his savings in South African gold mining shares—a loss all the more embarrassing because it came just as he got married and hoped to start a family. The South African gold rush of the late 1880s and '90s was, like the simultaneous ivory and rubber boom in the Congo, one of the great bonanzas of the Scramble for Africa. Tens of thousands of miners flocked to Johannesburg from all over the world—as did merchants, pimps, and prostitutes hoping to make money from them. Mine owners amassed huge fortunes. Meanwhile, the hardest, most dangerous and lowest-paid manual labor underground was done by Africans. Pushed off their land and desperate for money to survive, they died by the thousands in mining accidents, were forced to leave their families behind in distant rural areas, and were deliberately provided with few recreation facilities except drinking places, which recycled much of their meager earnings back to mine owners, several of whom owned the major distillery. How much of all this was Conrad aware of? How did he feel about his failed attempt to cash in on the gold rush? We will never know, but this may be yet another of those internal struggles which in the end added depth to an extraordinary book.

1998, 2012

TEN

On the Campaign Trail with Nelson Mandela

IN A HUGE EXHIBITION SHED the size of an aircraft hangar at the Pretoria fairgrounds, Nelson Mandela has arrived before most of his audience. This is not unusual in South Africa's first, tumultuous democratic election campaign. Few black South Africans have cars, and train routes are designed to move them between their workplaces and the distant townships where they have been forced to live, not to sites like this one. And so today's audience is being bused in, mostly in packed minivan taxis.

As the hall begins to fill, Mandela strolls about, smiling, joking, chatting, and shaking hands with supporters and the few journalists on hand. He wears a loose blue shirt with a white floral pattern, loafers, and dark red socks. Except for hearing aids in both ears, he looks younger and healthier than a 75-year-old who has spent more than twenty-seven years in prison. He stands erect. There is a majesty about him, but of a relaxed, not august, kind. Today he seems clearly buoyed by the electric ripple of excitement that follows him as he walks slowly through the crowd.

The African National Congress (ANC) is waging this historic campaign in alliance with the South African Communist Party (SACP) and the Congress of South African Trade Unions (COSATU), which has organized today's events. Several thousand of COSATU's more than 1.3 million members are filing into the hall this morning, singing, chanting, and doing the *toyi-toyi*, the shuffle-dance long associated with black protest gatherings. Close to 50 percent of South Africa's industrial and commercial work force is unionized—a figure many times the percentage in the United States. The unions have won major victories despite years of harassment and arrests of union leaders and firebombings of union offices. Today's audience includes metal workers, transport workers, and local government employees. Some of the latter have been bused in from Bophuthatswana, a nearby black "homeland," where, to the ANC's great delight, the longtime dictator installed by the apartheid regime, Lucas Mangope, has just been toppled by a popular revolt. "Bop," as it's called, is now officially part of South Africa again and will vote largely for the ANC.

The audience is almost entirely African. But there is an occasional white face in this black sea. Ever since South African blacks first won the right to organize trade unions some fifteen years ago, they have employed many whites as office staff. That hundreds of young white radicals, many of them Jewish, have been able to spend their lives working for black unions is one piece of evidence for the liberation movement's remarkable transcendence of racial feeling.

The lineup on the speaker's platform is interracial. Four others are sharing the stage with Mandela today. Two are African: Tokyo Sexwale, a rising young star in the ANC who is a candidate for regional premier of the country's industrial heartland around Johannesburg and Pretoria; and Charles Nqakula, general secretary of the SACP. One, Geraldine Fraser, is Coloured (mixed race); and one is a white labor economist wearing a bright red baseball cap, Alec Erwin. Fraser and Erwin are both running for the national parliament. Like many ANC candidates, both are also members of the SACP.

The ANC owes some of its nonracist tradition to its longtime links with the SACP, which has always been determined to see the world in terms of class rather than race; in Africa, promoting that viewpoint is usually uphill work. The Communist Party was one of the first political organizations in South Africa open to all races. Then came forty years underground and in exile until it was legalized, along with the ANC, in early 1990. But the Party is a paradox. Despite the bravery and nonracism of many of its leaders, for nearly three quarters of a century they have loyally, uncritically followed every twist and turn of policy laid down by Moscow. They backed every Soviet intervention, from East Germany to Hungary to Czechoslovakia to Afghanistan, until there was no Soviet Union to back any more.

What, then, does it mean today that many top ANC leaders are also Party members? The ruling National Party of State President F. W. de Klerk, which thunders endlessly about this in its propaganda, would have you believe it is all very sinister. But in the end, it may not mean much at all. When communist spokespeople appear on television in this campaign they wax as enthusiastic as everybody else about Christianity, tolerance, and the need for foreign investment. They have little choice. The Party still theoretically favors democratic socialism farther down the road. But that prospect, however appealing to many, is clearly a receding one in a world economy increasingly dominated by multinational corporations.

By now the Pretoria fairgrounds hall has filled with several thousand people. Although more are still arriving, the program begins. Today's event is what's called a "worker's forum": union members file up to two microphones and ask questions. After half a dozen or so, one speaker gets up and answers them. Then the process repeats.

This morning, as at several similar events later in the day, some questions come in English, some in Tswana or Sotho, and one or two in Afrikaans—the home language of most Coloured South Africans:

"How are we going to get that money of ours?" (This is from a Bophuthatswana municipal worker worried that the deposed dictator Mangope has robbed pension funds.)

"Are the taxes we are paying now going to the ANC or to the National Party?"

"Will the ANC cater for the nurses?" (This from a woman in a nurse's uniform.)

"What about affirmative action?" (This is from a Coloured worker: the National Party has been whipping up fears that affirmative action means Africans will be jumped ahead on the job ladder.)

"Will there be maternity leave . . . "

" . . . On full pay? For how long?"

"What will they do with the statue of Andries Pretorius?" (Pretorius was the Boer leader who defeated the Zulus at the pivotal Battle of Blood River in 1838, setting the stage for white rule of what would become South Africa. The new post-apartheid country is in for a long series of tussles over statues, monuments, and holidays, many of which commemorate similar victories.)

"How is the land going to be shared among the rightful owners and the invaders of it?"

For about an hour the four speakers other than Mandela take turns answering. The questioners are always addressed as "Comrade," which is sometimes shortened to "Com," or, for an older woman, "Com-momma." Some answers are colorful and specific. Alec Erwin assures the Bophuthatswana worker, "If you've paid pension money into any government fund, that will be secured. Even if we have to go and take it from Mangope's pocket!" But most answers follow the rule of politics the world over: if you're about to win an election, don't put your foot in your mouth. "Comrades, that matter will be reviewed!" "Affirmative action will not be at the expense of dropping standards!" And so on. Asked about socialism, Charles Nqakula promises that his Communist Party will "defend the working class"; asked about redistributing wealth through taxes, he says, "We will look into the question."

By now the hall is filled with perhaps five thousand people. It is time for Mandela. The audience greets him with a song and a massive foot-stomping ovation. Everyone is dressed in work clothes, except for one man in a Zulu warrior outfit with club, spear, feathers, and a sort of fur skirt who bursts out of the crowd and prances exuberantly up and down. He carries a small satchel full of coins and knick-knacks, and in what seems to be a traditional gesture of homage he spills the contents on the floor and lays down his club and spear near Mandela's feet.

Mandela speaks slowly and solemnly and in no way talks down to his audience. He reviews the situation in Bophuthatswana and then sharply condemns the crowds who looted shops during the recent turmoil there. "We understand that people are poor and the temptation is there. But you don't behave like that! We appeal to our people in Bophuthatswana to respect the property of others."

He then talks about a sense of "insecurity among whites, Coloureds, and Indians. There are some people, Africans, moving from car to car in trains, saying to members of the Coloured community, 'Your time is up!' This is something extremely dangerous. We condemn this in the strongest possible terms."

Finally, he also condemns ANC supporters who have been harassing National Party candidates. "Don't disrupt meetings of any party! Mr. de Klerk is going to Soweto, and I'm going to request the deputy president of the ANC, Walter Sisulu, to ensure that Mr. de Klerk does not encounter any problems. We are all fellow South Africans! In the course of this campaign, we should not open up wounds that would be hard to heal."

All this moderation is not what these thousands of labor unionists have traveled for hours sardined into minivans to hear, and their applause is more polite than enthusiastic. But Mandela segues smoothly into what pleases the crowd more:

"We want you to give de Klerk a chance to put forth his policies. Because unless you do, people will not see that he has no policies! Why does the National Party say now they'll create a better life for you? What have they been doing for these last forty-five years?"

He runs through the basic promises in the ANC election manifesto. They are all very down-to-earth. "Our task is to get each and every one a job!" Schoolbooks will be free. Education will be free and compulsory for the first ten years. "Any parent who fails to send his or her child to school in those first ten years, we will lock him or her up!" This line draws wild applause, perhaps because it is an indirect attack on the black teenage gangs who terrorize townships.

He speaks of electricity, clinics, hospitals, running water, of the seven million people who now live in squatter camps, and of the ANC's plan to build a million new homes for them. "We want flush toilets. We want to pave the roads in our country. We want proper sports stadiums. These things cannot be achieved overnight. You must be patient."

Finally, as happens at every event during this campaign, Mandela methodically goes through the voting procedure, since voting will be a new experience for almost everyone in this hall. Go to the first table, show your ID, get the ballot for the national parliament, mark it in private. Do this all over again for the ballot where you choose provincial legislators. And he reviews what to look for on the ballot itself. Because more than half of South Africa's new voters are illiterate, each party line will also show a logo and a photo of the party leader. "Look for a handsome face!" he says, pointing to his own, and the crowd roars.

. . .

Mandela's small entourage includes surprisingly few security men—half a dozen at most. As his motorcade leaves the Pretoria showgrounds and speeds out of the city, cars on side streets are held up by traffic police, both black and white. The white ones are expressionless behind sunglasses. The black ones grin and salute.

The next stop, an hour east, in the veld beyond Pretoria, is the Premier diamond mine. The world's largest diamond, the 3,106-carat Cullinan, was found here in 1905. Premier is owned by the Anglo American–De Beers conglomerate, the corporate giant that controls, depending on how you calculate it, between 30 and 50 percent of the value of companies traded on the Johannesburg Stock Exchange. Anglo/De Beers, *Business Week* once wrote, "looms larger in its home economy than does any other company in any country."

This corporate empire owns businesses of every sort, but gold and diamond mining is its core. These mines are worked by black migrant laborers;

if there is one thing in South Africa that cries out for change more than anything else, it is the migrant labor system, which forcibly separates some two million men from their families for most of the year, for all of their working lives.

Waiting to hear Mandela speak, close to a thousand miners are sitting or standing on a hillside next to the grim barracks, called "hostels," where they live. The hostels are lined up in drab gray rows, their prisonlike look reinforced by an architectural quirk that seems deliberately sadistic: the only windows are above head level, too high to look out of. (You see exactly the same thing in the floor of servants' quarters that sits atop many a high-rise apartment building in the white residential areas of Johannesburg.) On the hillside beside the barracks, some miners have been sleeping all night so as to be sure of a place from which they can see Mandela. Waiting for his arrival, they blow whistles, dance, and sing in the broiling sun. As they hear his motorcade approaching, several hundred of them, in orange safety helmets and orange jumpsuits, race down the road to meet his car and escort it into the mining compound. ANC flags flutter from their helmets.

When the cheers subside and Mandela takes his place before the microphone, he tells them, "I arrived in Johannesburg in 1941 and my first job was in the mines!" He was a security guard: "I had a khaki outfit! Big boots! I had a whistle. And I had a knobkerrie [a club]." Then, realizing that few in his audience know much English, he switches to his native Xhosa. But you can tell when he gets to the part about voting for the ballot line with the handsome face, for he points to his own, smiles, and the miners roar. He ends in English: "The National Party is a mouse. We are the elephant!"

Scattered throughout the country in these weeks leading up to its first democratic election are signs that this is an event not for South Africa alone: reporters from around the globe, observers from the United Nations in blue baseball caps, observers with the European Union's circle of gold stars on their shirts or jackets, and today, as we visit the diamond mine, several Australian mine workers in union T-shirts. They scramble to get a good vantage point to take photographs as Mandela speaks. The black miners here, far out on the veld, like everyone else in South Africa, can see that the whole world is watching.

This hillside, however, is not the only stop Mandela's caravan makes at the Premier mine. Another is perhaps more revealing. For lunch, the party goes to the mine's guesthouse, a luxurious, carpeted building with a lounge, dining room, patio, and bar. Its walls are hung with photos of mustachioed white faces from the turn of the century onward, all of them past Premier executives. There are also group portraits like "Chairman and Mine Staff, June 1926"—white men in suits and ties, lined up, seated and standing on a columned portico.

At the entrance of the guesthouse, white mine executives wait to meet Mandela and his party. He introduces those with him, drawing out Charles Nqakula's title with obvious pleasure, "General Secretary of the . . . South . . . African . . . Communist . . . Party!" The executives smile and shake hands with Mandela's group, and then they all enter the dining room together.

The press and lower-ranking members of today's campaign team must make do with hors d'oeuvres in the bar. But from there we can see through the door into the dining room. At Table No. 1 are seated Mandela, Nqakula, the manager of the Premier Mine, and Nicky Oppenheimer, deputy chair of De Beers and heir apparent to control the entire Anglo/De Beers empire, which was founded by his grandfather.

What are they talking about at Table No. 1? The conversation looks convivial and lasts more than an hour. My guess is that the subject is less likely to be politics than this week's cricket match between South Africa and Australia. For the basic political agreement has already been made. And in a way, this Grand Bargain of South African politics, which has made this first free election possible, has been as much between the ANC and corporate giants like Anglo/De Beers as between the ANC and the National Party government.

The first signal that a bargain would be possible came more than eight years ago. Mandela and the other long-imprisoned top ANC leaders were still behind bars. South Africa was at war in Angola, in Namibia, and at home. Black townships were in revolt, suspected informers were being burned alive, soldiers shot at crowds from armored cars with high V-shaped hulls built to deflect land mine blasts. Police death squads roamed the country at night.

South Africa's largest corporations had had enough. The endless conflict and the growing international boycotts and embargoes were bad for business. The opening move in the chess game that led to the Grand Bargain came on September 13, 1985. Half a dozen of the country's top white businessmen, including the chairman of the Anglo American Corporation, climbed into an Anglo corporate jet and flew to Lusaka, Zambia. There they spent a day having a much-photographed meeting with the leadership of the exiled wing of the African National Congress. The one-day jaunt was a message from business to the South African government: boys, you need to make a deal.

The Grand Bargain took years more to come into being—years of much bloodshed and of long behind-the-scenes negotiations. Three things speeded up the process. One was the accession to power in 1989 of President F. W. de Klerk, the shrewdest politician on the continent, a canny pragmatist who understood that a deal had to be made, and the sooner the better.

The second key event was the collapse of the Soviet Union. This ensured that a post-apartheid South Africa had to stay part of the Western economic system. It could never count on being heavily subsidized by Moscow, as Cuba did for three decades, and go its own way.

The third factor was that South Africa's business elite and its white government took a close look into the rest of the continent. And they realized that whites could still make as much money as ever under black rule.

And so South Africa's Grand Bargain gradually fell into place: blacks got the vote; whites kept their control of the economy. This arrangement is, in part, spelled out very explicitly in the country's transition-period constitution. An ANC-dominated government, for example, will still have to pay the pensions of the old regime's civil servants, hanging judges and police torturers included. Still more important are the constitution's tough clauses entrenching property rights. These provisions will make any redistribution of commercial and industrial wealth (whites own some 95 percent) or land (whites own more than 85 percent) agonizingly, glacially slow.

But much of the Grand Bargain doesn't need to be spelled out. Circumstances enforce it. The ANC seldom talks now about nationalizing the country's vast mineral deposits, as it did until recently, or about nationalizing much of anything, in fact. Such talk means capital flight, mass white emigration, no foreign investment, no help from the World Bank or the International Monetary Fund. And all of that means massive job losses for black South Africa, which already suffers from 50 percent unemployment. Jobs come first. And, sadly, the liberation movement's old, inspiring vision— land to those who till it, factories to those who work in them, the riches under the soil to all—will be put aside, perhaps for decades, perhaps forever.

Maybe Nelson Mandela and Nicky Oppenheimer are talking about all this in the Premier mine's guesthouse dining room, more likely not. As they are finishing their meal, a public relations man for De Beers wanders around the outer room, distributing a press release to the small gaggle of reporters. Its contents underscore the economic realities behind the Grand Bargain. Diamond sales are on the rise, the release says. Overall annual profits to shareholders of De Beers and its European holding company have gone up nearly 20 percent, to $595 million. Taxes took less than $200 million. The market value of all De Beers' assets is more than $9 billion. It's a measure of the confidence the white South African business world has in retaining its full power that the company can so routinely trumpet news of such high profits and low tax payments just weeks before this historic election. The press release doesn't add that the assets of South Africa's Anglo/De Beers group as a whole are worth more than the annual gross domestic product of the other nine nations of southern Africa combined.

This concentrated corporate might is what Nelson Mandela and his soon to be victorious ANC will be up against. Matching this harsh reality with the millenarian hopes raised over seventy years of struggle will be the ANC's most painful task. It is why, when he spoke earlier today, Mandela warned against unrealistic expectations and talked about schoolbooks, paved streets, clinics, and flush toilets. All of today's ANC leaders share the awareness of the great gap between the transformational dream of the century's oldest liberation movement and the tight constraints they will face the morning after the election. And they worry about it.

. . .

The same issue arose again, in a very different setting, a few days after Mandela's visit to the Premier mine. At a film festival in Cape Town, the German director Margarethe von Trotta showed her excellent 1986 feature film *Rosa Luxemburg*. Afterward she took questions from a small multiracial audience.

One man rose to say that he had been deeply moved by the film. Luxemburg's vision of social justice, her lonely fight against the madness of the First World War, had been such a noble and uncompromising one, he said. Was it still possible in the world today? Could such hopes of social transformation still exist? Had the ANC, in its long negotiations with the government, made too many compromises, negotiated away too many dreams?

What made these words so poignant was that everyone in the theater knew that the speaker was one of the ANC's key negotiators. His face, pitted with shrapnel wounds, is familiar to millions of South Africans. Albie Sachs is a veteran white anti-apartheid campaigner who spent many months in solitary confinement. When he then went to work for the ANC in exile in Mozambique, South African agents tracked him down and planted the car bomb that cost Sachs his right hand and forearm and the sight of one eye. A lawyer, he is now studying constitutions around the world for the ANC. He will be deeply involved in writing a new one for South Africa after the April elections.*

Sachs spoke from the heart. And there are no easy answers to his questions. Except, perhaps, to say that today we live in a world of small steps. Paved streets, free schoolbooks, and flush toilets are not Rosa Luxemburg's dreamed-of socialist commonwealth. But if the ANC can deliver them, it will touch the lives of millions. To those who've never had them before, it is out of such things, and of people's belief in their right to have them, that democracies are made. And on that foundation, so harshly denied to most South Africans until now, much more can be built.

1994

---

* Later in the year, he was appointed a justice of the Constitutional Court, the country's highest court.

India

FIGURE 4. Coffeehouse designed by Laurie Baker, Trivandrum, India.

ELEVEN

India's American Imports

A FEW DAYS AFTER ARRIVING in India for the first time, I went to see a big Hindi-language hit movie called *Dil To Pagal Hai*, "The Heart Is Crazy." The film was showing in a small, desperately poor town in the northern state of Rajasthan. Outside the theater, hundreds of people were arriving on foot, on bicycles, in pedicabs, on motor scooters carrying three or four men each, on packed carts drawn by camels or oxen with painted horns, and on wagons towed by farm tractors.

Parts of the film's plot are loosely borrowed from *A Chorus Line*. The director of a musical is loved by a woman in his troupe but he is attracted to someone else: the star of his new show. Various subplots, dance numbers, and smoldering glances fluff things out to several hours. In the end the director gets the new star and the other woman pairs up with the new star's old fiancé, so everyone lives happily ever after. But the curious thing about this film was that although it was made in India, and the producer, director, and actors were all Indian, and the audience and theater could not have been more Indian, there was, on the surface, little Indian about what was on the screen. The film showed virtually no Indian clothing, food, signs, furniture, or anything else.

There were no street scenes in India. There were, however, scenes in a European Disneyland-like amusement park, and in London, where one character is making his fortune. When he thinks he has won his woman, he makes the victorious downward jerk of the clenched fist that American pro athletes make after scoring a basket or touchdown. Interior shots showed a modern airport, film studios, a Japanese restaurant, and a luxurious hospital with private rooms. The musical numbers were American disco, not Indian. The stars used a conspicuously displayed variety of cell phones and new cars.

They sipped bottles of mineral water, wore blue jeans, leotards, and mini-skirts and drank copious amounts of Pepsi—the company must have paid hefty product placement fees. But the West itself, paying no fee, was the real product placement, from the California-sleek furnishings of the characters' homes to the distinctly unIndian rolling green pastures of the hero's imag-ined dream landscape, through which the heroine runs in a gauzy white dress. So: an Indian film without India in it.

Except that India was in the story. The spurned woman curses the gods for setting the man she loves on the wrong track. The other woman, who falls for the director, is escaping a planned marriage she is under great social pressure to make, for she is a poor orphan and her fiancé is what the government here calls an NRI—a non-resident Indian—prospering in Europe. Plus, although the film was as chaste as could be (no nudity, barely a kiss), the audience, except for our small, much-stared-at group of Indians and foreigners, was entirely male. Evidently local women don't come to the late show.

I began thinking about this curious blend of India and non-India as we left the theater and made our way through the camels and pedicabs and farm tractors, and the contradictions remained in the back of my mind for the rest of the five months my wife and I spent living in the country. You normally think of travel as a way of getting to know something unfamiliar. But travel anywhere for an American today involves getting to know a combination, often an uneasy one, of the unfamiliar and the familiar.

For the Indians who watched this film, and the hundreds like it that their country produces each year, glamour lies in a dreamworld where everything is smooth and clean and electronic, where the artifacts that surround you are American or European. Consumer goods are always advertised in ways that emphasize their foreignness. In the ads in India's slick newsweeklies promot-ing clothes, cars, cigarettes, and computers, there are no dark-skinned models. Either by birth, makeup, or the retoucher's brush, the features of most Indian models are ethnically ambiguous—hair dark enough to be Indian, skin light enough to be white. The implicit message is: buy this object that the model is holding or wearing or riding in and it will bring you closer to America.

But what's being imported here is not what we might like to consider admirable in America: informality and skepticism toward authority, for example, or schools that value individual creativity more than rote learning. Instead, cultural imports are mainly those things that someone can make money selling. Ideas travel slowly. The desire for objects travels at the speed of a TV transmission.

Through India's importing of such yearnings, the West, mostly the United States, has conquered the country far more conclusively than the British ever did. The British left some monuments and street names and, to the business, academic, and governing classes, the English language. But then they went home. Earlier conquerors left lighter traces: I saw squatters living inside sepulchers in an old overgrown Dutch graveyard in the port city of Cochin. But the signs of the new conquest are everywhere—on billboards, on movie and TV screens, in the armloads of gadgets that Indians who live or work abroad bring when they come home. No guns or tanks or ships are strong enough to keep this conquest at bay, for it is a conquest not by the sword but by religion: the religion of consumption.

The new religion outdraws the old. The one other movie we saw while in India was a James Bond film. The theater was huge, just across the street from a small Hindu shrine that had few visitors. I tried to watch the film through the eyes of the shrine keeper. The religion Bond represents provides tough competition. Bond braves, unscathed, some of the classic elements that impede mortal beings: air (he flies a jet fighter and does free-fall parachuting), water (he wears scuba gear), and fire (through which he dashes unharmed while the villain's lair goes up in flames). The chariot of this new god is a remote-controlled BMW whose electrically charged door handles and other secret weaponry make it impervious to harm. Additional devices—which look like Western consumer products such as wristwatches or cell phones, but have other powers as well—serve Bond as amulets, with a supernatural destructive force as strong as any thunderbolt hurled by Shiva.

This is the shape of the new conquest. For many an object to be desirable to the Indian consumer, it must have a Western aura, even if it is Indian-made. For example, the house we rented came equipped with an electric water purifier called an Aquaguard—something manufactured in India and sold by the millions. When running, the Aquaguard played music to remind you it was on, so you wouldn't let the bottle it was slowly filling overflow. And what music did it play, in ovenlike weather, only six hundred miles from the equator? Two tunes, over and over: "Jingle Bells" and "Santa Claus Is Coming to Town."

. . .

For a week, as part of our work as Fulbright lecturers, Arlie and I are teaching at something called the American Studies Research Center (since then renamed the Indo-American Centre for International Studies), in Hyderabad. This institution gives courses of various sorts on American history and culture, but its heart is a superb library. It contains, we are told, the largest collection of books and periodicals about the United States to be found anywhere outside that country and one library in Europe. A reader can feast on the complete works of hundreds of American authors and on back issues of more than seven hundred magazines and journals. From poetry to architecture to national parks, you could find enough material here to write a doctoral dissertation on innumerable aspects of American life, and hundreds of Indians have done so. The Center was founded some thirty-five years ago by the U.S. Information Agency; it is now scrambling for money elsewhere, because the end of the Cold War means no more government funds.

There is something unreal about this perfectly reproduced piece of an American university campus, complete with mowed and watered lawn, a green, carefully manicured island in the middle of scorched India. Thousands of yards of library shelves house such volumes as *The Papers of John Marshall* and *Interior Department Reports,* while across the road squatters are living in the bushes, and throughout this huge city tens of thousands of people are sleeping under tarpaulins or sheets of plastic or no roof at all—on the sidewalk, in vacant lots, at construction sites, and beneath freeway overpasses.

I have a similar feeling of disjuncture when I lecture to the Indian college teachers at the Center's American civilization course. Few have been to America, and almost all are eager to go. Many are leftists who believe—correctly, I think—that the way the United States is using the new global trade regime to reshape the world to its liking makes life harder for poor countries like India. But at the same time, America beckons: it is the source of travel grants, scholarships, and what appears to be cutting-edge culture. These teachers sit eat with us in the Center's cafeteria and shyly launch conversations, usually on subjects about which I feel abysmally ignorant. "Can I talk with you about symbolism in John Barth and William Faulkner?" asks one. Another, from Nepal, speaks movingly about the burden of illiteracy and the oppression of women there, but as a scholar he is entranced by Thomas Pynchon.

Am I jealous that these people have been able to make more sense of Barth and Pynchon than I have? Probably. But why are they attracted to the most abstruse and difficult of our writers? Is it because these seem the highest peaks to scale in the American cultural landscape? Do they see it as a path to getting a scholarship in the United States? Or is it because the complexity and sophistication of Barth and Pynchon are a substitute for the complex and sophisticated personal computers, video cameras, and other consumer goods that are beyond the financial reach of so many Indian college teachers?

I'm left feeling that if there's anything useful being imported from the United States at this particular spot, it is neither our lectures, nor John Barth and Thomas Pynchon, nor the judicial opinions of John Marshall and the other contents of the library. Rather, it is the example of how the library itself is run. Unlike those in most other libraries in India, and, indeed, elsewhere in the world, the stacks are open. The catalogue is well organized and up-to-date, and it matches the books on the shelves. The shelved books are upright and in their proper places. There are no dusty, moldering piles that have been waiting to be reshelved for months. And, above all, the librarians—who are all Indians, incidentally—smile. They make eye contact. They offer to help you find what you're looking for. They don't treat library users as unwelcome, lower-ranking intruders. Indeed, when we meet Indian academics who have been to Hyderabad to use this library, it is these things, not the actual books, that they marvel over. With reason: to my mind an open-stack American university library with a skilled staff is one of the great cultural treasures on earth.

Was this the key part of American culture that Congress thought would be imported by India when it appropriated funding for this place during the Cold War? I'm sure not. They were doubtless thinking instead about the glories of free enterprise and the evils of communism. A paradox of the strange business of cultural imports is that what one country imports may be quite different from what another country thinks it is exporting.

．　．　．

One of the most pervasive of all cultural imports—something reinforced unconsciously by every minute spent looking at *Baywatch* or *NYPD Blue,* or at any newspaper photo that shows the West—is the idea of what constitutes a proper building. It is built of materials that are inflexible and permanent. They are usually costly and often brought long distances. These notions are American and European in origin, not Indian. More than half of India's structures are made of mud, and in some parts of the country the roofs are likely to be palm thatch. If you own even a small plot of land, both materials may be plentiful, close at hand—and free.

In the south Indian state of Kerala, where we are based for our five months, I visit a small settlement of "tribals," as they are called, members of one of the many indigenous groups that live close to the land throughout rural India. The people in this settlement are from the Kani tribe, and they live beneath a rocky mountain ridge in a bamboo forest, raising and eating fruits and vegetables. To reach them requires walking a mile and a half from the nearest dirt road, along a forest trail.

I'm being given a tour of this area by the president and several members of the *panchayat,* or city council, of the municipality that includes the bamboo forest. A hard-driving, energetic man, the president wants to show me the primitive conditions in which the tribals live, "so that you can really understand the need for changes." But the visit has the opposite effect on me.

At the settlement of half a dozen homes, we go to the house of Malian Kani, the chief. He gives me sliced pineapple and a coconut with a hole to drink from. Malian Kani wears only a loincloth. He doesn't know his age, but the officials believe him to be between eighty and eighty-five. We find him with his two daughters and two daughters-in-law. A son arrives, returning from an expedition into the forest to gather firewood. Everyone is barefoot.

Almost everything that surrounds us is made of the versatile bamboo, from the thatch of the roof (which lasts three years before it needs to be replaced), to the walls of split bamboo, to the woven mats that cover the dirt floor. On three sides, the house is open to the cooling breeze. The only furniture is a bamboo cot with another woven mat. More rolled mats are stored in a rack hanging from the ceiling, reached by a bamboo ladder. In the kitchen, bamboo racks of various shapes hold tin pots and plates and spoons. One of the chief's daughters demonstrates a bamboo bow, used to shoot not arrows but small stones—to force away bothersome wild elephants. Even the settlement's chicken house is made of bamboo, as are a trap for catching fish from a nearby stream, and a rat trap, whose spring utilizes the tension of a bent piece of the wood.

All this bamboo has been cut within a few minutes' walk. Gathering it cost no money, depleted no limited resource, required no fossil fuel, added nothing to global warming. To look at a house where everything has been so ingeniously made of one material is breathtaking. It is like looking at a visual piece of music: bamboo theme with variations. I am awed by the beauty. One of the local officials with me seems to experience an unexpected twinge of the same feeling and says, "It's a pity we have to change all this."

Under a new development plan, the *panchayat* president explains to me proudly, they are building houses for these people—solid, durable houses of concrete, with tin roofs. However, one of the Kani tells my interpreter that many of them don't want the new houses the *panchayat* is so eager to build. Even in daytime, it will be dark inside, and under the equatorial sun the tin roofs will get broiling hot. If the *panchayat* insists on building these concrete structures, he says, the Kani will use them to store farm tools, and they'll keep on living in the bamboo houses. But the next generation, will they continue? I doubt it. By then the imported idea of what a house is supposed to be will be irrevocably in place.

· · ·

One of the things I do in India, in four different cities, is give two- and three-day workshops in nonfiction writing for students and working journalists. What am I importing? It is not anything uniquely American about writing techniques. The best students know what I mean when I talk about narrative strategy. And some of the published examples of good writing that I've picked for us to read and discuss are Indian. I think what I'm importing most effectively are some strong beliefs about chairs. Each time I arrive at a university for one of these workshops, the chair I'm supposed to sit in is on a platform, behind a table or podium, and everyone else's chairs are lined up in rows facing me. Each time, I enlist the puzzled class in rearranging the chairs in a circle. I have noticed the same kind of thing in classrooms in Africa; there, also, the legacy of colonialism lives on in ossified form. And thus school classrooms in Africa or Asia are not like the British or French classrooms of today, which are sometimes as informal and non-hierarchical as American ones. Rather, they are like the British or French classrooms of a sixty or seventy years ago, or the British or French classrooms of someone's imagination.

Rearranging the chairs helps, but it is still like swimming in molasses to get a discussion going, to get anyone to speak up or to argue with someone else—especially me. In one workshop it is Day Two before a student finally says, "I think I disagree with your point about . . . " I let go an inner sigh of relief. The right to dispute the teacher: one American import I wholeheartedly like.

· · ·

Something else American visitors import to India is their own expectations. You expect the unfamiliar, and you certainly find it. What strikes me, though, is not the occasional elephant in the street or the processions of brilliantly costumed people on a Hindu holy day. These I'm prepared for; they are the unfamiliar made familiar by postcards. More striking are the ways in which all kinds of things that in Western society are usually more hidden suddenly become visible.

The vast yard where old cars are carefully taken apart—hubcaps in one pile, steering wheels in another, axles in another, and so on, right next to a big complex of butcher stalls where taken-apart animals are also sorted into their separate body parts. The gigantic switch with a six-inch handle, such as one imagines the on-off switch in a nuclear power plant to have, that controls the electrical line entering the vast fuse box that takes up many square feet of prominent wall space in the house we have rented. Our backyard pit for burning garbage. The vacant lot next door where our neighborhood's unburnable garbage ends up. The fact that, yes, our house has a gas-burning stove as advertised, but we ourselves have to go to the gas dealer's office (where the manager's desk has an offering to the gods on a banana leaf) and collect the gas—contained in metal canisters that clank and rattle together ominously beneath our seat in a rickety three-wheeler auto-rickshaw on the way home. The way social ranks are laid bare: a person's degrees and the universities they are from, one's profession and title, are all displayed on the nameplate in front of one's house and, in the case of a government official, on a little red sign on his car, such as: VICE CHANCELLOR, KERALA UNIVERSITY.

Living in India also lays bare the material expectations we import. I may think of myself as nonmaterialistic and deplore the Indian attachment to Western consumer goods, but I'm forced to realize how many of them I take for granted myself. Our standard of living in India is far higher than that of most people around us. We told house rental agents that we were just looking for something simple. But simplicity is relative. For we expect electricity, a telephone, flush toilet, hot and cold water.

We are assured that the house we've rented will have all these things. And after a fashion that's true. But it takes five weeks for the telephone to be installed, sometimes it goes dead, and we can't use it to call abroad. There is hot water, but not in the kitchen. The electricity goes out for a scheduled half an hour every evening, and often for longer stretches during the day. The voltage is high enough to work the e-mail modem only before 9:00 a.m. The municipal water supply shrinks to a trickle in the dry season, and sometimes the pump to our backup well fails. When there's water, the toilet flushes, but you can hear it gurgling into the backyard septic tank (which is, strangely, uphill from the well). So: all of these basic things exist, but most of them come and go unpredictably.

This is a healthy lesson. For one thing, it connects us with others. If one or another of these services isn't working, we share with neighbors, or do without for a few hours, or for a day or two. They take buckets of our water if they have none; they bring us candles if we have no electricity. At first I am frustrated when something breaks down—and my impatience makes me feel embarrassingly American, since a few houses away there are people who live by kerosene light and get water from a public faucet down the road. What right do I have to complain? Yet complain I do.

Eventually, I come to be more relaxed. To learn that we can survive temporarily without phone or water or e-mail, makes us feel a little more hardy and self-reliant. But that's only because we're doing without things to which we secretly feel entitled. In this way, I'm much more American than I'd like to be.

. . .

Among the strongest American imports to India are fears. At the beginning I am afraid of getting sick, of being taken advantage of, of being robbed. We bring lots of medicines and vitamin pills; I examine all food suspiciously for signs of germs or spoilage. I fear being taken for a naïve tourist by shopkeepers. And it seems that people here are also afraid of robbery: windows throughout India are covered with bars, even on the upper floors of apartment houses. Thieves must be resourceful, I think, climbing up from below or rappelling down from the roof.

However, we don't get sick. The first time I leave our neighborhood fruit and vegetable stall after buying food, its keeper comes racing after me from a hundred yards away, with my change—because I had misunderstood him and left fifty rupees (about $1.25) on the counter instead of fifteen rupees. And after a month or two, it dawns on me that the window bars everywhere are not against thieves but against India's vast population of aggressive, hungry crows, whose taste for human food scraps has been honed feasting on the omnipresent roadside garbage. It takes a few weeks more before I realize that virtually nobody in our part of India worries about street crime. The rare policemen I see are unarmed. Why does it take so long to let go of my fears? What's most foreign, most unknown, is what we're most afraid of, even when we seek it out. Maybe that's why we seek it out.

I can date the moment I let these fears go. It is about eight o'clock one evening, and I'm making my way home from a workshop for Kerala local government officials in a distant, unfamiliar neighborhood. The isolated building where the workshop took place is on top of a big hill. There are no taxis outside, no buses. The nearest place I have any chance of finding an auto-rickshaw that can take me home is a mile or so away, a traffic circle at the bottom of the hill. I head off down the road. There is no moon, and everything is pitch black. There are no streetlights. Either the electricity is having its nightly shut-down or the houses in this neighborhood don't have any. Here and there, a far-off kerosene lamp flickers faintly, most likely in someone's window; it is too dark to tell. Occasionally, a pair of very dim headlights zooms up or down the road, and I step quickly aside, but not too far, for fear of unseen ditches. I'm wearing dark clothes; the drivers of passing vehicles can't see me. I should have brought a flashlight, worn a white shirt. I should have one of those red reflective safety vests. Dumb, not to have thought about this. In vain, I anxiously try to flag down what may or may not be a passing taxi that looms suddenly out of the darkness and then disappears. The driver can't see the furled black umbrella I'm waving. The only way I can tell I'm on or off the road is by the feel of the asphalt underfoot.

Partway down the hill, I become aware of the rattle of metal wheels ahead of me on the road, accompanied by a rhythmic clinking. Finally, I'm close enough to make out, just barely, the outline of a food vendor's cart. The man pushing it, judging from the sound, is continually stirring something—I can't see what—in a frying pan or wok. But standing upright on the front of the cart, his protection against being run over, is a candle. That's all it takes. I realize that the candle can be my protection, too. Flooded with a sudden sense of safety, I follow twenty paces behind this mysterious, candlelit stir-frying the rest of the way down the hill.

2000

TWELVE

Palm Trees and Paradoxes

DURING THE FIVE MONTHS THAT I lived in Trivandrum,* the capital of the south Indian state of Kerala, I went for a run every morning. My neighbors were thoroughly amused at the spectacle of someone eccentric enough to voluntarily work up a sweat in their sauna-like climate. Laborers gathered at a roadside stall for a cup of milky tea laughed and called out "Where coming from?" Children heading down the narrow dirt lanes to school giggled and raced alongside.

India overwhelms the senses, caress and assault together. It was all there for me each dawn: The bat trapped in the telephone wires. The beautiful vista over a pristine, green valley floor filled with coconut palms (which hid, I discovered before long, thousands of small houses). The border of garbage lining every roadside, dotted with bright plastic shopping bags. The luminous multicolored sari worn by each older woman, and the salwar kameez by each younger one—a long dress, sometimes embedded with bits of mirror that flashed in the sun, accompanied by a gauzy, flowing scarf. The strings of fiery-hot red peppers for sale at the roadside food stands. The massive, gated house of the neighborhood money-lender (36 percent interest for six months, compounded thereafter, with gold jewelry as security): "Maximum discretion. If a woman brings me her bracelet, her husband will not know. If a police chief needs money, he sends his servant."

And the sounds: The soft chant of a Hindu prayer meeting coming through an open door. The muezzin's amplified dawn call to prayer from the mosque. The hymns on Sunday from the Salvation Army hall down the street.

---

* As with many Indian cities, in recent years its name has been restored to its original form in the local language, Thiruvananthapuram.

The calls from a man selling squawking ducks out of a box on the back of his bicycle, from a woman selling fish from a flat basket on her head, and from the "ironing man," with his wheeled cart and clothes iron, heated by charcoal. The *whump! whump!* of coconuts dropping to the ground while, forty feet above, a harvester clung to a tree with his legs, a loop of rope, and one arm and wielded a machete with the other.

All of these sights and sounds can be had elsewhere in India, but there was one thing that an early morning jogger could see far more of in Kerala. Even in the very poorest homes in my neighborhood—two-room mud houses without even a chimney, so that cooking smoke rose through the roof thatch—someone would often be sitting on the doorstep reading a newspaper. The newspaper would usually not be in English but in Kerala's language, Malayalam. A written tongue since before Chaucer, it has its own alphabet of more than fifty beautifully looping letters. In a country where roughly half the population is illiterate, Kerala is the only state where more than 90 percent of adults can read and write.

Equally impressive was what I did not see on my morning neighborhood jog. There were no children with the swollen bellies of the severely malnourished. There were no people living under miserable, makeshift tents of plastic sheeting or sleeping on the sidewalk, such as you see by the millions elsewhere in India. (In Trivandrum, a city about the size of San Francisco, there were also no sidewalks, which made pedestrian life challenging). And there were no beggars. There were a few in the city's downtown, but not as many as you might see in Boston or New York.

Kerala has the highest immunization rate in India and more than three times as many hospital beds per capita as the rest of the country. The average person born in Kerala today lives to be seventy-two, nearly a dozen years longer than someone born elsewhere in India. The infant mortality rate is less than a quarter that of the country as a whole. These statistics approach American and European levels; they are better, in fact, than those for black Americans. Only thirty years ago, Kerala had the fastest-growing population in India, but today the state's birth rate is 1.7 children per woman. A generation from now, Kerala's population will level off and begin to drop.

Figures like these are all the more striking because Kerala has a per capita income that, on paper, is only about one seventieth that of the United States. Furthermore, a population roughly the size of California's is crammed into an area smaller than San Bernardino County: a long, thin strip of coastal land laced with rice paddies and internal waterways. For doing so much more with less, the state has drawn praise from assorted radicals and greens everywhere, who are eager to find a juster, gentler way of development than the cruel gaps between rich and poor that prevail throughout most of the global South.

Does Kerala provide some answers? To explore these issues, my wife and I lived there when we went to India as Fulbright lecturers. The state turned out to be far more complicated than the rosy picture of it gleaned from our reading beforehand. The statistics are real and indeed indicate an achievement. But Kerala, we found, is also a place of many paradoxes.

· · ·

The first is that credit for Kerala's accomplishments is strangely divided between a strong labor movement and communist politicians, on the one hand, and some feudal monarchs, on the other.

Despite at least one infusion of CIA campaign money to the opposition, over the past forty years Kerala has had several long stretches of rule by coalitions led by one or the other of two communist parties (the old Indian party split into pro-Soviet and pro-Chinese factions in the 1960s). Kerala's communists are somewhat like those in Italy: however unsavory their past affiliations overseas, they've won a reputation at home for good government and for being noticeably less corrupt than other parties. Besides near-universal literacy, the changes they have brought to Kerala include public health clinics, shops that sell staple food at controlled prices, and South Asia's most substantial land reform.

However, the communists built their welfare state on foundations provided by an amazingly enlightened series of hereditary rulers. In colonial times about half of what is today Kerala lay in two princely states, which, to a greater degree than most of those elsewhere in India, were largely left alone by the British. Furthermore, Kerala's royal families were markedly different from their counterparts. For example, in 1817 the maharani of Travancore, whose domain covered most of today's southern Kerala, issued an edict declaring that "the state should defray the whole cost of education of its people." At that time few, if any, European kings and queens would have embraced so radical an idea. Later in the century, Travancore was the first princely state to set up a legislative council and to begin a halting transformation into a constitutional monarchy.

Other members of these royal families started schools and a university and studied medicine, both traditional and Western. One maharaja in the

Travancore dynasty was a noted painter and another, who reigned in the early 1800s, was a polymath who spoke eight languages and was famous as the composer of many hymns and songs, some of which are still sung today. (Although a researcher recently claimed that it was a court musician who wrote the songs.) Because of their unusual enthusiasm for universal literacy, the maharajahs welcomed Christian missionaries, who started what are still the state's best schools. By the first decade of the twentieth century, the literacy rate in Kerala was more than twice that of India as a whole.

At the time we lived there, Kerala was once again under a coalition government dominated by the largest of India's left parties, the Communist Party of India (Marxist), whose red flags flew everywhere. But the current maharajah, today without political power, still lived in a small palace in downtown Trivandrum, where I went to see him.

A roof of traditional red tile kept out the broiling sun, and beautifully carved wooden grillwork around the tops of the palace walls let the breezes flow through, making the rooms comfortably cool without air conditioning. A generator roared in the background, providing royal independence from Kerala's anemic electric grid. An elderly Mercedes was parked under a portico.

His Highness Sree Uthradom Thirunal Marthanda Varma, the fifty-fifth maharajah of Travancore, was a slight, lithe, upbeat man with a small mustache. He wore a short-sleeved shirt, a dab of yellow paint, signifying devoutness, in the middle of his forehead, and a *mundu*. This standard Kerala male attire is a loose combination of pants and skirt that wraps around and between the legs. In a way I could never quite fathom, it can be instantly readjusted by its wearer to reach either just down to knee height, for coolness, or, as a sign of respect to someone you meet, all the way to the ankles.

When a servant ushered me into the large reception room where the maharajah was sitting, he was still busy with his preceding visitors. He pointed cheerfully to a large portrait on the wall and called out, "That's my doctor ancestor. Take a look at him!"

After a few minutes, he motioned me over and showed me a genealogical chart of his forebears. "In 1809, we were the first to rise against the British, and when you are the first to get out of hand they are more severe with you. They start breaking up all your forts, disbanding your army, doing away with the police. And then they say, 'You people are not very well behaved, so we will keep two British regiments here, for your protection, for which you will pay!'"

The maharajah went on to describe his childhood, his face lighting up with pleasure every time he could get off a bon mot: "I'm a graduate of the University of Travancore, in '41. But I never went to college. The college came to me!" Fourteen tutors, some British, some Indian, appeared at the palace regularly.

Although he reportedly made and lost considerable money as a business-man while waiting to inherit the maharajah's position from his elder brother, the activities he wanted to talk about were, in his family tradition, scholarly, religious, and philanthropic. Just that morning, he said, he had had a Sanskrit lesson and had gotten his weekly homework assignment. He said he was in the middle of writing a book of religious philosophy. "The Queen of England is Defender of the Faith. I'm an Attender of the Faith! I go to Padmanabhaswamy Temple every day, early in the morning, and that makes me fit for the next twenty-three hours."

Today there are no more tax revenues for "people of our breed," as he put it, but the family's wealth is still there, much of it in a group of trusts, which give money to schools and hospitals. Benefactions are carefully divided among Kerala's different religious groups. Roughly 60 percent of the state's people are, like the maharaja, Hindu; 20 percent are Muslim; and 20 percent are Christian. "When I was a little boy, every Christmas Eve, Christians would come to the house and sing carols. Only after that would they go on to the town. Then, on the birthday of the prophet, the imam would come, and only after that would he go to the town." Does the maharajah feel in conflict with Kerala's current communist government? Not particularly, it seems. "The other day, about a month back, they organized a youth festival. The education minister sent word to me, 'Would you go and inaugurate it?'" He did so. But, with a laugh, he implied that his own family had originated most of Kerala's social reforms. When I asked how many children he had— he is seventy-seven—he answered triumphantly, "Two! We thought of the limited family well in advance!" He was right: a history of the state I later read reported that a member of the dynasty had helped bring the birth con-trol pioneer Margaret Sanger to Trivandrum in 1934.

. . .

In few places on earth today are the outward signs of left-wing politics as flamboyant as they are in Kerala. Beside almost every major workplace, even the temple the maharajah attends, a sign marks the office of a union of its employees. Hammers and sickles, or sometimes a sickle and sheaf of grain, are painted on walls everywhere. Rare was the day when a group of people was not sitting in or fasting in protest against something in front of the main state office building. Posters of Marx and Engels abounded; once in a while their bearded faces were joined by Lenin and Stalin. Almost every day some chanting group carried red banners through downtown Trivandrum, incongruously crossing paths with the occasional temple elephant. When a taxi I was in came upon a march of labor unionists one morning, I expected them to be hostile. But foreigners are a great rarity in the city; one marcher peered through the cab window curiously, then threw me a grinning salute.

It took several months for another of Kerala's paradoxes to fully dawn on me: the state's vocal politics of the Left coexist with a deep-rooted social conservatism. Even more unexpected, most Keralites, as they call themselves, don't see this as a paradox. There is no notion that the personal might be the least bit political. Few people thought it surprising, for example, that the late E. M. S. Namboodiripad, the longtime Kerala chief of the Communist Party of India (Marxist), plus all four of his children, had all had arranged marriages within their own Brahmin caste.

For centuries, Kerala had the most rigid and complex caste hierarchy in India. When Dutch fortune-seekers killed more than four hundred members of the Nayar warrior caste in battle in 1662, a Dutchman was startled that "fishermen, and other classes, apparently of the same nation and country, looked on with indifference." Kerala had not only untouchables, but unseeables: people considered so polluting that they could not even be seen close-up by a Brahmin. In 1924, a missionary reported that he saw a Brahmin walking along a road with a man in front of him armed with a stick, to ensure all outcastes would be more than thirty yards away when the Brahmin passed. Gandhi himself came to Kerala the same year to join a massive protest against laws that kept lower castes from using roads near certain temples.

Today, all this has long since been reformed; untouchables are officially no more, and one speaks of "former untouchables." Indeed, the current president of India, the ceremonial head of state, is a former untouchable from Kerala. But, as with slavery and segregation in the United States, no heritage of centuries can be legislated out of people's minds in a generation or two.

Gradually I began to understand how important these divisions were. A bitter factional dispute in the ruling Communist Party that made headlines, for instance, was partly connected to conflict between its mostly lower-caste rank and file and mostly upper-caste leadership. And my wife and I came to see some caste scars in our own neighborhood, an area where many former untouchables lived.

A few weeks after we moved in, the power line outside our house was struck by lightning. Wires sparked and sizzled, light switches leapt out of the walls, and everything went dark. We needed an electrician. Happily one lived with his extended family just three houses away. After he fixed the wiring, he and his wife came for tea several times. He was a former untouchable and seemed immensely pleased to be visiting this house we were renting from a Brahmin doctor. But he keenly felt a vast gulf between the "little people," as he put it, and his upper-caste neighbors, the "big people." Recently, he said, his father had suffered an accident and needed to be rushed to the hospital. The electrician had no car and no telephone to call an ambulance. He had raced from house to house on our street, begging for someone with a car to drive his father to the hospital. No one would do so, he said, even though perhaps a third of the homeowners on the street were doctors or nurses at a nearby complex of hospitals. He had to run a mile to the nearest taxi stand.

The worst effect of any kind of discrimination is the way it gets internalized. Another former untouchable in the neighborhood was a young man who often visited our house to talk. But when we offered him something to eat or drink, I noticed, he always took it outdoors, as if he would somehow offend us by eating in our presence.

Sometimes you see how pervasive something is in one society when people make the assumption that it exists everywhere. For many people, we were the first Americans or Europeans they had met, and once we got talking with a man who came to install some screens on our windows. He asked, "Are the two of you of the same caste?" We explained, of course, that America did not have castes. But after he left, it occurred to me that yes, we really *were* of the same caste. Castes in India have their roots in ancient occupations: priests, farmers, scribes, warriors, and so on, and we both do indeed belong to the caste of scribes. A marriage between a scribe and a warrior in California would be as rare as one between a Brahmin and an untouchable here.

Kerala is also deeply conservative when it comes to gender. Any time I went to lecture to a university class, the women always sat on the left side of the room as they faced the speaker, the men on the right. The same was true at a large political rally I attended where, despite its being staged by the state's left-wing government, among more than a dozen speakers over the course of three hours, not one was a woman.

Women factory workers are routinely paid less than men. (When a researcher friend of ours asked a union official about this, he said disapprovingly, "Comrade, you are criticizing us!") At construction sites, women do the hardest labor, carrying baskets of dirt and sand on their heads. And women do much of what looks like the toughest work of all in Kerala, sitting by the side of the road in the unbelievably hot sun, using hammers to break large rocks into gravel. Kerala women hold few high political posts and constitute only a small percentage of the membership of the ruling Communist Party.

As in all of India, someone is expected to marry a person of the same caste, and the vast majority of marriages are arranged. Kerala may vote for the Left, but the Sunday newspapers' matrimonial advertisements were classified by caste. We heard innumerable stories of people being ostracized by their families for marrying someone from another caste or for a marriage that was not arranged. One woman told me that an uncle of hers "simply will not come" to any wedding that is a love match, no matter who is getting married. This woman, now a graduate student, got to meet her own husband only once before her wedding, and that in the presence of many other people. "This will not happen to *my* daughter," she said.

All these practices, curiously, cut across political and educational lines. One Kerala friend of ours, a professor who was once head of the international scholarly association in his field, was busily arranging his son's marriage. (In this case, the bride and groom were allowed to spend part of a day together before the wedding, a liberal-minded gesture unheard of in older times.) Arundhati Roy's best-selling 1997 novel *The God of Small Things* is about a Kerala community's violent reaction to a love affair across caste lines. And it makes no difference that the woman involved is Christian and therefore supposedly without caste, or that her brother, who is horrified by the affair, is an Oxford-educated communist. On this score, Roy got Kerala exactly right.

A defiant young man in a magazine advertisement for a line of clothing says: "My parents chose the girl. Her parents chose the date. No one chooses my suit."

. . .

Another Kerala paradox is this: its citizens have no patience for foreign admirers who praise their state for its ability to do more with less. They would like to do more with more.

We may compare them with the rest of India, but they don't. They compare themselves with Europe and the United States, where hundreds of thousands of people of Kerala origin are living. And the comparison hurts. Even closer at hand, they compare themselves with the oil-rich nations of the Persian Gulf, where an estimated five to eight hundred thousand Keralites, from neurosurgeons to stevedores, are contract workers. Indeed, the number of Kerala men away from their wives in "the Gulf" may be part of the reason why the state's birth rate is so low.

Economically, Kerala is less a part of India than of the Arabian Peninsula. From Trivandrum there is one plane a day from New Delhi, the national capital. But four to six planes a day make the longer trips from Kuwait, Bahrain, and other Arab countries, their disembarking passengers bringing home baggage full of radios, video cameras, TVs, and computers. In Trivandrum's equivalent of a yellow pages phone book, there are twenty-one pages of Gulf listings, plus street maps of Abu Dhabi and Dubai. Depending on the job market in the oil states, anywhere from 15 to 30 percent of Kerala's income, it is estimated, is sent home by Keralites working abroad. People at every class level go to the Gulf for a few years at a time, sometimes for several such stints during their lives: the returned migrants we met just in our neighborhood ranged from doctor to army officer to construction worker and more.

Whatever your trade, the chances are that you can make three to eight times as much by plying it across the Arabian Sea as you can in Kerala. Competition for Gulf jobs is fierce, and the agents who arrange these positions charge high fees and occasionally abscond with the money. Some attracted to the Gulf get caught up in a sort of Gold Rush mentality. Throughout Kerala stand thousands of "Gulf houses": huge, concrete, fortress-like structures, occasionally even with crenelated ramparts, that dwarf their neighbors. One I passed on my morning run had a large outbuilding of concrete—servants' quarters? a guest cottage?—molded in the shape of a houseboat, with bow, stern, a deck, deckhouse, portholes. Construction on a couple of gigantic Gulf houses near us had mysteriously stopped; perhaps the owner had lost that overseas job and now had to make do with a lowly Kerala salary.

Throughout the world, children are told to stay in school if they want a job; countries invest in schools and universities if they want their economies to grow. This brings us to the next paradox of Kerala: the state, which spends proportionally more on education than any other in India, has the country's highest unemployment rate, three to four times the national average.

For one single advertised job opening as a municipal laborer some years back, there were 59,014 applications. At every Kerala shop, office or building site, people with time on their hands cluster about: friends, relatives, job-seekers, people on a waiting list for jobs. When I took a taxi to visit a news-paper editor friend, a dozen people, it seemed, lounging in the building's courtyard, leapt up to signal to the driver how to turn around. Economic growth per capita is near zero. Although Kerala grows a lot of coconuts, rice, cashews, and rubber, it has very little industry. Indeed, fully half the state's trade unionists, like those I often saw marching so militantly through Trivandrum's streets, are directly or indirectly government employees. The Keralites who've gone abroad or to other parts of India are not just going for the Gulf-level salaries; they're going because there's no work for them at home.

What happened? Business-oriented critics say that Kerala's powerful trade unions have priced the work force out of the market. An industrialist can find workers, even literate ones, who'll work for half as much money in the poverty-stricken state of Tamil Nadu next door. To some extent this is true, and Tamil Nadu and Kerala's other neighbor, Karnataka, have higher growth rates. But it doesn't seem the full explanation, for, despite all the marches and red flags, Kerala loses fewer days per factory worker to strikes and lockouts than does the rest of India. And, despite its name, the ruling Communist Party of India (Marxist) is eagerly putting money into incentives for foreign investors. I was told that it had quietly instructed its union allies that, at a new industrial park in Trivandrum, there were to be no strikes.

One obvious drag on economic growth is bureaucracy. Government drowns in a sea of paperwork. Getting a telephone installed in our house, for instance, required an odyssey of visits to four separate offices of the telephone company in different parts of town, and waiting for them to send reports to each other. Over the course of our five months in Trivandrum, we had to pay an astonishing ten visits to something called the Foreigners Registration Office, to register, unregister, and get various stamps and signatures and per-missions. The dusty, dimly lit room was a scene out of "Bartleby the Scrivener": Ceiling fans turned lazily above high stacks of ledgers and bun-dles of files tied with string, some papers spilling out of the bundles. The files had turned limp and moldering in the humidity and looked as if they con-tained the registration documents of every foreign visitor to Kerala since Marco Polo, who stopped here on his way home from China.

Besides bureaucracy, there is a routine system of under-the-table payments. The scarcest commodities, jobs, are for sale. It's an open secret, for example, that it costs you anywhere from two to five hundred thousand rupees (about $5,000 to $12,500) to get a teaching post at a private college, where your salary is paid by the government. Then, if you're the college president, a high-ranking, frustrated Kerala state official explained to me, "you really can't fire the fellow, no matter how incompetent he is, because he paid you for the job! Meanwhile, he's opened a private tutoring business on the side, so he can earn money to pay back the person he borrowed that payment from."

However, the paperwork thicket is just as dense everywhere in India, and public opinion surveys rate Kerala as less corrupt, by quite a large margin, than any other state. In our many dealings with officialdom, no one ever asked for a bribe.

One clear source of Kerala's economic troubles is its skimpy and uneven supply of electricity. Stagnant tax revenues have left the state government painfully short of money to improve the basic infrastructure, and nowhere has this been more crippling than with power. The proliferation of Gulf houses and modern appliances has surged far ahead of the supply. In much of the state the current goes off for half an hour each night, a blackout that rotates by schedule through different neighborhoods. There are many unscheduled outages as well. Furthermore, the voltage starts going down when thousands of offices put on their air conditioners in the morning and drops still further when millions of homes turn on their lights at night. The ceiling fans in our house moved ever more sleepily as the evening wore on, and revved up to top speed only as midnight approached, when the city's residents turned off their lights and went to bed.

Keralites cope with this in a variety of ways. When the state's governor arrived at a conference I attended, his staff carried a portable generator so that the microphone would not go dead while he was speaking. Our house came equipped with something that looked like a swollen car battery, which (when it was working) captured incoming electricity during the day and then fed it back to certain lights during the nightly power cuts. But you can't have such a device for an entire factory or have an assembly line that slows down during brownouts.

Another reason for Kerala's low growth is the state's extreme social conservatism. One curious way this shows up is the statistics on what happens to the money Keralites earn overseas and then send home. Less than 6 percent gets invested in any sort of business. More than half of it goes into land or into building or improving homes. There's no telling what proportion of that is spent by people merely trying to put decent roofs over their families' heads for the first time (those roofs of coconut palm thatch, however picturesque, have to be replaced after every monsoon season) and what proportion goes for Gulf houses. A glance around any Kerala city tells you that a goodly share goes to the latter. And this conspicuous consumption can't be blamed entirely on the evils of global advertising. Some of it in Kerala comes from a reaction to the even more caste-bound society of the past, where lower castes were not permitted to wear gold jewelry or, sometimes, even clothing above the waist.

What else does the Gulf money get invested in? One study found a startling 22.8 percent of it going into "marriage of daughters," a euphemism for something nominally illegal but still pervasive: dowries. Our electrician neighbor was shortly planning to go off to the Gulf to start earning money he could put away for the dowry of his daughter—who was now just ten months old. Dowries make having daughters a financial liability. And a huge one, for Indian dowries sometimes can amount to a year or more of a parent's income. And in Kerala, under the impact of Gulf money, the price is going up. Any "Gulf boy" can command a far higher dowry from a bridal candidate. Furthermore, much of that dowry is likely to be in gold and jewels, which creates jobs for miners in Africa but not for workers in Kerala. In these ways, the feudal past still hobbles Kerala today.

. . .

What's the next step for Kerala? Each new left-wing state government introduces a program to be its hallmark; the last time around it was a big adult-literacy campaign. The current effort, praised highly in a recent World Bank report, is a radical change in the way India usually does business. Of Kerala's state planning budget—money spent not for recurring expenses like teachers' salaries or road maintenance, say, but for economic development and new infrastructure—35 to 40 percent is now being turned over to the state's tens of thousands of villages to spend, within broad limits, as they like. Elsewhere in the country, these funds are jealously monopolized by state governments. For Kerala's villages, this is the first time they've gotten control of such large sums. Village and neighborhood meetings have been held up and down the state, and citizens have worked on inventories of their communities' needs.

"Economic development" can include everything down to getting a goat or some chickens or a coconut seedling for your backyard, so hundreds of thousands of Keralites have applied for grants.

I spent a day accompanying the guiding spirit of this program, a charismatic, likable, upbeat, bearded economist named T. M. Thomas Isaac, a member of the state planning board, on a visit to a mountain village named Vithura, where doormat-sized sheets of whitish, freshly harvested rubber were hung on roadside fences to dry. Isaac thought Vithura was making particularly good use of these funds and was a model that could inspire other villages. Officials had assembled several hundred people for an afternoon of speechmaking, tree-planting, and ceremonial handing out of some of the fruits of the program to the town's citizens: envelopes of money for the construction of latrines, packages of vegetable seeds, and a dozen pairs of pickax and hoe blades (you go into the forest to cut your own handle).

Isaac gave a speech to the open-air crowd, in which he told the story of a smuggler. Each day the smuggler showed up at a border post wheeling a bicycle with a sack of sand on it. Each day the police inspected the sand, poked at it, sifted it, and finally laughed at this fool who thought he could make money by smuggling sand. But, Isaac said, he was not smuggling sand, he was smuggling bicycles! Thus with the new program: the real change is not what the money gets spent on, it's that this massive transfer of funds will bypass the huge, creaky state bureaucracy, will be less likely to be siphoned off by crooked contractors, and will be spent in a more accountable way. All grants and grant applications must be public and everyone at the village level knows one another. The sand is the money, the bicycle is grassroots democracy.

I went back to Vithura myself several months later to see how things were going. It was not only members of the ruling party who were enthusiastic about the program but also members of the rival Congress Party on the village council, one of whom accompanied me for much of the day. Was there less corruption at the village level than the state level? I couldn't tell, although members of both parties claimed this was the case.

But in talking with them I began to realize that there was a contradiction at the heart of this new program. State government paper-pushers, who will lose control over tens of millions of dollars' worth of spending, have every reason covertly to oppose it. Yet these are the very people who, through their trade unions, are the core of the ruling party's political base. And so a deal was cut: the government employee unions are giving their grudging support to the big change, but in return none of their members will lose their jobs. Thus an already bloated bureaucracy lives on, with even less to do than before.

. . .

Kerala's many paradoxes make it hard to view it as the eco-sensitive paradise that so many Western progressives would like to find. Few Keralites themselves view it this way. There is a widespread sense that a genuine idealism of thirty or forty years ago has been lost. The first half of *Mukhamukham* (Face to Face), a film by the Kerala director Adoor Gopalakrishnan, shows a heroic young labor organizer, Sreedharan, in the early 1950s. An austere, self-denying revolutionary, he puts up a portrait of Lenin, organizes workers to fight miserable conditions at a tile factory, and rejects an attempt by the factory owner to buy him off. Police wreck the union office. Sreedharan is beaten severely. Then the factory owner is murdered and police try to pin the blame on Sreedharan. He vanishes, and his friends assume he is dead. More than a decade later he returns, aged, bent, alcoholic, silent. In trying to get him to speak, his old union comrades reveal the various ways they have changed. One has become a sectarian guerrilla; another has various businesses on the side and tells Sreedharan not to believe all the things he will hear about him. All want Sreedharan to inspire them again, but he cannot. Then he is mysteriously murdered, and only this event once again draws the workers together, to solemnly march under their red flags, chanting "Long Live Comrade Sreedharan!" It has proven much easier to celebrate Sreedharan in death than to live out his ideals in life.

Someone else who has thought about Kerala's malaise is Dr. K. A. Kumar, head psychiatrist at Trivandrum's Medical College. He is concerned by the rapid rise of alcoholism in the state. Sixty percent of Kerala's road accidents are related to alcohol, he says, as are one third of its industrial accidents and more than 20 percent of male hospital admissions. "When I was a medical student [in the 1960s], when we saw advanced alcoholism with cirrhosis, the age of the patient would be late forties, fifties, or even sixties. Now we find it occurring in the late twenties and thirties." Another ominous symptom that he sees is suicides: Kerala's rate, nearly three times India's national average, is growing fast, and, at 27 per 100,000 people, is matched by few countries anywhere.

Dr. Kumar feels that Kerala "took a wrong turning" in the 1970s. These were the years large numbers of Keralites first began going to the Gulf. It was also when unemployment grew worse and when it became painfully clear that a high school or college degree would not guarantee you a job. Kerala was affected by changes throughout India during this time, when the idealism of the Nehru years had been replaced by deep-seated corruption and the increasing authoritarianism of Indira Gandhi and her 1975 declaration of emergency rule.

What else lies behind the soaring rates of alcoholism and suicide? My own guess is that Kerala's near-universal literacy, its extraordinary percentage of people with higher education, its millions of citizens who have worked abroad, and its millions more who live in families with one member overseas have all given its people an unusually wide window onto the outside world. And that world is one where others seem to have much more.

The men I would see on my morning jog, sitting on the steps of their two-room mud houses reading newspapers, were seeing pages tailored, as everywhere, to the upscale readers advertisers are seeking: articles about vacation travel ideas or tips on "How to Choose Your Child's First Computer." Yet Kerala's economic woes have made it impossible for many people easily to buy even a child's first bicycle, much less a computer. From that disparity between the dreamed-of world summoned up by the newspaper page, or the TV screen, or the letters of the relative in Chicago and the mud-walled reality arises a kind of despair, a sense of being on the periphery. And it's no comfort to hear either an Indian Gandhian or an American environmentalist saying that you shouldn't be coveting material things to begin with.

Everywhere today, the borders between the global North and South are no longer between continents; they are within countries and cities: the white suburb and black shantytown in South Africa; the beachfront condo and the hillside *favela* in Rio; the sprawling slum and the fenced, guarded compound for diplomats and other foreigners in Dakar or Nairobi. In Kerala, that border lies everywhere; it even zigzagged between the homes on the streets where I ran each dawn, where vast Gulf houses sat side by side with thatched-roof ones whose residents had to get their water from the roadside tap that flowed only early in the morning, if at all. Goats, cows, and bullocks drawing creaky carts plodded past garages holding shiny new Toyotas. Sometimes the line bisected a home: one Muslim family not far from us had electricity, TV, and a radio but had to walk more than half a mile a day for water.

Furthermore, in Kerala, the border between worlds does not divide people of different nationalities, religions, languages, or skin colors. A family trapped, economically, in a dirt-floored hut may have greatly better-off neighbors who have an aunt or brother or uncle with a job in London or Dubai who is sending money home. The border between them is of agonizing thinness. Almost all of us define our sense of being rich or poor not by absolute standards but by comparison to people we can see. And if we see them every day that can make envy worse.

Yet for all its troubles, and in a world where the World Bank and the International Monetary Fund are pressing governments to slash social spending, Kerala has managed to provide a basic safety net under everyone: access to education, to medical care, to low-priced staple food, and to a welfare system that works. And it is a society where civic spirit is very much alive. Kerala regularly produces some of India's highest voter turnouts, ones that far surpass the United States—more than 70 percent in the last national election. My morning run took me past the Recreation Center for the Handicapped, one of innumerable institutions for the blind, the deaf, and the disabled proclaimed by large signs around town. It took me near the Medical College auditorium where, for a conference that I attended, Dr. Kumar assembled 173 high school teachers from throughout the city for a workshop in how to recognize and help the children of alcoholics. It took me near a medical research institute developing a program on learning disabilities that will be part of retraining for every teacher in the state. Kerala has its problems, but it does not forget the disadvantaged—something that can't be said for many parts of the world that are far wealthier.

1999

THIRTEEN

_____

The Brick Master

THE FIRST THING THAT INTERESTED me in the bold and unconventional architect Laurie Baker was my roof. During the five months my wife and I spent living in Trivandrum, the sweltering, leafy capital of the south Indian state of Kerala, the house we rented, like thousands of others in the city, was built largely of concrete. It would have looked at home as a row house in California. A flat roof lay directly above our kitchen, bedroom, and living room, and it was rain-proofed with tar.

Trivandrum is almost at the bottom tip of India, an hour's flying time from the equator. After a few minutes' walk in midday, you were drenched in sweat. Even people who had lived in Trivandrum all their lives complained about the heat. We were not the first visitors to India overwhelmed by this; one nineteenth-century British governor-general felt "as though one were passing through the mouth of a foundry." But with this lunatic black roof soaking up the blaze of the tropical sun and then radiating it down at us like a broiler for twenty-four hours a day, it seemed as if we had gone from the foundry's mouth into its flaming innards. Because of the roof, at almost any time of day or night, it felt cooler in the shade outside our house than inside.

We soon noticed that it was also much cooler whenever we visited friends living in the attractive brick homes designed by Laurie Baker, who although British-born has lived in India for more than fifty years. None had air conditioning, but some Baker houses had strange, irregular, pyramid-like structures on their roofs, with one side left open and tilting into the wind, to funnel it into the house. These seemed inspired by the air intakes on early steamships' decks that funneled cool air below; I had never seen an architect do something like that on land. And unlike our rental house, Baker's homes invariably had sloping roofs in traditional Indian style, with gables and vents where rising hot air could escape.

Gradually, I realized that the flat, black California-style roof on our house was not an isolated piece of insanity but a small example of a much larger pattern. In architecture, as in so much else, Indians want to be like us. But Baker's work, most unusually, combined Western and traditional Indian ways. Furthermore, his great passion in life was not building the grand museums or concert halls by which architects usually make their mark but low-cost housing for the untold number of Indians who, quite literally, do not have a real roof over their heads. And on a subcontinent whose educated classes have by the millions emigrated to Europe or North America, Baker was that great rarity: a Westerner who had chosen to spend his life living and working in India. I was curious to meet him.

Long before I did so, I got a taste of life in Baker buildings at Trivandrum's Centre for Development Studies, a research institute and graduate school where Arlie and I were Fulbright lecturers. The ten-acre campus, stretching across a hillside heavily wooded with coconut palms, is Baker's masterpiece. The offices, classroom clusters, and dormitories are all brick, with seldom a straight line; each structure curls in loops and waves and intersecting semi-circles. Almost all staircases are circular as well. The trees and folds of the hillside hide the Centre's buildings from each other; I was never able to find a spot from which you could see all or even most of them. The main building has a majestic entrance thirty or forty feet wide, whose ceiling rolls out and up toward the sky and whose sides roll outward onto an even wider set of steps. But, symbolic of an institution whose aim is to apply economics to helping the poor, the building has, amazingly, no front door. Anyone can walk up the steps and through the wide entrance and down the corridors at any hour of the day or night. If you want to lock your office door, that's up to you. But you can't lock the front door, because there isn't one.

Not only is this campus one of the country's most beautiful, but Baker built it for roughly half the normal cost per square foot of Indian university buildings. And the Centre's buildings were oases of coolness on even the most ferociously hot days. Some of that was due to the breezes blowing through the *jalis* that fill many outside walls. A Baker *jali* is a brick version of traditional south Indian patterned wooden grillwork: Gaps between bricks let air and daylight through a wall, while diffusing the glare of direct sunlight. Some of the Centre's coolness also came from open breezeways and some from tiny courtyards around pools whose evaporation helped fight the heat. And some came from the shade of the many palms overhead: Baker designed the campus so he would have to cut down as few trees as possible, curving some buildings around the trees. And with only one or two exceptions, such as the campus computer center, none of the Centre's offices have the Indian bureaucrat's normal status symbol, an air conditioner. In a world whose warming is speeded by electricity generation, Baker was intent on creating buildings whose construction and use required as little energy as possible.

· · ·

Although largely unknown outside India, Baker is a legendary figure in Kerala. One influential admirer was the late C. Achutha Menon, communist former chief minister of the state, who hired Baker to design public housing for the poor. Another enthusiast is the decidedly noncommunist maharaja of Travancore, who has no more political power these days, but who told me that he greatly respected Baker's work, because "he's very practical, down to earth, and I think he's quite right: You need not build a house that's a copy of one in Manhattan. It doesn't suit."

A droll, unassuming man with a handsome gray beard, Baker has the manner of an avuncular, absent-minded professor. His conversation rambles as if he hadn't a care in the world, and he wears no watch or socks—no one with any sense wears socks in south India. His voice is hearty, and he speaks slowly, always in complete sentences. A five-year-old granddaughter played quietly at his feet while we talked. He is still working at the age of eighty-three, and his most recent writings—two fifty-page pamphlets profusely illustrated with his own drawings—were published on his eightieth birthday. Although he has also written articles aimed at his fellow architects, most of Baker's writing is, like these pamphlets, aimed at a wider audience. Some have been translated into the local language, Malayalam. His key message is that building homes, schools, and community centers is too important, and too simple, to leave to architects and masons alone. Everyone can do it—and, indeed, almost everyone in rural India used to build their own homes. In one article Baker calls for "honest" building. He has a particular meaning in mind: the avoidance of "unnecessary architectural fashions, frills & finishes." But the word carries an echo of another part of his life as well, for he is a longtime Quaker, and the Quaker tradition of plain living helped lead him to the southern tip of India.

Baker grew up and studied architecture in the British industrial city of Birmingham. A conscientious objector, he joined an ambulance unit at the start of the Second World War, took care of bombing victims in London, then spent most of the conflict as a health care worker at a leper colony in China. On his way home, space for passengers in ships was hard to come by and he was stranded for several months in Bombay where, through Quaker friends, he came to know Mohandas Gandhi.

The Mahatma, it turned out, had a great interest in architecture. "He said, 'Please don't take any notice of this terrible stuff around us'—the four-, five-, and six-story buildings going up. There was a new telephone exchange, seven or eight stories high and covered all over with sheets of marble, stuck on, which he thought was terrible, gilding the lily." Gandhi sent Baker to see what he termed the "concrete slums"—the tenements for Bombay's workers, and then asked him, "What is the alternative? What can we do about it? We need people like you here."

Deeply inspired, Baker soon came back to India as an architect and began to build treatment centers for lepers. The British were still ruling, and he was horrified to find that he was assigned a bungalow with servants and was expected to dress for dinner and to ride a horse but not a bicycle. He promptly bicycled off to share quarters with an Indian staff member at one of the leper colonies. A few years later he married an Indian doctor, "and to begin with I was the rest of the hospital staff." Until 1962, they worked in a remote Himalayan region, then moved south to his wife's native state of Kerala. There they have lived ever since, with three adopted children, most recently in an eccentric hillside house of Baker's design, with no locks or burglar bars, protected only by a wall and a doghouse that sits atop the gateway. He did much of the construction himself, some of it using stone found on the site. Window grills in the house make use of scrap metal: parts of a bicycle wheel and a clutch plate from an old car. Baker also makes his own scratch pads of the backs of discarded envelopes, bills, and wedding invitations.

It was in the Himalayan foothills that Baker first saw how traditional Indian architecture reflects thousands of years of trial-and-error research in energy efficiency. "The rock they quarried for building the foundation and basement walls was ... from the same bedrock on which they would build," he has written, noting that timber "was always found within a few hundred yards, or at most a mile or two, of the house being constructed." Seeing this reminded him of one of Gandhi's beliefs—that all buildings should be made of materials found within a five-mile radius.

Baker has not always been able to follow this principle, but he has come close. He is profoundly hostile, for example, to glass and steel: Making each requires large amounts of fossil fuel, and in Kerala the steel has to come from other parts of India. He also hates plaster, which he regards as a costly prestige item that does nothing except cover up a handsome wall of bricks made from local clay.

Bricks he loves. Standard red bricks do require energy to make, but in the brick-makers' kilns of south India, he points out, much of the fuel would not be used for much else: brush, tree branches, and scraps of palm wood too small for lumber. On a construction site, Baker often lays a brick wall with his own hands. For him this is not a matter of Gandhian self-humbling but one of sensual pleasure: "Designing a house and getting someone else to build it is like preparing a menu with great care and then leaving it to someone to do the cooking and the eating. It's no fun."

Mortar for bricks normally would require cement—another Baker enemy, because it takes energy to produce, and until recently most cement in India had to be imported. He prefers local substitutes, such as lime. When building the Centre for Development Studies, he made lime on the spot. Sending people to gather bullock-cartloads of seashells on beaches a few miles away, he then had the shells baked in a mud kiln (its fan powered by someone pedaling a stationary bicycle) and ground up into powder. Few of the scholars from India and abroad using the graceful, sturdy brick buildings at the Centre realize that their office walls are partly held up by pulverized clamshells.

Nor do they know that they're walking on bamboo. Concrete floors and steps are ordinarily reinforced with steel rods, but Baker has found that a grid of split local bamboo, carefully lashed together in the right pattern, does just as well—and at less than 5 percent of the cost. Skeptics claim that the bamboo will rot, but Baker replies that if the contractor pours the concrete properly, the bamboo is sealed tight within it, protected against moisture, insects, and bacteria. Twenty-five years of footsteps on the concrete stairways at the Centre have proved him right.

Baker would like to work more with that greatest of renewable materials, wood, but widespread deforestation in India has made this impossible. He would love to see Kerala's devastated forests replanted with a traditional building wood, the jack tree, a fruit-bearing Indian member of the mulberry family—"a very beautiful wood, a nice rich amber color"—which can be rubbed with oil from local cashews that acts as a preservative. It would be so easy, he muses, gesturing plaintively, for the state forestry authorities to plant groves of jack trees: "They could do it with picnics for the foresters' children! Give them each a jackfruit and have them go wandering spitting out pips."

The trouble with Indian policy-makers is that "they haven't the faith in their own materials," he believes. Everyone who can afford it wants to use only concrete, steel, and glass. His own favorite building material of all is one that uses no fuel to produce, is usually only a few steps away, and is free: mud. To those who laugh, he points out that if you count everything from village house to New Delhi office towers, 58 percent of all buildings in India are built of mud, and a good number of those are more than a hundred years old. Mud is also completely reusable. You can tear down your old house, add water, and make a new one in a different design. Try that with glass and steel.

When building a mud house, he says, you have to put an overhanging roof above the outside walls and a drainage ditch around the outside of the house; otherwise, the monsoon rains will turn your walls back to liquid again. Sometimes also, depending on the composition of the local earth, you need to add a stabilizer to the mud—"to make it stick together, to act as a sort of glue or binder. There are dozens and dozens of stabilizers—from latexes to the wild cactus in the forest: If you cut the cactus stalk, a white milk comes out and it's a very good stabilizer." In his early years, he had one memorable lesson in stabilizers: "We used to go through a place on our way from the Himalaya to Delhi, where we had to wait for a train. There were *beautiful* mud houses, but the soil was totally unsuitable. So I tried to find out what the stabilizer was that they used. But they would not tell me! What was this nosy blighter from outside wanting to know this for? Eventually, I discovered that they were using pig's urine! We chased pigs and got their urine analyzed. The urea content is very high, and urea is a binder."

Unfortunately, few middle-class clients share Baker's enthusiasm for this building material. "I say, 'Have you thought of using mud? It would save you a lot of money.' And they say, 'Well ... no, you don't know our rain, Mr. Baker!'" Where he has most often been able to design mud buildings has been in public housing. A family sleeping under a tarpaulin or under nothing at all won't worry if its first real house doesn't look like one in the San Fernando Valley.

Baker has designed tens of thousands of low-income housing units in Kerala, but outside the state he has had few such commissions. There are too many enemies: his fellow-architects "feel that I'm somewhat of a traitor to the whole profession" because of the low fees he charges when designing housing for the poor. When Baker showed that homes could be built for a fraction of government estimates, contractors saw their opportunities for fraud diminished. And public works bureaucrats haven't liked the way Baker's plans fail to fit their idea a proper housing project: his homes are specifically designed *not* to all look alike; they are on winding, village-like streets, not an orderly cross-hatched grid; and there aren't separate living areas for Hindus, Muslims, and Christians.

. . .

Laurie Baker has not turned his back on the modern world; the homes and offices he has built have running water, electricity, telephone lines, and sometimes garages. But in his embrace of brick, mud, and bamboo, in his recognition that letting hot air escape is wiser than air conditioning, and much more, Baker has done what tragically few people in any field in the global South have done, which is to be *selective* about what they take from the North.

His ideas have caught the imagination of younger, environmentally minded Indian architects and engineers, and nearly a hundred of them now work for a Kerala nonprofit organization that practices his approach, COSTFORD, or the Centre of Science and Technology for Rural Development. In the past fifteen years, COSTFORD has built homes for ten thousand poverty-level families, for which it charges no design fee. It has also built government buildings and homes for fifteen hundred middle-class and professional families— which has helped pay for the other work. The organization's Trivandrum office is run by Shailaja Nair, a 34-year-old architect, and her engineer husband. Here in one of the most caste-conscious parts of India, the two of them, most unusually, come from different castes; their marriage caused much tension between Nair and her family. It meant a great deal to the couple that when this happened, at the outset of their professional lives, Laurie Baker, who also knows something about being an iconoclast, took them in and gave them space to work in an outbuilding of his own home. They have been with COSTFORD ever since. A picture of "Bakerji" is on the office wall. "He's half a century older than us," says Nair. "But he's one of us. How do you explain a man like that?"

Nair is a tall, fast-talking, dark-haired woman who wears a dazzling salwar kameez. She energetically sketches designs on a piece of scrap paper to describe forty-five primary schools COSTFORD is now building for the state government. All of these are four-room schools in rural areas, each built for the equivalent of about $15,000. Nair's quick drawings show me first the long, rectangular shape of most schools, "like a factory": classrooms in a row, opening off a corridor. Instead, the schools she is working on are all variations of a Baker-inspired design that looks like part of a sliced pie. The four classrooms are each shaped like the broader two-thirds of a slice. Normally each teacher will stand at the wide, outside end of the pie slice. But when need be, students can turn their chairs around to face the narrower, inside end of the slice, which has no end wall. The inside ends of all four slices open onto the center of the pie, a space that can be used as if it were the stage of an auditorium, with the classrooms as seating areas.

Over the course of a day, Nair takes me on a tour of COSTFORD projects. We end up in a rural village called Koliyacode to visit five recently completed mud homes of several rooms each. Government subsidies provided the equivalent of around $400 per house, and the village residents contributed more, in some cases their own labor. Most of the money went for wood (roof beams and window and door frames) and roofing tile. There is no glass in the windows, but wooden bars keep out the crows. Except for the roof tile and the wood, everything is dried brown mud: inner and outer walls, and even the large mud bricks that hold up some living room shelves. The earth in Koliyacode has just the right consistency and requires no stabilizer.

The weather has gotten hotter than ever since I arrived in Kerala, but today, inside these buildings, it is wonderfully cool. The one place inside where it's hot—the loft area underneath the tile roof, where the sun's heat has seeped through the tile and hot air from inside has risen—is used to dry grain or freshly washed clothes. The sturdy outer walls are about six inches thick. They do not crumble to the touch and feel hard as concrete when I bang my fist on them. As I tour the houses, an increasing flock of villagers and their children gather, curious that a foreigner would come all this way to punch a wall of mud.

· · ·

Sometimes Laurie Baker doesn't bother about blueprints; he prefers informal sketches and talking with construction workers on the spot. And so I ask if I can see a home he is now building. The house is for a government official and his wife, a poet. Appropriately, it is the poet whom Baker is mainly dealing with. She is, he says happily, his first client who is as eccentric as he.

"One of the things I'm noted to be crazy for is that I use old colored bottles set in cement—they give a nice light. In the drawing room, about half the main wall is going to be made of bottles only. And then we've got some holes in the roof to let sunlight in and air out." Baker seizes a piece of chalk from a pouch slung over his shoulder and uses the brick wall of the house as a crude blackboard: He shows how each roof hole will have a raised rim of bottles. The rim will support a concrete cap to keep the rain out, like that covering a chimney. And, he adds gleefully, these round skylight-vents will also function as sundials. An even more unexpected feature of the house is that—like many Baker buildings—it is in the form of a spiral. A rising ribbon of smaller rooms, interspersed with a few desk-sized nooks for writing poetry, curls around a central living room, whose ceiling is two stories high.

A spiral home with poetry-writing nooks is not likely to be reproduced en masse as housing for India's poor, as Baker himself would be the first to admit. But even here, at his zaniest, Baker has built a house that costs vastly less than one of the same square footage designed by a conventional architect. First of all, as any high school geometry student knows, a circle is the shortest line that will contain a given amount of space. The outer wall of a rectangular house would use far more brick. Second, the fact that most inside walls in the poet's house are also curved means some can be built with just a single thickness of brick, instead of the double thickness that straight brick walls of equal length would require to remain stable.

And finally, Baker is using a remarkable variety of recycled materials beyond the several hundred glass bottles. In the bathrooms, for example, bits and pieces of waste glass are put to work as tiles: "If you want a piece of glass to fit a window you go to the glass place and they cut your size, and there're always these little strips left that they throw under the table. So I said, 'Can I have some?'" In addition, several hundred chipped or broken roofing tiles are embedded every foot or two in this building's concrete roof, a signature Baker technique. As you look up at it, the inside of the roof looks like a checkerboard whose squares have been battered and then flown apart. These otherwise wasted tiles add so much reinforcement that Baker can use 30 percent less concrete in the roof.

Furthermore, once finished, the poet's house will consume far less energy than many homes half its size. Thanks to *jali* walls, cool air flows in; and thanks to the bottle-rimmed roof vents, hot air flows out. There are no electric ceiling fans (even modest Indian homes often have one in each room) and no air conditioning.

As we continue our tour through the house, Baker gives instructions to the workmen, who today are making windows—some of which, incidentally, will contain no glass, only rough vertical wooden slats which can be tilted one way or the other to catch the breeze. After several dizzying loops, we have spiraled up to the roof, and climb out onto it.

Here too, Baker says, "You can sit and write poems." The nearby trees tower another fifteen or twenty feet overhead, their breadfruit and coconuts dangling almost within reach. The real poetry of this house is that it respects its surroundings and doesn't try to overpower them.

The same cannot be said, unfortunately, for what we can see from here of the city skyline. A few older buildings in sight, such as the maharaja's palace, respect the ancient unwritten law that no building should be higher than one of Kerala's coconut palms. But dotting the horizon are the palaces of the new maharajas—slablike eight- and ten-story modern luxury apartment buildings for India's burgeoning business and professional class, all of them, Baker points out, requiring huge amounts of scarce electricity to run their elevators and air conditioning. Baker's poetry in brick and mud is, by contrast, in harmony with its surroundings, not only aesthetically but in its knowledge that the Earth will not forever permit us to be so profligate with its riches.

1999

FOURTEEN

The Impossible City

CITIES, LIKE COUNTRIES AND FAMILIES, have an official currency of power and a real one. The official currency is votes and laws: citizens elect mayor and city council members; politicians pass laws; police supposedly enforce them. But the real currency of power is always different. In the Mumbai of Suketu Mehta's dazzling book *Maximum City: Bombay Lost and Found* that currency is a combustible mix of threats, violence, bribes, sex, and glory. If someone owes you money and won't pay, you hire a gang to kidnap one of his children. If the cops capture a particularly dangerous gunman, they call up the gang leader and ask how much he'll pay to get his man released. In one district, plumbers bribe local officials to turn off the water to public taps so that people have to hire them to install private pipes. In another, drivers of water-tanker trucks pay off the government so that it installs no pipes at all. A group of traders calls a public meeting to complain that extortion costs are soaring; they threaten to stop paying sales taxes unless police death squads kill more extortionists. (The city's High Court has ruled that extortion payments are tax deductible as a business expense.) The huge local film industry, heavily financed by all this crime, completes the circuit. When some gangsters are hired to do crowd control at an outdoor shoot, they are thrilled to see the glamorous stars up close. An actress, in turn, is fascinated to meet real gangsters. She asks Mehta, "Can you point out someone who's killed?"

Mehta, who is happy to point out to readers more than a few people who have killed, seems to have known for a long time that his real subject was the city where he grew up, and he has been working on this book, his first, for many years. He lived mostly in Mumbai—then Bombay—until coming to the United States at the age of fourteen. As an adult, he has returned to

India ever more frequently to write about it, finally moving his wife and American-born children to Mumbai for several years. Being an outsider all his life—variously a Gujarati in a city dominated by Maharashtrians, an Indian in the United States, an American citizen in India, a secularist in a country brimming over with all the world's major religions, a writer in an extended family of diamond merchants—has made him a voraciously curious observer.

Because of his zest to put every byway of the Mumbai underworld on the page, his high-energy evoking of characters high and low, and the way his gaze settles on the newcomers trying to make it in the great city, Mehta's eye reminds me of no one's so much as Balzac's on Paris. He makes almost all other reporting on India, such as the overrated travel books of V. S. Naipaul, look pallid by comparison.

The first few of the dozen or so extended portraits in Mehta's gallery bring us inside the Hindu nationalist Shiv Sena movement, long powerful in the politics of Mumbai and the surrounding state of Maharashtra. (The old British-educated business elite of Gujaratis, Parsis, and others who once ran the city are as horrified by these lower-class Maharashtrians as Boston Brahmins were by the Irish who elected the machine boss James Curley as the city's mayor in 1914.) The movement's demagogic founder, Bal Thackeray—his father liked the novelist—professed an admiration for Hitler. In 1993, Shiv Sena mobs rampaged through the Muslim parts of town, burning, raping, and murdering. The police stood by and, before long, transcripts of radio traffic reveal, enthusiastically joined in. Over nine days, some six hundred people were killed and two thousand injured. Only a handful of the Hindu rioters were ever prosecuted, and ten policemen charged with murder were actually promoted. Some 215,000 Muslims fled the city on special trains, the homes and businesses of many of them blackened ruins.

Sometimes, in savoring a book's unexpected power, I imagine how a lesser writer would have handled the material. In sketching the shadow this communal violence has left on Mumbai, for instance, most would have spoken only to the victims or their families. Mehta, by contrast, goes straight for the killers. He gets a Shiv Sena member to walk him through the city, showing him the spots where the man set fire to a mosque, looted shops, and burned Muslims to death. "It was like a movie," the man tells him: "silent, empty, someone burning somewhere and us hiding." Mehta asks another such killer, whom he calls Sunil, "What does a man look like when he's on fire?" Sunil tells him, and describes how he and four other men killed a Muslim bread vendor. "We poured petrol on him and set him on fire. All I thought was, This is a Muslim. . . . That day we showed them what Hindu dharma is."

Why does someone get caught up in such killing? As with so many people drawn to fascist movements, Sunil remembers a childhood of humiliation. At one point both his parents were in the hospital and he would try to bring them hot food. But, after racing home from school, if he didn't make it to the hospital by 2:00 p.m., when daytime visiting hours were cut off, he would have to wait until evening visiting hours, vainly pleading. Those who had money to bribe the guard got let in. "I didn't have ten or twenty rupees, so I sat there thinking . . . If one has to live, one should live in a proper way." All is now different. "Now I can cross the door of any hospital. . . . I can talk to Balasaheb Thackeray, and he will phone the hospital, and they will fear him." Sunil's daughter goes to a top school, her admission arranged by a Shiv Sena minister in the state government. In return, Sunil is always ready to turn out his men for the minister when, he says, "they are needed to burn a train or break a car."

Sunil has risen in the movement and prospered from a cable TV franchise it arranged for him. But his very success may be loosening his ties to the Shiv Sena. When the government at one point barred Indian cable systems from broadcasting the programming of the country's archenemy, Pakistan, Sunil objected, saying, "The thing that someone pays for, you should give them." His business instincts are winning over his malice towards Muslims," Mehta writes. The city "is seducing him away from hate, through the even more powerful attraction of greed."

Hate, however, is still the key tool for the Shiv Sena leader, Thackeray, who himself opens up to Mehta with amazing candor about how he gets mobs to do his bidding: "Young blood, young men, youngsters without jobs are like dry gunpowder. It will explode any day." Part of the art of manipulating them is to convince them that their unemployment or any other problem of life in this city, where sewage leaks into freshwater lines and some two million people are without access to private or public toilets, is all the fault of Muslims. Thackeray would like to have visas required for anyone coming to Mumbai to live. He admires the strict border controls of the United States.

Mehta's quest to plumb every depth in Mumbai leads to an equally disturbing portrait of someone ostensibly upholding the law, a senior police officer whom he calls Ajay Lal. Lal is startlingly frank about his means of interrogation: bullets fired past an ear, electrodes to the genitals, a trip to a creek where cops tie a heavy stone to a prisoner and repeatedly bring him close to drowning. For Muslim militants, Lal says, other methods are necessary, because "those who have no fear of death also have no fear of physical pain. For them we threaten their family. . . . That usually works."

Hearing this, that lesser writer might have thought: I've got the incriminating quote; that's all I need. Mehta, however, asks Lal if he can sit in on a few interrogation sessions. Lal lets him do so. In one, Lal and his officers question two men just arrested with a stash of counterfeit money. "Both speak English and are well dressed. They are uncomfortably familiar. A little more money, a little more education, and they would be People Like Us." Lal's constables go at them with fists and "a thick leather strap, about six inches wide, attached to a wooden handle. One of the cops takes it and brings it savagely down across the fat man's face. The sound of leather hitting bare human flesh is impossible to describe."

Yet in the midst of watching this beating, Mehta still manages to notice that, just as the Hindu and Muslim gangsters he has interviewed don't let go of their religion, neither do these counterfeiters let go of India's deep respect for rank. "As they are being beaten, they address their tormentors as 'sir.' Thus we addressed our teachers in school. . . . Not once do they fly out; not once do they scream an obscenity." One man finally yields the name of a mistress, a dancer; she is quickly arrested and leads Lal to the rest of the counterfeiters' ring. (Such questioning is routine; when Mehta visits another police station, he hears agonized screaming coming from behind a closed door.)

One feels a guilty, voyeuristic horror at even reading such a scene on the page. But then that horror becomes slowly, uncomfortably tempered as we learn more about Lal and see that this picture is far more complicated than merely a brutal man at work. Lal takes no bribes. He plans arrests in secret to prevent corrupt superiors from tipping off gangsters in advance. He knows exactly which senior police official has received what—women, money, a free apartment—from which gang chief. He suspects that one junior officer working for him is a gang mole. If he doesn't threaten or beat information out of a suspect as soon as he's been arrested, a gang boss will bribe someone to get him out of jail, or stand by and let him take the fall for those higher up. In court, appeals can take twenty years or more; each judge has more than three thousand cases pending, and, thanks to payoffs, the conviction rate for criminal offenses is a mere 4 percent.

Lal has devoted his life to the vain struggle to break the power of the gangs, too often getting home after his children have gone to sleep. Gang leaders have threatened to kill him, to kill his wife, to blow up his sons' school. He needs bodyguards even to come to Mehta's apartment for dinner. His boys need them to go to school. He can relax only when he travels abroad. He is fearless about raiding the houses of Shiv Sena officials, including Bal Thackeray's son, and his career has suffered as a result. He has turned down offers of jobs outside the police department at far higher pay. Despite everything, this torturer is one of the few honest high officials in the book.

. . .

It is exhilarating to plunge so deeply with Mehta into the lives of his characters, but at times you have the uneasy feeling that his lust to know everything about them is so intense, it's reckless. The currency of power he wields is the writer's coin: the knowledge of secrets. Only once does he openly flaunt this wealth, when he talks about a bar dancer and prostitute who shares with him stories of her childhood, her hopes, her struggles with her family, her attempt to end her life, her clients, and how she lures them. "I know what color and type of underwear she wears. I know how she likes to make love. I know when she is sad, when she is suicidal, when she is exuberant." Mehta's relationship with the dancer is only platonic, he claims, but, he exults, "What is sex after such vast intimate knowledge?"

Just for that reason I wonder how this woman, and the other people who so readily confide their stories to him, feel when these are read by family and friends. Mehta is disturbingly foggy about when he has changed names and identifying details and when he has not. And even the changes he does make seem to be minor: the brutal, incorruptible, and supposedly pseudonymous Ajay Lal, for example, is transparently recognizable to any reader of Indian newspapers as Rakesh Maria, a longtime Mumbai police official. A senior cop is surely experienced in the dangers and rewards of talking to journalists, including those careless about protecting sources, but most of the others who so opened their souls to Mehta probably have never spoken to a writer before. Are their identities any better hidden? I hope so.

Part of Mehta's ambitiousness—and here is where his characters remind me of Balzac's provincial immigrants to Paris—is that he knows that today every great city in the global South is simultaneously a destination and a jumping-off point. Village Indians crave a foothold in the vast metropolis. Those living on the sidewalk want a shack. Shack dwellers dream of a proper apartment. The upper classes want to emigrate to London, Toronto, New

York. *Maximum City* abounds with long, vivid sketches from this entire array: a teenage runaway who sleeps on planks in the open air; the bar dancer who fled a violent mother and whose great dream is to win the Miss India contest; a slum family who finally scrape together enough money to buy their first apartment; a group of professionals planning to move together to Vancouver.

The entire city is packed with people trying to claw their way up. Mehta glues himself to them, never content just to interview and go away. He rushes to the scene when the runaway's father comes to find his son; he follows the bar dancer back to a reunion with her family; he's there when the slum family move into their first apartment building—where a shady contractor has put in an elevator shaft but no elevator.

Some people open up to Mehta because he's from America, the land of dreams; even just speaking to him raises their status. Sunil, the Shiv Sena thug, talks more readily when Mehta brings him to a friend's high-rise flat, a great luxury for someone who grew up in a slum; he notices Sunil's "sense of well-being whenever I take him to a high floor." And some of the gangsters tell him their stories because they know he writes movie scripts, and they imagine making the greatest migration of all: having their lives on the screen, to be seen the world over.

It is all the more striking, then, that Mehta's final portrait from this city of people on the make is the story of a family—and here I can recall no equivalent in Balzac—that renounces every form of its currency of power. A wealthy diamond merchant, his wife, and their three children decide to follow the most honored custom in the Jain religion by giving away all their money to become wandering barefoot pilgrims, begging for their food, allowed to eat only once a day, with no possessions but the simple clothes on their backs. The husband and two sons, the wife and the daughter, must wander the roads of India separately, for man and woman must renounce not just all their worldly goods but each other.

Fellow Jains praise the family for taking this holiest of steps. But for others, this act is deeply upsetting, a challenge to the whole basis of the city's modern life. A critical onlooker believes the family only did it because "the Dawood gang must have been after them." Someone else mutters that things are not as they seem, that there is a trust fund in case the family changes its mind. Mehta's Westernized, cosmopolitan friends "shudder even more when hearing about them than when I talk about the hit men." Mehta is there when the family gives away its wealth, throwing endless handfuls of bills and gold and silver coins into a vast crowd from carts drawn by elephants—a gesture that reminds him of a picture he has already shown us of patrons showering rupees on his bar dancer.

Not content to let the story rest with such an extraordinary scene, months later Mehta tracks down the former merchant to see how he is doing in his life of pilgrimage. The soles of the man's bare feet are "cracked, calloused, split, and blackened" from walking through the villages of India; his heart, he says, is at peace.

. . .

It is certainly hard to feel one's heart at peace in visiting this overwhelming city. My first visit to Mumbai stands out in memory with unforgettable vividness. An afternoon sky dark with pollution, like premature dusk; streets, parks, buses, and sidewalks jammed with people—holy men, beggars, cripples, cricket players, hawkers of every conceivable item of food or clothing; shantytown huts packed together in unimaginable denseness; the smell of human waste, rotting fruit, diesel exhaust, sweat, perfume; the layer of oily dust that rapidly covered every object, even indoors. It was numbing, paralyzing, insurmountable.

Late in the day, coming back to the university guesthouse where I was staying, I was peering out through a car window, which, like everything else, was covered with grime. We passed a flatbed cart, pulled and pushed by a dozen or so men in white knee-length kurtas, leaning far forward with the strain. Suddenly I realized it was a funeral procession. A man's body dressed in white lay on the cart, wreathed with garland upon garland of white flowers. The moment seemed transcendent, the sorrow of the procession softened by the flowers, a touch of beauty under a dark and smoky sky. *Maximum City*—gritty and unsentimental, but by its breathtaking boldness and scope a paean to this impossible city—is a garland for Mumbai.

2005

Europe .

FIGURE 5. Republican militiawomen, Spanish Civil War.

FIFTEEN

Our Night with Its Stars Askew

SOME YEARS AGO I WAS AT A CONFERENCE of writers and journalists from various countries. In a group of a dozen or so, someone suggested that we go around the circle and each of us name the political writer he or she most admired. When my turn came, I named Victor Serge. A man I did not know leapt to his feet, strode across the room, and embraced me. He turned out to be Rafael Barajas of Mexico, who under the pen name of El Fisgón (the Snooper) is one of Latin America's leading political cartoonists.

It is rare when a writer inspires instant brotherhood among strangers. A prolific novelist, poet, journalist, and author of one of the twentieth century's great memoirs, Serge began and ended his life in exile and spent much of it either in prison or in flight from various governments trying to put him there. He was born Victor Kibalchich in 1890; his parents were Russian revolutionaries who had fled to Belgium. With little formal schooling, as a child he often had only bread soaked in coffee to eat. In Brussels, he recalled, "On the walls of our humble and makeshift lodgings there were always the portraits of men who had been hanged."

As a teenager, in a leftist political group, he was one of the tiny handful of people in Belgium who boldly criticized King Leopold II's avaricious rule over the Congo. But he went farther than others in taking a stand against colonialism itself—a rare position in Europe at that time. He soon left home, lived in a French mining village, worked as a typesetter, and finally made his way to Paris. There he lived with beggars, read Balzac, and grew fascinated by the underworld. But soon the revolutionary in him overcame the wanderer. He became an anarchist and the editor of one of the movement's newspapers. For refusing to testify against some comrades he was sentenced, at the age of twenty-two, to five years in a French maximum security prison. Released in

1917, he eventually managed to make his way to Russia—the ancestral homeland he had never seen.

He arrived there in early 1919, in the midst of the Russian Civil War. This brutal conflict, which took several million lives, was between the Bolsheviks and the counterrevolutionary White forces—mostly led by former tsarist generals, and supplied by England, France, Japan, the United States, and other countries wary of revolution spreading to their own territory.

Writing, as he did for the rest of his life, under the pen name of Victor Serge, he spent most of the next seventeen years in Russia. Among the shrill and dogmatic voices of that time, his still rings clear and true today. Although a supporter of the Russian Revolution, Serge never abandoned his sympathy for the free spirits who didn't toe the Bolshevik line. "The telephone became my personal enemy," he wrote. "At every hour it brought me voices of panic-stricken women who spoke of arrest, imminent executions, and injustice, and begged me to intervene at once, for the love of God!"

Yet the White armies were attacking on several fronts; Serge felt it was no time for intellectuals, however just their criticisms, to be on the sidelines. "Even if there were only one chance in a hundred for the regeneration of the revolution and its workers' democracy," he later wrote, "that chance had to be taken." He served as a militia officer fighting the Whites and then at one point was put in charge of examining the captured archives of the Okhrana, the tsarist secret police. At the same time he continued to be appalled by the growth of a new secret police regime around him, and, once the Russian Civil War was over, argued ceaselessly against the straitjacketed press, the arrests, the closed trials, and the death penalty for political prisoners.

In a sense, Serge never resolved the tension between his ardent hope for a revolutionary new society and his passion for civil liberties. What do you do if most people are more concerned about staying alive and having enough to eat than living in a new utopia? Was that utopia still worth fighting for if there was "only one chance in a hundred" it could be achieved? And was the suppression of all opposition built in to the millenarian confidence in that utopian dream? Serge never fully sorted out the contradiction in his own soul between the revolutionary and the democrat. Despairing as he watched the Soviet bureaucracy grow ever more oppressive, he and some like-minded friends tried to build a miniature version of the society they believed in by founding a communal farm on an abandoned estate where "we would live close to the earth." But, surrounded by turmoil, famine, and distrustful villagers, the experiment didn't last.

His protests against the regime's actions got Serge expelled from the Communist Party. In 1928, Stalin clapped him in jail. Always alert to irony, Serge talked to one of his guards and found that he had served in the same job under the last tsar. When he was released some weeks later, the janitor at his Leningrad apartment building said that it was "the same under the old regime. The intellectuals were always arrested like this, just before the first of May." A few days after being freed from prison, Serge wrote, "I was laid out by an unendurable abdominal pain; for twenty-four hours I was face-to-face with death.... And I reflected that I had labored, striven, and schooled myself titanically, without producing anything valuable or lasting. I told myself, 'If I chance to survive, I must be quick and finish the books I have begun: I must write, write...' I thought of what I would write, and mentally sketched the plan of a series of documentary novels about these unforgettable times."

And write he did. In all of his books, his prose has a searing, vivid, telegraphic compactness. His style comes not from endless refinement and rewriting, like Flaubert's, but from the urgency of being a man on the run. The police are at the door; his friends are being arrested; he must get the news out; every word must tell. And he is not like the novelist in a calmer society who searches and experiments to find exactly the right subject at last; *his* subject—the Russian Revolution and its aftermath—almost killed him. During Stalin's dictatorship, it is estimated today, somewhere between ten and twenty million people met unnatural deaths: from the deliberate famine brought on by the collectivization of agriculture, from firing squads, and from the vast Arctic and Siberian gulag of labor camps that devoured the victims of mass arrests. Driven by Stalin's increasing paranoia, these arrests and executions peaked in the Great Purge of the late 1930s, when millions were seized in midnight raids, many never to be seen by their families again.

Serge's opposition to Soviet tyranny meant that his work could never be published in Stalin's USSR, but his radicalism long kept much of it out of print in the United States as well. George Orwell felt akin to Serge and tried unsuccessfully to find him a British publisher. Today, however, he has won increasing recognition. Recent decades have seen books and articles about him by many writers, a biography, and the translation of a number of his novels into English for the first time. Older editions of other Serge books have been reprinted, and some admirers founded a Victor Serge Library in Moscow.

Serge was part of the generation that, at first, believed the Russian Revolution was an epochal step forward. Millions of people in many countries were ready to see it that way after the First World War, which took the lives of more than nine million soldiers, wounded twenty-one million, and left millions of civilians dead as well. His great hopes make all the more poignant his clear-eyed picture of the gathering darkness as the Revolution turned slowly into the equivalent of a vast, self-inflicted genocide. It was the era when, as a character in his novel *Conquered City* says, "We have conquered everything, and everything has slipped out of our grasp." A poem Serge wrote captures the same feeling:

> If we roused the peoples and made the continents quake,
> ... began to make everything anew with these dirty old stones,
> these tired hands, and the meager souls that were left us,
> it was not in order to haggle with you now,
> sad revolution, our mother, our child, our flesh,
> our decapitated dawn, our night with its stars askew ...

Serge's eyewitness account of this decapitated dawn is nowhere more tragic than in his *Memoirs of a Revolutionary*, a book that ranks with Orwell's *Homage to Catalonia*, Koestler's *Darkness at Noon*, and Primo Levi's *Survival in Auschwitz* as a great act of political witness. He describes, for example, coming back to Russia in 1926 after a trip abroad: "A return to Russian soil rends the heart. '*Earth of Russia*,' wrote the poet Tyutchev, '*no corner of you is untouched by Christ the slave*.' The Marxist explains it in the same terms: 'The production of commodities was never sufficient.'" In the countryside, the hungry poor have taken to the roads. The streets of Leningrad are filled with beggars, abandoned children, prostitutes. "The hotels laid on for foreigners and Party officials have bars that are complete with tables covered in soiled white linen, dusty palm trees, and alert waiters who know secrets beyond the Revolution's ken." One after another, people Serge knows and admires—labor organizers, poets, veteran revolutionaries—commit suicide.

In 1933, Serge was arrested again. He asked friends to take care of his wife and young son if he were executed. Instead, however, he and his family were exiled to the remote city of Orenburg in the Ural Mountains. People were starving; children clawed each other in the streets for a piece of bread. Serge became fast friends with the other political exiles there, a small group of men and women who shared food and ideas, nursed one another through illnesses, and kept each other alive.

Fluent in five languages, Serge did almost all his writing in French. By the time of his exile in Orenburg, his books and articles had found him a following among independent leftists in the West who were alarmed by both fascism and Stalinism. In 1936, protests by French intellectuals finally won him the right to leave Russia. This was the year that the Great Purge began in earnest, with mass arrests and executions on a scale unmatched in Russian history, indeed, in almost any country's history. Serge's release from the Soviet Union almost certainly saved his life. The secret police seized all copies of the manuscripts of four books he had written, including the novel he thought his best. Thanks to his exile, Serge said wryly, these were "the only works I have ever had the opportunity to revise at leisure." Since the collapse of the USSR, people have searched repeatedly for these manuscripts in Russian archives, but with no success.

When he arrived in western Europe, Serge's politics again made him an outsider. Neither mainstream nor communist newspapers would publish his articles, and the European communist parties attacked him ferociously. His primary forum was a small labor paper in Belgium. There, and in a stream of new books, pamphlets, speeches, and defense committees, he railed against the Great Purge, defended the Spanish Republic, then in the midst of a losing war against Francisco Franco and his Nationalists, and spoke out against the Western powers for accommodating Hitler. These ideas were not popular. To make ends meet he went back to work at a trade he had first learned in his youth. As a typesetter and proofreader, he now found himself sometimes correcting the galleys of newspapers that would not publish his writing.

Meanwhile, Stalin's agents roamed Europe, on occasion assassinating members of the opposition in exile. Back in the Soviet Union, things were still worse: Serge's sister, mother-in-law, two brothers-in-law, and two sisters-in-law disappeared into the Gulag. His wife, Lyuba Russakova, became psychotic and had to be put in a French mental hospital. The Germans invaded France; when Nazi tanks reached the suburbs of Paris and shells were falling on the Fontainebleau woods, Serge fled the city. He was stranded for many months in Marseille, then under the control of the Vichy government, sharing a house with others in flight, including his friend the French surrealist André Breton, while American sympathizers lobbied desperately to find countries across the Atlantic that would accept them as refugees. As always, he was writing, now, even in these circumstances, working on the novel that would be his best-known, *The Case of Comrade Tulayev.* The United States refused him a visa. The Nazis burned his books. It was, Serge wrote, "a world with no possible escape." Just ahead of the Gestapo, he and his teenage son were at last able to leave Marseille on a ship to Mexico. When it stopped in

Martinique, Vichy French officials grilled the passengers, wanting to know who was Jewish. "I do not have that honor," Serge told them.

. . .

Although Serge's novels provide a vivid picture of the tumultuous era he lived through, his greatest work is his *Memoirs of a Revolutionary*. The book he thought he was writing, however, is not exactly the one we admire him for today. In both this volume and some twenty others—fiction, nonfiction, biography, history, and poetry—his driving passion was to rescue the honor of the idealists who participated in the Russian Revolution from the Stalinists, who turned it into a horror show. "The scrupulous and the just, the noble, humane, and devoted . . . the unselfish and the intelligent may begin a movement," Joseph Conrad wrote in his prescient *Under Western Eyes*, "—but it passes away from them. They are not the leaders of a revolution. They are its victims." Serge wanted to celebrate just those people.

Noble and humane some of the Bolsheviks may have been, but looking back on those times today, it is hard to believe that anything promising could have emerged from a movement that so early made clear its contempt for democracy. It was January 1918, after all, only two months after their coup, that Bolshevik soldiers with fixed bayonets broke up the first day's meeting of the Constituent Assembly, the national legislature chosen in the first reasonably free election Russia had ever had. Nor can we share Serge's hope that the fractious Left Oppositionists who loosely coalesced around Leon Trotsky in the following decade could have created the good society in Russia, even though surely none of them would have constructed a charnel house as murderous as Stalin's. Once again, Serge's revolutionary dreams were in conflict with his shrewd assessment of the people around him, for the brilliant capsule portrait of Trotsky in his memoirs shows both the man's wide-ranging intellect and his harsh, authoritarian streak.

What moves us now in this book, and Serge's others, is not so much his vision of what the Revolution might have been. It is, rather, two qualities of the man himself. The first is his ability to see the world with unflinching clarity. In the Soviet Union's first decade and a half, despite arrests, ostracism, theft of his manuscripts, and the near starvation he faced for a time, he bore witness. This was rare. Although other totalitarian regimes, left and right, have had naïve, besotted admirers, never has there been a despotism praised by so many otherwise sane intellectuals. George Bernard Shaw traveled to Russia in the midst of the man-made famine of the early 1930s and declared that there was food enough for everyone. Walter Duranty, the Pulitzer Prize-winning *New York Times* correspondent in Moscow, whitewashed the famine as well. In Soviet Russia the great muckraking journalist Lincoln Steffens saw, in his famous phrase, a future that worked. An astonishing variety of other Westerners, from the Dean of Canterbury to the U.S. ambassador, Joseph E. Davies (see p. 181), saw a society full of happy workers and laughing children. By contrast with all these cheerful visitors, Victor Serge had what Orwell, in another context, called the "power of facing unpleasant facts."

Serge's other great virtue is his novelist's eye for human character. He never lets his intense political commitment blind him to life's humor and paradox, its sensuality and beauty. You can see this in photographs as well, which show his kindly, ironic eyes, behind steel-rimmed glasses, that seem to be both sad and amused by something, set in a modest, bearded face. "I have always believed," he writes, "that human qualities find their physical expression in a man's personal appearance." In what other revolutionary's autobiography could you find, for example, something like this thumbnail sketch of a French communist Serge knew in Russia?

[Henri] Guilbeaux's whole life was a perfect example of the failure who, despite all his efforts, skirts the edge of success without ever managing to achieve it. . . . He wrote cacophonous poetry, kept a card index full of gossip about his comrades, and plagued the Cheka [the Soviet secret police] with confidential notes. He wore green shirts and pea-green ties with greenish suits; everything about him, including his crooked face and his eyes, seemed to have a touch of mold. (He died in Paris, about 1938, by then an anti-Semite, having published two books proving Mussolini to be the only true successor of Lenin.)

In *The Case of Comrade Tulayev,* three members of the Trotskyist opposition meet on skis in the woods outside Moscow. They talk of the injustices around them, agree that things are hopeless and that what probably awaits them is prison and early death; then they have a snowball fight. In *Memoirs of a Revolutionary,* Serge describes fighting White saboteurs on the rooftops of Petrograd in 1919, during the "white night" of the far northern summer, "overlooking a sky-blue canal. Men fled before us, firing their revolvers at us from behind the chimney pots. . . . The men we were after escaped, but

I treasured an unforgettable vision of the city, seen at 3 a.m. in all its magical paleness."

. . .

After I first discovered Serge's writing, I tried to look for traces of him in Russia. In the summer of 1978, some dozen years before the Soviet Union began to crumble, I visited what he had called "this city that I love above all." When he first arrived there it was Petrograd, then Leningrad, and later once again it would become, as it was more than a century ago, St. Petersburg. I began at the Smolny Institute. Before the Revolution, the Smolny was Russia's most exclusive girls' finishing school, under the personal patronage of the tsarina. In 1917, the Bolsheviks took it over as their headquarters and planned their coup d'état from classrooms where daughters of the aristocracy had once studied French and Latin. Serge had his office here, as the infant Revolution defended itself against the attacking White armies. In one of his novels, he describes how the barrels of cannons poked out between the Smolny's majestic neoclassical columns.

Now the building was closed to the public; the grounds were a park. Fountains played and a warm breeze rustled the trees. Two old men talked on a bench. There was no suggestion of the history that had taken place at this spot; it felt ghostly by its absence. By 10 p.m. the sun had just set, but the sky still glowed with the same mysterious "magical paleness" that had caught Serge's eye, even while he was being shot at, so many decades before.

In October 1919, when the Revolution was menaced from all sides, Serge took up arms in defense of the city. He fought in the decisive hillside battle that turned back the White Army at Pulkovo Heights, site of an old observatory on the outskirts of the city. Some sixty years later, a puzzled cabdriver waited while my wife and I climbed the hill at Pulkovo. A beech grove shaded us from the hot sun. A woman in a red kerchief walked slowly around the edge of a field, in search of something—wildflowers? mushrooms? From the hilltop we could see the distant city. On the horizon was a gleam of gold from the towers of the Fortress of St. Peter and St. Paul. This hill was as far as the White Army advanced. When the Whites fell back, the tide of the Russian Civil War turned, the battles died away, but the Russia that took shape was not the one that Serge had risked his life for.

On another day we went in search of the apartment where he and his family had lived. It was on a street lined with weathered stone buildings where gates to enclosed courtyards seemed to open onto another century. I found the right building and mounted marble steps still lined by a prerevolutionary wrought-iron railing and banister. Outside the large wooden door on the top floor, there was no telling which bell to ring, because it was a communal apartment, with seven doorbells for the seven families who lived there. I picked one, and the woman who answered said, "Wait. I'll get someone. She has lived here many years."

We remained on the landing. Finally, a woman came out: stocky, broad-faced, with gold teeth and slightly suspicious eyes. She said she was sixty years old and that she had lived in this apartment since she was seven. No, she said, defying my arithmetic, she did not remember the man I was asking about in my clumsy Russian—although, oddly, she did recall the Russakovs, Serge's wife's family. But when asked about Serge, she shook her head firmly, arms crossed on her chest. Another *nyet* came when I asked if we could come in. Evidently she feared getting into trouble if she allowed a foreigner into the apartment. Anyway, she added, the whole place has been remodeled, so it is not the same as when this man—is he a relative of yours?—lived here.

Despite the noes, she was happy to talk, and we chatted on the landing for more than half an hour. I peered past her, trying to glimpse inside. According to Serge, the apartment had been hastily abandoned by a high tsarist official and still had a grand piano. In the bookcase had been the many volumes of *Laws of the Empire*, which, savoring the symbolism, Serge burned for heat one by one in the winter months of early 1919.

I brought up his name again, and suddenly her eyes narrowed. "This man—was he an anarchist?"

"Aha, so you *do* remember him!"

"No." Her arms crossed again firmly and she shook her head. "Absolutely not."

That evening, back at our hotel, I checked some dates in his memoirs. If she told me her age correctly, this woman was ten when the police knocked on that same door at midnight and arrested Serge the first time. And she was fifteen when, in front of a pharmacy still standing on a nearby corner, he was arrested again and sent into exile in the Urals. Fifteen years old. A family she shared a kitchen with. Could she really have forgotten? Did she only remember the "anarchist" from some later denunciation? Then I noticed another passage in the memoirs. Serge says that in the mid-1920s, the Soviet authorities moved a young secret police officer "plus his wife, child, and grandmother" into the communal apartment to keep an eye on him. The dates fit. Was this woman the child?

. . .

Even crossing the Atlantic to Mexico, on the final flight of his exile-filled life, sleeping on a straw pallet in the airless hold of a freighter hastily converted to hold several hundred refugees, Serge never allowed himself to *feel* exiled. An internationalist always, he was at home wherever there were people who shared his beliefs. He recorded the clenched-fist salute his shipload of anti-Nazi refugees got from Spanish fishermen; he organized political discussions even at sea: "Out in the Atlantic, past the Sahara coast, the stars pitch up and down above our heads. We hold a meeting on the upper deck, between the funnel and the lifeboats."

In Mexico he stayed true to his vision as both a radical and a believer in free speech, and again met resistance. Communist Party thugs at one point shot at him; on another occasion they attacked a meeting where he was speaking, injuring some seventy people. His young daughter was covered with blood from stab wounds to a man who had bent over her to protect her. At the same time, even though he was denied entry to the United States, the FBI kept him and his children under surveillance and copied his correspondence with Americans. His FBI file—or at least as much of it as the agency was willing to release to his biographer Susan Weissman—is 331 pages long. Serge's politics cut off his access to both the mainstream and pro-Soviet Mexican press. Book publishers were no better. He wrote anyway, finishing both his panoramic novel of the Purge, *The Case of Comrade Tulayev,* and *Memoirs of a Revolutionary.* He tried and failed to find an American publisher for the memoirs; neither book appeared before he died of a heart attack, in the back seat of Mexico City taxi, in 1947. He was fifty-six years old.

One portrait in the memoirs is of Serge's friend Adolf Joffe. A Russian Jew, Joffe was a revolutionary whose desire to change the world was matched by a deep, free-ranging curiosity about it. He read widely, and as an exile in Vienna before the First World War, underwent psychoanalysis by Freud's disciple Alfred Adler. From a wealthy family, he donated his entire inheritance to the revolutionary movement. Originally trained as a doctor, he "reminded one," wrote Serge, "of a wise physician . . . who had been summoned to the bedside of a dying patient." After the Revolution, Joffe became a Soviet diplomat. In 1927, he returned to Moscow from his post as ambassador to Japan, seriously ill and in despair at the repressive direction the regime had taken. As an act of protest, he committed suicide.

Serge came to Joffe's apartment and helped organize the procession that, despite harassment from the authorities, accompanied his body to the Novodevichy cemetery. Even the most pessimistic of the mourners could not have imagined that theirs was to be the last antigovernment demonstration permitted in Moscow for the next sixty years.

In 1991, sixty-four years after Joffe's death, a friend and I go to see his daughter Nadezhda at her apartment in Moscow. Stalin had wiped out his opponents and their family members with such thoroughness that it is amazing to find one of them still alive. Nadezhda Joffe had spent some two decades of her life in prison camps and internal exile. A vibrant, gray-haired woman of eighty-five, she may be the last person alive in Russia who had once known Victor Serge. As the spring sun streams through her window, we spend a morning talking about him and her father and the Russia that might have been if people like them had prevailed. Just before we leave, she tells us a story.

A descendant of the Decembrists [reformer aristocrats who rebelled against the tsar in the 1820s] sees a crowd demonstrating in the street and she sends her daughter outside: "Masha! Go and see what's going on."

Masha returns and says, "Lots of people are out on the street."

"What do they want?"

"They're demanding that no one should be rich."

"That's strange," says the woman. "My grandfather went out onto the street and demanded that no one should be poor."

The artist in Victor Serge would have liked this parable, I think. And the idealist in him would have liked its hint of the path not taken, of a revolution leading to a gentler society and not to one drenched in blood. He would have been in the grandfather's crowd and not the later one. In his life he saw both types of crowds—humans at their best and at their worst—and left us a record of the world he knew in a voice of rare integrity.

. . .

One last visit, this one in 2002, in Cuernavaca, Mexico. Outside the open door, bursts of lush green vegetation climb everywhere; sunlight reflects dazzlingly from whitewashed walls. Inside, this one-room building seems almost the size of a small gymnasium. The ceiling is dotted with more than a dozen skylights. Oil paintings lean against the walls; a table is piled high with black-and-white prints; and to one side is a large, old-fashioned, iron printmaking machine, with a big wheel that must be turned by hand. At the far end of the room, against the back wall, is a work in progress, a giant canvas more than twenty feet high, a symphony of brilliant colors.

This is the studio of Vlady Kibalchich, Victor Serge's son, now eighty-one. A spry, sturdy man with a warm face bisected by a wide gray mustache, he wears a belted Russian peasant's blouse and a flat Russian cap such as Lenin has in photographs. Depending on who comes in and out of the studio this morning, he speaks in Russian, French, or Spanish. Among the books on shelves at the side of the room are volumes by his father, in many languages and editions, and from time to time as we talk, he goes over and retrieves one to make a point. Vlady was born in revolutionary Petrograd in 1920 and was dandled as a baby on Lenin's knee. He shared the first twenty-seven years of his life with his father: hunger, the arrests of family and friends, exile in Orenburg and western Europe, and then the final, last-minute voyage to Mexico. Like his father, Vlady has had troubles with the authorities. The Mexican government, long proud of the country's muralists, commissioned him to do four big paintings for the Interior Ministry headquarters, which were unveiled with great public fanfare in 1994. Several months later, they disappeared. Officials had judged one of them to be too sympathetic to the Zapatista peasant rebels in the state of Chiapas.

Vlady remembers well his childhood years in the 1920s and early '30s, as darkness closed over Russia. Two rooms in that Leningrad communal apartment where he grew up were occupied by families of policemen (one possibly including the woman I met), and "each time Serge went to the telephone, someone opened a door" to listen. Serge told his young son Russian fairy tales at night and took him skiing on the snow-covered ice of the Neva River. But a normal childhood became difficult as arrests mounted and newspapers filled with articles demanding death for traitors. The translation work on which Victor Serge depended for his income dried up. Vlady was twelve when his father was arrested for the second time.

> He telephoned me, from his prosecutor's office. He told me that I was now the man of the house, that I had to take care of my mother, to study, to brush my teeth, to speak French, to draw.
> Things were very tense at home. I went out one evening, and I passed the building of the GPU [the secret police]. I ran in the door. There were two soldiers with bayonets, and a red carpet on a big staircase.

"Stop!"

There was a door, and a man there, in uniform, who asked, "What's going on?"

"You've arrested my father!"

I remember he had a corner office. He picked up the telephone, talked, and then said, "Your father is in Moscow."

"It's not true!"

He telephoned Moscow, and then said, "He's in the Lubyanka [national secret police headquarters]."

At home, Vlady's maternal grandparents were aghast that he had entered the secret police building. Ten months later the family finally received permission to join Serge in exile in Orenburg. Vlady and his mother sold their books and furniture and left for the Urals. "We had a particularly hard time with hunger there. People were dropping like flies." But Orenburg was where, with strong encouragement from his father, Vlady really discovered himself as an artist.

When Vlady speaks of Victor Serge as a human being, what he remembers most warmly is his father's calm, optimism, and equanimity. "He never swore—even though he had been long in prison, with some terrible people." And, wherever they were—at home, in exile, on shipboard—whether there was hope of publication or not, Serge wrote. He and Vlady were stuck in an internment camp for some weeks in Martinique in 1941, trying to get to their promised haven in Mexico. Even in the camp, Serge kept writing, prose and poems—Vlady makes the motion of a writer's hand holding a pen and crossing a page—"he worked just as if he were at home."

Have his father's beliefs influenced Vlady's art? One answer lies in the giant canvas on the end wall of his studio, which he has been painting and repainting for many years, interrupted by a public viewing at an exhibition. The painting shows the Persian emperor Xerxes, who invaded Greece in 480 BCE. When a storm destroyed the pontoon bridges he had built to cross the Dardanelles, the narrow strait between Asia and Europe, the enraged Xerxes ordered his soldiers to whip the sea in punishment. Xerxes is a cyclops in Vlady's painting, mounted on a dragon the color of fire; the soldiers whipping the stormy, deep green sea are tiny figures, in keeping with the hopelessness of their task. More than half a century after Victor Serge's death, his artist son has gone back two and a half millennia to find an image for the lesson that Serge's own life taught them both, about the arrogance of an autocrat's grasping for absolute power.

1979, 2012

SIXTEEN

Shortstops in Siberia

THE MOUNTAINOUS REGION OF KOLYMA, some five hundred miles west of the Bering Strait, is the coldest inhabited area on earth. During Joseph Stalin's dictatorship, some two million prisoners were sent to mine the rich deposits of gold beneath its rocky, frozen soil. In 1991, researching a book on how Russians were looking back at Stalin's rule, I traveled there to see some of the old prison camps, legendary as the most deadly part of the Soviet Gulag. I had interviewed survivors from them. In a country beset by shortages of building materials, all the hundreds of former Gulag camps that anyone could drive a truck to had long since been stripped bare. The only ones still standing were those reached by roads that had washed away or reverted to wilderness, and to get to them you had to rent a helicopter. Amazingly, since the slowly collapsing Soviet Union had not yet let the ruble float against the dollar, you could do this for the equivalent of about $30 an hour, less than a taxi would cost in New York.

I spent a full day flying across desolate Kolyma, its gravelly mountainsides streaked with snow even in June (see the photograph on p. 243). We descended into three of the old camps, finding rickety wooden guard towers, high perimeter fences of rusted barbed wire, and, in one camp, an internal prison of punishment cells. Its wooden roof was rotted away, but thick stone walls still stood; within them were small windows crossed both vertically and horizontally by heavy bars, the intersections further cinched with thick iron bands. A photograph of the view through one of these cell windows is this book's cover. At the end of the day, as we flew back to the town where I was staying I sat in the helicopter cockpit between the pilot and co-pilot. Beyond every jagged ridge, it seemed, in every hollow or valley, were the ruins of yet another camp, the crumbling wood blackened by decades of exposure.

No one knows exactly how many Soviet citizens perished outside of war during the quarter-century that Stalin wielded absolute power, but like the similar horror show unfolding in German-occupied Europe in the same period, the Soviet story was one of death on an almost unimaginable scale. But in its first two decades, the Soviet Union was idolized by millions of people the world over, who fervently saw it as the just society of their dreams. *The Forsaken: An American Tragedy in Stalin's Russia* by Tim Tzouliadis is a poignant reminder of this. For he looks at this period through an unusual prism: the experience of Americans who emigrated to the USSR in the 1930s and who, like so many of the Soviet subjects they lived among, fell victim. Bits and pieces of this story have been told before, mainly in the memoirs of a few survivors. But his is a more comprehensive history, and a fascinating and tragic one it is.

Like the tens of thousands of western Europeans who arrived in the same period, these immigrants were driven by the Great Depression at home and the hope for a better, fairer way of life in the Soviet Union. A quarter of the U.S. labor force was out of work, another quarter underemployed, and millions of Americans were standing in line at soup kitchens or living in "Hooverville" shantytowns after losing their homes, farms, or jobs. Was it not possible to build a better world than this? Of course it was—and in Russia, apparently, they were doing it. Factories were hiring from abroad—particularly skilled workers and engineers, who were being offered lucrative contracts. And these factories were said to have nursery schools, clinics, libraries. Although many of the American immigrants to Russia had been socialists or communists in the United States, you didn't have to be one to believe that somewhere on Earth people had been able to build a more sensible economy than the Depression-ridden one of the Western world. An English translation of something originally written for Soviet schoolchildren, *New Russia's Primer: The Story of the Five-Year Plan,* spent seven months on the U.S. bestseller list in 1931.

When the Soviet foreign trade agency advertised jobs for skilled workers in Russia that year, a hundred thousand Americans applied. Ten thousand were hired; untold thousands more headed for the country on tourist visas, hoping to find work when they got there. By early 1932, the *New York Times* was reporting that up to a thousand new American immigrants were arriving in Moscow each week—and that the number was increasing. This may have been an exaggeration; nonetheless, that year the total climbed so high that the English-language weekly *Moscow News* turned daily. The American immigrants brought their children, and soon there were English-medium schools in at least five Soviet cities. For $40 million, Stalin bought 75,000 Model A sedans from Henry Ford, plus an entire Ford factory—which required expert technicians to run it, and so more Americans came.

With them, the eager newcomers brought baseball. *The Forsaken* includes a group photograph of smiling young American players at Gorky Park in the summer of 1934, with the initials on their jerseys identifying the teams: the Moscow Foreign Workers' Club and the Gorky Auto Workers' Club. One of the teams named Paul Robeson, who had been a star college athlete before becoming a communist and famous singer, honorary catcher. Other American baseball teams sprang up everywhere from Kharkov in the Ukraine to Yerevan, Armenia. The motif of baseball threads through the book, and some of its pages trace what happened to the men who played that day in Gorky Park.

Baseball caught on with Russians, and they began joining the American teams or starting their own, although they considered the practice of stealing bases somewhat capitalistic. Then suddenly it was 1936, and the Great Purge had begun. Having already shot, jailed, or exiled all his real political opponents, a paranoid Stalin now went after imaginary ones, in the process tapping a deep vein of Russian xenophobia. Waves of mass arrests swept across the country. Millions were seized in the space of a few years. At the show trials of high Communist Party officials, the charge was usually espionage for a foreign power. Kept awake for days at a time and brutally interrogated, one person after another was made to confess to having been a spy or saboteur for Britain, Germany, the United States. And so foreigners, or anyone connected with foreigners, were suspect. No more Russians joined the American baseball games. Very soon, there was no more baseball.

From Alexander Solzhenitsyn and other Russians who have borne witness, we know about the midnight arrests, the forced confessions, the trains hauling boxcars packed with emaciated prisoners to labor camps scattered across the Arctic, Siberia, and Kazakhstan. Tzouliadis traces the story of the Americans who got caught up in this madness through a wide range of letters and documents and the published memoirs of two men who played on American baseball teams in Moscow in the mid-1930s, Victor Herman and Thomas Sgovio. Unlike many of their fellow players, whom they occasionally encountered in the Gulag, they survived their imprisonment, Herman in central Russia and Sgovio in Kolyma. No one knows how many of the American immigrants were caught up by the Purge and perished either in execution cellars or in the camps, although one mass grave with more than 140 American bodies was found in 1997 near the Finnish border. My own guess would be that the total of American deaths might approach a thousand; if we add victims among other Westerners living in USSR at the time, their ranks increased by refugees from Nazi Germany and Fascist Italy, the total would be far higher.

The testimony of Herman and Sgovio has found its way into some books about the Gulag, including my own, for which I was able to interview Sgovio. But Tzouliadis's most unexpected contribution is the sorry tale of how desperate pleas for help from captive Americans, some smuggled out of prison, some made by family members still at liberty who risked their lives by walking into the closely watched U.S. embassy, were ignored by diplomats in Moscow and officials back in Washington. Old State Department correspondence files reveal this evidence, which includes even a wooden tag smuggled out of a camp with the words, in English, "Save me please and all the others." Even though the conservative ambassador of tiny Austria was able to protect more than twenty Austrian left-wingers by sheltering them in his basement, the U.S. embassy staff, contemptuous of the Americans who had come to Russia out of naïve idealism, did virtually nothing. Yet they could have saved many lives if they had tried, for Stalin was shrewd enough to want to please a valued foreign trading partner. Again and again, the diplomats turned aside those begging for help, generally with the excuse that there was no proof that the prisoner involved was a U.S. citizen. This was often literally true, for when Americans arrived to work in the Soviet Union, the Russians usually confiscated their passports—the better to exert control and also to acquire a stash of passports they could later doctor and use to send Soviet spies abroad.

Why were the officials so callous? For one thing, making too much noise might get you expelled from what was, for a rising young Foreign Service officer, a plum post. Beyond that, diplomats temperamentally are seldom troublemakers; the exceptions, like Raoul Wallenberg, are rare. And finally, behind those who played it safe at the U.S. Embassy in Moscow in the late 1930s was another factor: their boss.

In the American practice of handing out ambassadorships to presidential chums and campaign contributors, never was there a more ill-fated choice than Franklin D. Roosevelt's selection, in 1936, of Joseph E. Davies as U.S. ambassador to Moscow. Davies knew nothing about Russia; he had made a small fortune as a lawyer, defending corporations against tax collectors during the boom times of the 1920s. He had then married the owner of a much larger fortune, the cereal heiress Marjorie Merriweather Post, known for her array of extravagant homes, one of which was the world's largest private yacht, the three-masted *Sea Cloud,* with a crew of sixty-two.

Davies "loved bigness," Justice Louis Brandeis once said, criticizing him for his failures when serving on a government commission that was supposed to curb monopolies. In Stalin's Russia, Davies found plenty of highly satisfying bigness. To the horror of other envoys, he attended several of the Purge show trials and told the State Department that justice had been done. It did not seem to bother him when Russian acquaintances vanished. One Soviet diplomat had taken Davies's daughter and some friends out for dinner and dancing when two men came to their table and tapped him on the shoulder. "He was never seen again," Tzouliadis writes. Nor was Mrs. Davies much disturbed by any of this, even though, she said years later, from their bedroom at the U.S. ambassador's residence in central Moscow she could sometimes hear women and children screaming in nearby apartment buildings as men were arrested in the middle of the night. Her main interest was in collecting art, jewelry, and china that had belonged to the prerevolutionary Russian aristocracy, something she was able to do on a lavish scale as the government sold off confiscated collections.

In 1937, the peak of the Purge terror, Davies managed to spend most days of the year outside Russia, some of it cruising the Baltic on the *Sea Cloud,* with his astonished Soviet secret police guards along as invited guests. At the end of his stay in Moscow, he was overjoyed when Stalin granted him a two-hour audience, after the dictator had refused to meet other Western ambassadors. "He is really a fine, upstanding, great man!" Davies told an underling at the embassy. Of all the foreign deniers who turned an unseeing eye to Stalin's mass murder this staunchly capitalist couple were certainly the strangest.

Soviet officials who dealt with Americans during the 1930s are by now all dead, as are almost all the surviving Purge victims themselves. Russian archives, once briefly accessible in the early 1990s, when I was able to read the transcripts of interrogations of half a dozen Americans arrested in the Purge, are again now mostly closed. This is an American as well as a Soviet story, and in telling it skillfully from a wide variety of rarely used and mostly American sources, *The Forsaken* etches a small piece of a great historical cataclysm and reminds us of how Stalin's regime devoured not just human lives but hopes, dreams, trust. Those American baseball players who came to Russia found themselves in a tragic game with no umpire, either in the Kremlin or the U.S. embassy. Their story made me wonder whether the several mass grave sites I saw in Russia—one of them full of exposed bones bleached white under an electrical transmission tower on a foggy, rocky, wind-swept hillside in Kolyma—might have contained any of my countrymen who were once catchers, pitchers, or first basemen.

2008

SEVENTEEN

A Homage to Homage

FOR ANY IDEALIST WHO DREAMED of forging a more democratic and equitable world, the late 1930s were a grim time. Not only did Adolf Hitler and Benito Mussolini rule as dictators in Germany and Italy, but half a dozen other countries, from Portugal to Lithuania, Hungary to Greece, were under regimes of the far right, some of them, like the Nazis, making dark threats against Jews. Even in England, the British Union of Fascists boasted fifty thousand members; wearing black tunics, black trousers, and wide black leather belts, they paraded through Jewish neighborhoods of London under a flag with a lightning bolt, shouting insults, giving the straight-arm salute, and beating up anyone in their way. "Fascism has spread its great black wings over Europe," wrote the French writer André Malraux.

Nowhere were those wings spread more ominously than over Spain. After centuries of monarchy, it had become a republic in 1931 and was Europe's newest democracy. In early 1936, Spanish voters had elected a coalition of liberal and leftist parties, which promised reforms that would begin to rectify the country's vast imbalance of wealth between industrialists and workers and between a small elite of large landowners and a great mass of miserably poor, often illiterate peasants. Months of unrest followed the election, and then, in July of that year, a large group of right-wing army officers made a brutal grab for power, igniting civil war.

In the first weeks of fighting, the plotters and their troops occupied roughly a third of Spain. Quickly emerging as the dominant figure among them was a tough-talking young general, Francisco Franco—ambitious, puritanical, devoutly Catholic, and possessed by a fierce belief that he was destined to save his country from a deadly conspiracy of Bolsheviks, Freemasons, and Jews. He spoke of Germany as "a model which we will always keep before us" and kept a photo of Hitler on his desk. "It is necessary to spread terror," declared another general, Emilio Mola. "We have to create the impression of mastery by eliminating without scruples or hesitation all those who do not think as we do."

And eliminated they were, with a violence far greater than anything seen when Hitler or Mussolini first seized power. As Franco's armies advanced through Spain, they showed a ferocity that Europeans had assumed as their right in colonial wars but that had seldom been unleashed in Europe itself since the Inquisition. Trade union leaders and Spanish Republic officials, including forty parliamentary deputies from the governing coalition, were shot or bayoneted to death. Torture was routine. Killings mounted into the tens of thousands, some carried out with the *garrote*, a medieval instrument with which the executioner slowly, if he is so inclined, tightens a metal band around the victim's neck.

As with many fundamentalist movements, for Franco's followers, women became the object of particular savagery. Many who had been union members or supporters of the Republic were branded on their breasts with the military rebels' symbol, also drawn from medieval times, of yoke and arrows: the yoke of obedience to an all-powerful kingdom, and the arrows for shooting down heretics. Others were gang-raped by entire platoons of Franco's soldiers—something that officers actually boasted about to foreign reporters covering the war.

As such news spread, tens of thousands of Franco supporters in Republican-controlled territory, including many clergy, were massacred in revenge. Anticlericalism, demands for regional autonomy, and animosity between Spain's rich and poor, all of which had been building for centuries, boiled over. For the first time since 1918 a western European country was at war.

As the Republic fought back against the attempted coup, it faced great odds: most regular army officers had joined Franco, and Hitler and Mussolini quickly began supplying his forces with the most modern weaponry, including airplanes, tanks, and the crews to man them. Italy sent entire divisions of infantrymen. Against these forces the Republic mustered a smaller number of loyal officers and soldiers and, trained hastily or not at all, badly armed militias organized by trade unions or left-wing political parties. Even though Spain was a highly patriarchal society, many militia units included women. Desperately short of rifles, artillery, tanks, and warplanes, the Republic tried to buy these arms overseas. But Britain, France, and the United States were leery of the Republic's left-leaning government and loath to fuel a war that might engulf the whole continent. They refused to sell weapons to either side in the Spanish Civil War and pressured smaller countries to follow their lead.

Ironically, the only major nation that finally did sell arms to the Spanish Republic was not another democracy: it was the Soviet Union, just then beginning at home the enormous bloodletting of the Great Purge. In return for providing weapons, pilots, and military experts, Joseph Stalin demanded high positions for Spanish communists and Soviet advisers in the Republic's army and security services. He also instructed communist parties around the world to begin recruiting foreign volunteers to fight in Spain. Before long, more than 35,000 came, from some fifty countries.

Besides these International Brigades, as they were called, several thousand additional foreigners came to Republican Spain, both to volunteer as soldiers and for other work. These men and women were leftists but not communists. And they were drawn not just to the battle against fascism but to something else as well. Throughout the northeastern part of the country, particularly in Catalonia and neighboring Aragon, after the popular militias had swiftly defeated Franco's attempted coup, there spontaneously erupted the most widespread social revolution ever seen in western Europe. Peasants occupied dozens of large estates; railway workers took over the train lines and trolley drivers the urban transport systems. Workers took over factories, including Ford and General Motors plants. The Ritz Hotel was Barcelona's most elegant; cooks, waiters and busboys took over its dining room, converting it into People's Cafeteria #1 for the poor. The anarchist trade union federation occupied the city's Chamber of Commerce building and began using stock certificates as scratch paper. Garbage trucks sported anarchist slogans. Some villages abolished money and issued coupons, with more coupons going to families with more children. Exhilaratingly, this was a revolution that came not, as in Stalin's Russia, from the top down but, something many radicals had long dreamed of, from the bottom up.

The upheaval's epicenter was Spain's second-largest city, Barcelona. A few days after Christmas 1936, a foreign volunteer, a young American economist named Charles Orr, was working in the office of the POUM—Partido Obrero de Unificación Marxista, or Workers' Party of Marxist Unification—a group with its own militia at the front. "A little militiaman, in his blue coveralls and red scarf, trudged up the stairs to my office on the fourth floor," Orr remembered later. "The lifts, as usual, bore the familiar sign NO FUNCTIONA....

"There was an Englishman, he reported to me, who spoke neither Catalan nor Spanish. . . . I went down to see who this Englishman was and what his business might be.

"There I met him—Eric Blair—tall, lanky and tired, having just that hour arrived from London. . . .

"Exhausted, but excited, after a day and a night on the train, he had come to fight fascism. . . . At first, I did not take this English volunteer very seriously. Just one more foreigner come to help . . . apparently a political innocent." The newcomer spoke of a book he had written, about living as a tramp in England and washing dishes in Paris restaurants. But Orr had not heard of it, nor of the several novels by this "gawky" figure.

"To us he was just Eric . . . one of a small band of foreigners, mostly British, fighting on the Aragon Front." This was where Blair would be sent, northwest of Barcelona, when he promptly joined the militia of the POUM. He "was tongue-tied, stammered and seemed to be afraid of people," Orr wrote. But however inhibited the newcomer was in conversation, he was anything but that in print, where he wrote under the name George Orwell.

Like Orr, few people anywhere had then heard of the 33-year-old author, who had been supporting himself largely as a part-time bookstore clerk and by running a tiny grocery shop out of his home. (He put "grocer" as his occupation when he applied to join the POUM militia.) He had finished the book that would first bring him wide notice, *The Road to Wigan Pier,* a close-up look at poverty in the industrial north of England, but it had not yet been published.

Along with other foreigners with whom he crossed paths in Barcelona— one, for example, was 23-year-old Willy Brandt, who three decades later would become chancellor of West Germany—Orwell quickly found himself under the spell of the revolutionary city:

> Waiters and shop-walkers looked you in the face and treated you as an equal. Servile and even ceremonial forms of speech had temporarily disappeared. Nobody said *"Señor"* or *"Don"* or even *"Usted";* everyone called everyone else *"Comrade"* and *"Thou.".* . . . Almost my first experience was receiving a lecture from an hotel manager for trying to tip a lift-boy. . . . The revolutionary posters were everywhere, flaming from the walls in clean reds and blues that made the few remaining advertisements look like daubs of mud. . . . Practically everyone wore rough working-class clothes, or blue overalls or some variant of the militia uniform. All this was queer and moving. There was much in it that I did not understand, in some ways I did not even like it, but I recognized it immediately as a state of affairs worth fighting for.

Within a week, Orwell was on his way to the front. A photograph of his militia column shows him a head taller and some fifteen years older than the Spanish teenagers he is surrounded by. The book he would write about the following six months, *Homage to Catalonia,* is the one in which for the first time he fully found his voice. In 1940 he would refer to it as his "best book," and for many of us that judgment still holds.

Orwell was always an acute, deeply thoughtful observer of everything he saw—even when, as would be the case in Spain, it didn't fit the script he had expected. Indeed, part of the moral drama of this book lies in the way we can see him find the politics around him far more complicated than the black-and-white picture in his mind at the start. After more than three-quarters of a century, this quality still makes his account a lasting piece of literature. And we now know more about an eerie backstory to his experiences in Spain that Orwell only dimly sensed, and about the odd way his explicit instructions for revising the book were, for decades after his death, ignored.

. . .

In Spain, Orwell never stopped examining everything that happened to him. Who can forget his description of exactly what it feels like to be hit by a bullet? "It was the sensation of being *at the centre* of an explosion." Yet part of what makes *Homage to Catalonia* one of the great nonfiction books of its age is that he managed to write in the first person without ever sounding self-centered. You can look at almost any page and see how deftly he amasses rich, sensual detail, but always in the service of a larger point. For example, after that sniper's shot almost severed his carotid artery, he was put on a hospital train to the rear. As it pulled into one station, a troop train filled with Italian volunteers was pulling out for the front, "packed to the bursting-point with men, with field-guns lashed on the open trucks and more men clustering round the guns."

> I remember with particular vividness the spectacle of that train passing in the yellow evening light; window after window full of dark, smiling faces, the long tilted barrels of the guns, the scarlet scarves fluttering–all this gliding slowly past us against a turquoise-coloured sea.
> ... The men who were well enough to stand had moved across the carriage to cheer the Italians as they went past. A crutch waved out of the window; bandaged forearms made the Red Salute. It was like an allegorical picture of

war; the trainload of fresh men gliding proudly up the line, the maimed men sliding slowly down, and all the while the guns on the open trucks making one's heart leap as guns always do, and reviving that pernicious feeling, so difficult to get rid of, that war *is* glorious after all.

Within the Spanish Civil War was another civil war. An odd-bedfellows alliance between communists and the Republic's mainstream parties was determined to crush the social revolution. Several of their reasons were understandable: they thought it was folly to try to build a new utopia in the midst of a desperate war for survival; they felt that the best hope of defeating Franco was with a disciplined army under a central command, not a hodge-podge of militia units reporting to political parties and labor unions; and, still hoping to buy arms from Britain, France, or the United States, they feared this would never happen if Republican Spain were perceived as revo-lutionary. (As it turned out, these countries would refuse to sell arms to the Republic even after the revolution was finally snuffed out.) But another fac-tor was the long reach of the Soviet Union's Great Purge. In Stalin's eyes, any dissenters from the world communist movement were traitors. He was far less angry at the driving force behind the social revolution, Spain's powerful anarchist movement, which came from a different political tradition, than he was at the anarchists' allies, the much smaller POUM. Several POUM lead-ers were former communists, one of whom had lived in the Soviet Union and had known Stalin, who had broken publicly with the USSR and denounced the Purge. To the Soviet dictator, this was unforgivable heresy.

Orwell first became aware of how intense these conflicts were when, after the several months at the front described so vividly in his early chapters, in late April 1937, he returned to Barcelona on leave. Within a few days of arriv-ing in the city, he was unexpectedly caught up in a deadly outburst of street fighting between the communist-dominated police on one side and the POUM and its anarchist allies on the other. Although Orwell himself was unharmed, several hundred people were killed. Deeply distressed, he returned to the front line. Some weeks later, after he was wounded, hospitalized, and discharged from the militia, his voice was still hoarse from the bullet that had passed through his neck, grazing his throat; it sounded, his commanding officer wrote, like the grinding brakes of an old Model T Ford. Orwell then made his way back to Barcelona again, to meet his wife, Eileen O'Shaughnessy Blair, who had for several months been working in the POUM office, and to head home with her to England to recuperate.

It was then that he discovered, to his horror, that the POUM and its newspaper had been banned and many of its supporters thrown in jail. He stayed out of sight for several days—once on the street meeting Willy Brandt, who was also lying low, and once sleeping in a vacant lot—while he and Eileen arranged to slip out of the country before they, too, could be arrested. She told him how, several days before, six plainclothes police had burst into her hotel room and taken all the couple's letters, books, and documents, including the extensive notes and diaries Orwell had sent her, and she had typed up, from his first four months at the front. (He "was always writing," an Irish fellow soldier remembered. "In the daytime he used to sit outside the dugout writing, and in the evenings he used to write by candlelight.") This must have been a particularly painful loss. Yet even in describing the theft of his own writing Orwell was alert to a curious human detail of the search of Eileen's room:

> They sounded the walls, took up the mats, examined the floor, felt the curtains, probed under the bath and the radiator, emptied every drawer and suitcase and felt every garment and held it up to the light. . . . In one drawer there was a number of packets of cigarette papers. They picked each packet to pieces and examined each paper separately, in case there should be messages written on them. Altogether they were on the job for nearly two hours. Yet all this time they never searched the bed. My wife was lying in bed all the while; obviously there might have been half a dozen sub-machine-guns under the mattress, not to mention a library of Trotskyist documents under the pillow. Yet the detectives made no move to touch the bed, never even looked underneath it. . . . The police were almost entirely under Communist control, and these men were probably Communist Party members themselves. But they were also Spaniards, and to turn a woman out of bed was a little too much for them.

During his brief visits to Barcelona, Orwell wrote, "you seemed to spend all your time holding whispered conversations in corners of cafés and wondering whether that person at the next table was a police spy."

Sometimes he *was* a spy, and today we can read *Homage to Catalonia* side by side with these agents' reports. For more than half a century, all such records were tightly locked up, but since the collapse of the Soviet Union some have become accessible.

Certain documents, including the papers removed from Eileen Blair's hotel room, are believed to remain in closed files in Moscow. But among what we can now see is a two-page inventory of what the police took that day. This includes such items as "correspondence exchanged between Eileen and Eric BLAIR," "correspondence of G. ORWELL (alias Eric BLAIR) concerning his book 'The Road to Wigan Pier,'" and "checkbook for the months of October and Nov 1936." There were also letters to and from a long list of people and "various papers with drawings and doodles."

Some reports, as well as a translation of one letter to Eileen whose English original has disappeared, are in German. This was evidently the work of Germans involved in running Soviet espionage in Barcelona. One German communist agent in the city, Hubert von Ranke, subsequently had a change of heart: before the end of 1937 he would leave Spain, leave the Party, and declare that the people he had spied on and interrogated "were not 'agents of Franco' but honest revolutionaries." Someone else may have been reporting to André Marty, the much-disliked French communist chief of the International Brigades, for the list of materials confiscated from Eileen is in French.

A British communist, Walter Tapsell, meanwhile was reporting to London, writing to Party superiors there that Orwell was "the most respected man in the contingent" of Britons fighting with the POUM militia but that "he has little political understanding." Another member of this farrago of agents was Hugh O'Donnell, the British Communist Party representative in Spain. Orwell and his wife knew him, but what they almost certainly did not know was his Party code name, O'Brien—which, by an uncanny coincidence, Orwell was to give to the sinister villain of his novel *1984*.

In *Homage*, Orwell wrote, "You had all the while a hateful feeling that someone hitherto your friend might be denouncing you to the secret police." This was even more true than he knew. David Crook, for example, another British communist, posed as a POUM sympathizer but meanwhile was reporting everything to his Soviet handlers, including his suspicions that Eileen Blair was having an extramarital affair—information potentially useful for blackmail. Crook claims in his memoirs that during the long Spanish lunch-and-siesta, he used to slip into the office used by Eileen and the handful of other Britons and Americans working in the POUM building, purloin documents, and quickly photograph them at a Soviet safe house. By design Crook was even briefly jailed during the crackdown on the POUM, so he could report on POUM prisoners and offer to help smuggle their letters out. He would die at ninety in the year 2000, having lived his last five decades in

China, his faith largely unshaken despite five years' imprisonment during the Cultural Revolution.

. . .

Almost all journalists who try to explain a complex conflict in a foreign country assume an air of authority. Even if just arrived in a new war zone the day before, an opinion columnist will rarely say he or she is unsure what the causes of violence are and what should be done about them. By contrast, one of the more subtle virtues of *Homage to Catalonia* is its humility. "It is difficult to be certain about anything except what you have seen with your own eyes," Orwell writes in one of several such cautionary notes. ". . . . Beware of my partisanship, my mistakes of fact, and the distortion inevitably caused by my having seen only one corner of events." He published his book in 1938, less than a year after he had left Spain and while the war was still raging. But he never forgot that he had seen "only one corner of events," and as time passed, to his enormous credit, on some points he was not afraid to change his mind.

In *Homage,* for example, he blames the Republic's military defeats on its internal conflicts and the suppression of the social revolution he had so admired in Barcelona. He declares that if the government "had appealed to the workers of the world in the name not of 'democratic Spain' but of 'revolutionary Spain,' it is hard to believe that they would not have got a response"—in the form of strikes and boycotts by millions of workers in other countries. For Orwell, however, this was a rare moment of wildly wishful thinking. Most "workers of the world" had long since shown themselves not to be the revolutionary internationalists that radical intellectuals hoped for, something most notably demonstrated by their willingness to slaughter each other in huge numbers in the First World War.

But by the time he published a long essay, "Looking Back on the Spanish War," in 1943, six years after he had left Spain and four after Franco's troops had won the war, Orwell had come to feel that "disunity on the Government side was not a main cause of defeat." Instead he believed, as do most historians today, that "the outcome of the Spanish War was settled in London, Paris, Rome, Berlin." Rome and Berlin had supplied Franco with a flood of troops, aviators, advisers, and advanced weapons, like the latest Messerschmitt Bf-109 fighter planes and Stuka dive bombers, each of which had its combat debut in Spain. And not just London and Paris, but Washington as well, had refused to sell arms to the democratically elected government of the Republic.

The "Trotskyist thesis that the war could have been won if the revolution had not been sabotaged was probably false," he wrote in his 1943 essay—somewhat misleadingly, for this belief was not limited to Trotskyists; it was exactly what Orwell himself had said in *Homage*. But he was completely right when he continued: "The Fascists won because they were the stronger; they had modern arms and the others hadn't." And in the scope of the larger struggle against fascism, he told a friend, the suppression of the POUM, however unjust, was something that had "had far too much fuss made about it."

Because these thoughts reflected a somewhat different view of the war than the one he had taken in *Homage,* Orwell wanted changes in the next printing, first outlining them in 1946, eight years after he had published the book. Before he died in 1950, he typed out corrections and marked up a copy. Most important, he asked that two long chapters, comprising roughly a quarter of the text and dealing with the factions on the Republican side and claims and counterclaims about the Barcelona street fighting, be relegated to appendices—a rearrangement that did not unsay anything he had written but that significantly altered the book's political emphasis.

Most of these changes were made when *Homage* appeared in French several years later—Orwell had also been corresponding with his French translator. But, surprisingly, his British publisher ignored his wishes and the marked-up copy, and it is not clear if his American publisher even knew about them. An English edition in the form Orwell intended did not appear in Britain until thirty-six years after his death in 1950 and until sixty-five years after it in the United States.

. . .

Barcelona today is a very different city from the revolutionary one full of armed militia members, defiant songs, militant posters, and workers in blue denim that Orwell first saw in 1936. The foreigners strolling the Ramblas— the city's central, tree-lined pedestrian boulevard where so much of the action of Orwell's memoir takes place—are not soldiers in uniform but tourists in baseball caps snapping cellphone photos and young people from elsewhere on the continent who have taken advantage of European Union migration rules to live here. The former Communist Party headquarters is now an Apple computer store, and the POUM building Orwell was assigned to protect in the 1937 street fighting is no more, although across the street remains the theater on whose roof he stood guard for three days and nights. Yet today's

Spain is a democracy and in that sense is far closer to the Spanish Republic that Orwell fought to defend than it is to the harsh military dictatorship, marked by repression and torture, that Francisco Franco imposed for three and a half decades after his victory.

As with many books that matter, the reactions to *Homage to Catalonia* have changed over the years. When it was published in England in 1938, it was largely ignored. This memoir of fighting against Franco was of course anathema to right-wingers, who shunned it. Many readers on the Left, however, had no appetite for its indictment of the communist-dominated Republican police hounding and imprisoning members of the POUM. This complicated the image of the war as purely a battle between democracy and fascism. The book sold a mere eight hundred copies in the dozen years between its publication and Orwell's death.

When it first appeared in the United States two years later, however, the Cold War was under way, and *Homage* soon found an enormous audience. Most critics on both sides of the Atlantic seemed unaware of Orwell's important 1943 essay, and none of them knew of his unheeded instructions for the revising of *Homage*. Ignoring the failure of the Western democracies to help stop Franco, they were eager to point to Orwell's portrayal of Spain as an example of Soviet perfidy. The poet Stephen Spender, for instance, called the book "one of the most serious indictments of Communism which has been written." And to the critic Lionel Trilling, *Homage* was in large part "about disillusionment with Communism." But Orwell had very few such illusions to begin with, and despite his well-founded hostility to the Soviet Union, he would almost certainly not have agreed that this was his main message in *Homage*.

Many of the young Americans who headed to the South as civil rights workers in the 1960s carried *Homage* in their backpacks or had read it. For us, Orwell was above all an example of someone willing to risk his life for what he believed in. He remained convinced until his death that it had been worth fighting to defend the Spanish Republic. "Whatever faults the post-war Government might have," he says in *Homage,* Franco's regime was "infinitely worse." He repeated that conviction in his later essay. If the Spanish Civil War "had been won, the cause of the common people everywhere would have been strengthened. It was lost, and the dividend-drawers all over the world rubbed their hands. That was the real issue; all else was froth on the surface." And not only did he write this; he lived it. Where did he go, after his upsetting experience of the fratricidal street fighting in Barcelona? Back to the front.

2015

EIGHTEEN

On Which Continent Was
the Holocaust Born?

LIKE MANY OF THE MOST ORIGINAL WRITERS, Sven Lindqvist is hard to pigeonhole. He is not exactly a historian, for his graduate degree is in literature. He is not exactly a travel writer, for he has little interest in the colorful details that make a place seem exotic; he always wants to direct our attention back to our own culture. He is not exactly a journalist, for when he travels to far points on the globe, he is less likely to tell us about his conversations with anyone than about his own dreams. His work does not come in neatly tied packages: he travels through Africa meditating on Joseph Conrad's *Heart of Darkness* but never reaches the Congo River; he goes all the way to Australia to write powerfully about what its native peoples endured but chooses not to interview a single Aborigine. And, for that matter, he's not someone on whom I, or almost any American writer, can have the last word, for the great majority of his thirty-three books have not been translated from Swedish.

If there is an English-language writer whom Lindqvist reminds me of, it might be James Agee: also hard to categorize, also working in many genres, also at times forcing painful detail on his admirers; his masterwork *Let Us Now Praise Famous Men* (1941) can be highly difficult reading. Yet that book changed and expanded forever our sense of how to see the world, and, at its best, so does the work of Lindqvist.

If you asked almost any American or European, for example, to date the great tragic turning points of the modern era, they might say 1914, when the First World War began and we saw the toll industrialized slaughter could take, or 1945, when the United States carried this to a new level by dropping two atom bombs on Japanese cities. If you asked Lindqvist, I think he would say 1898 and 1911. Why?

These dates, too, have to do with industrialized warfare; the difference is where the targets were. The year 1898 saw the Battle of Omdurman in the Sudan, when a force of British and colonial troops, Winston Churchill among them, in a few hours killed more than ten thousand Sudanese and wounded another sixteen thousand, some fatally, many of them falling victim to half a million bullets fired by Hiram Maxim's latest machine guns. It was the first large-scale demonstration in warfare of what this horrific new weapon could do. Thirteen years later, on November 1, 1911, during another long-forgotten war, an Italian lieutenant named Giulio Gavotti leaned out of his single-engine open-cockpit plane and dropped several hand grenades on two oases near Tripoli, Libya. It was the world's first bombardment from an airplane.

In both cases, the victims Lindqvist draws our attention to were outside of Europe. This perspective is the driving passion at the core of two of his books available in English, *Terra Nullius* and *"Exterminate All the Brutes"* and the same point of view is visible in several others, particularly the remarkable *A History of Bombing*—where he traces the genealogy of British terror-bombing of German cities in the Second World War back to similar targeting of civilians in a colonial war in Iraq more than twenty years earlier.

We think of the 1937 bombing of Guernica in the Spanish Civil War as another one of those historical turning points: for the first time, it seemed, bombers had tried to raze an entire town with no military targets. We remember Guernica, of course, because of Picasso's great painting, which Lindqvist himself saw as a child when it traveled to Stockholm in 1938. But he points us toward other bombings, a decade earlier, which the rest of the world didn't notice, because the victims were not European. During years of colonial rebellions in Morocco in the 1920s, for instance, Spanish and French aircraft (some of the latter flown by American mercenaries), dropped high explosives on many Moroccan towns and villages, severely damaging several of them, including Chechaouen, considered a holy city for its many mosques. But "Chechaouen," writes Lindqvist, "had no Picasso."

. . .

To read such books is to be reminded of how incredibly Eurocentric most historians are. We are accustomed to thinking, in the famous phrase of British Foreign Secretary Sir Edward Grey, of "the lamps ... going out all over Europe" in 1914 as a catastrophic war began, but we forget that they were extinguished decades earlier for people on other continents as they experienced European conquest. Almost all of us educated in North America or Europe grow up learning that there were two great totalitarian systems of modern times, each with fantasies of exterminating its enemies: Nazism and communism. Lindqvist reminds us that there was a third: colonialism. And, most provocatively, he makes connections between it and one of the others.

"*Exterminate All the Brutes*"—the title is the phrase scrawled by Conrad's Mr. Kurtz at the bottom of his report to the International Society for the Suppression of Savage Customs—takes us deep into the history of Western consciousness in a search for the sources of the very *idea* of extermination. An early "kindergarten for European imperialism," for example, was the Canary Islands, where some five hundred years ago diseases and weapons brought by conquering Spaniards reduced an estimated eighty thousand indigenous inhabitants to zero in less than a century. How many people who have visited these lovely islands as tourists ever learned this? Not me. Lindqvist also introduces us to Lord Wolseley, commander in chief of the British army at the time of Omdurman, who, in this era when British wars were colonial ones, spoke of "the rapture-giving delight which the attack upon an enemy affords. All other sensations are but as the tinkling of a door-bell in comparison with the throbbing of Big Ben." Then there is the nine-teenth-century birth of scientific racism, which eagerly twisted Darwin's discoveries to justify the idea that "inferior" races were fated to disappear from the Earth, just like species of plants and animals gone extinct—and implied that there was no sin involved in helping them vanish.

And finally, along came plenty of thinkers and politicians who saw this as inevitable. In 1898, the year of Omdurman, one of them declared, "One can roughly divide the nations of the world into the living and the dying." This was no fringe racial theorist speaking but Lord Salisbury, prime minister of Great Britain. And then comes Lindqvist's most unexpected discovery: a German thinker, Friedrich Ratzel, an ardent enthusiast of colonialism, believed that there was a "demonic necessity" for the "superior race" to see to it that "peoples of inferior culture" die out. And who were these inferior people? They included "the stunted hunting people in the African interior" (tens of thousands of Africans—neither stunted nor hunters, incidentally—would die in the notorious 1904 German genocide of the Herero people of today's Namibia), Gypsies—and Jews. Hitler had a copy of Ratzel's book with him in 1924, when he was in prison writing *Mein Kampf.*

"Hitler himself," writes Lindqvist, "was driven throughout his political career by a fanatical anti-Semitism with roots in a tradition of over a thousand years, which had often led to killing and even to mass murder of Jews. But the step from mass murder to genocide was not taken until the anti-Semitic tradition met the tradition of genocide arising during Europe's expansion in America, Australia, Africa, and Asia."

Can we prove this beyond doubt? Not without knowing exactly what was in Hitler's mind. But I defy anyone to read *"Exterminate All the Brutes"* and not see the Holocaust in a somewhat different light and the Jews, as Lindqvist suggests, as the Africans of Europe. His bold contention has riled some more traditional scholars, deeply wedded to the idea of the Holocaust's uniqueness. Unique it certainly was in scale, technology, and speed, but Lindqvist makes us realize that it was but one of an appalling series of attempts—the others almost all outside of Europe—to exterminate entire peoples from the face of the Earth.

Terra Nullius has also not been without its critics, chief among them white Australians who feel that all this history of the shameful treatment of Aboriginal peoples is familiar news by now. To some extent that's true, but unfortunately, as Lindqvist shows us, not true enough. He reminds us of how people in a country we normally consider enlightened thought so much like Nazis. What would we say, for instance, about a German theorist who, a mere half-dozen years before Hitler took power, wrote, "The survival of the Jews will only cause trouble"? We'd say that this person paved the way to Auschwitz. In *Terra Nullius,* Lindqvist introduces us to George H. L. F. Pitt-Rivers, a British anthropologist, who wrote in 1927 of Australia, "The survival of the natives will only cause trouble." By contrast, Pitt-Rivers added, "there is no native problem in Tasmania for the very good reason that the Tasmanians are no longer alive to create a problem." Hauntingly, Lindqvist quotes an earlier report from similarly minded researchers who described the typical Aborigine as "a naked, hirsute savage, with a type of features occasionally pronouncedly Jewish."

In other ways as well, he subtly examines how white Britons and Australians have looked at Aborigines, showing us how their perceptions and theories are so often a projection of white fantasies. Because women used the same form of address in talking either to a husband or his brother, for example, early anthropologists theorized that the Aborigines practiced group sex, with brothers owning several women in common. Because Aborigines, unlike whites, used no corporal punishment on their children, their child-rearing was judged inexcusably lax, and their children, half-castes in particular, were often seized and taken from them in order to be reared in state institutions in ways less "primitive." That practice was replicated in the notorious Indian boarding schools of the United States and Canada.

Above all, whites eagerly promoted the reassuring illusion that, because so much of central and western Australia looked like desert, it couldn't possibly belong to anyone and so was *terra nullius*—no one's land. "There was little appetite for admitting that every stone, every bush, and every water hole had its specific owner and custodian, its sacred history and religious significance." It was far more convenient to believe that the land was no one's, which meant it could be used for everything from open-pit mining to testing long-range missiles and British atomic bombs.

Lindqvist's work leaves you changed. *"Exterminate all the Brutes"* first made me fully aware of one of the real-life models for Joseph Conrad's Mr. Kurtz and set me looking for more. Two books later, I found myself writing about the Battle of Omdurman as a step on the way to the First World War. And no one who reads *A History of Bombing* will ever again feel that the Allies of the Second World War, ignoring international law and dropping bombs that killed some half million German civilians, fought the "Good War." Lindqvist opens a world to us, a world with its comforting myths stripped away. You read him at your own risk.

2014

NINETEEN

Sunday School History

FROM THE MID-1700S ON, roughly half the captive Africans taken to the Americas in chains were transported by ships based in Liverpool, Bristol, London, and a few other English ports. And so when Britain abolished its Atlantic slave trade in 1807, it was a historic turning point. Parliament's votes to end the ocean traffic in human beings and then, a quarter-century later, to end British slavery itself—which affected, above all, those who worked the lucrative sugar plantations in the British West Indies—have long fascinated historians, because the country acted against its economic self-interest. According the scholars Chaim D. Kaufmann and Robert A. Pape, these two steps cost the British people roughly 1.8 percent of their gross national income annually over some six decades. How can they be explained?

For many years, almost all the credit for ending the slave trade and British slavery was given to William Wilberforce, the eloquent, widely respected leader of the abolitionist forces in the House of Commons and a convert to the new evangelical strain of Anglicanism. Centering the story on Wilberforce offered great comfort. It allowed Britons to acknowledge that their ancestors had been involved in something horrendous, while at the same time giving Wilberforce credit for inspiring an unprecedented act of national benevolence. From throughout the nineteenth century you can find paintings and engravings showing the kindly figure of Britannia on her throne, in her gown, proclaiming to the world the end of slavery. At her feet are often one or more grateful, kneeling slaves receiving the news of this wonderful gift. Forgotten are the whips, the chains, the twelve-hour days of being worked to death in the sugar fields. For the Victorian age and after, Wilberforce, the inspiration behind Britannia's great gift, made a good schoolbook hero. He was rich, philanthropically generous, and deeply religious; and in a raucous, hard-drinking, high-living era, he was faithful to his wife, with whom he had six children.

Many American politicians of the Christian right have adopted Wilberforce as a model. Republican Congressman Mike Pence* of Indiana calls Wilberforce one of his personal heroes, often quotes him, and has declared that Wilberforce's "words hold equally true to abortion as they did to slavery." Congressman Frank Wolf, a Virginia Republican, says, "If we can get the word out about Wilberforce's life and legacy, we can change this country." Senator Sam Brownback of Kansas talks about the man so much that the *Economist* recently dubbed him and others "Wilberforce Republicans." Their agenda is much the same as that of many on the far right, with a few twists, such as an interest in prison reform (Wilberforce himself used to visit prisoners and ask them to repent).

Even the unsavory political consultant Dick Morris portrays himself as an admirer. Of Wilberforce, Morris told Fox News, "His whole crusade was a reformation of manners. No cock fighting. No dog fighting. No bull baiting. No abusing of horses. . . . And of course no slavery." (Morris did not mention various other things Wilberforce opposed, which ranged from the theater to bathing in the Thames to "the progressive rise of Wages.")

In 1933, England marked the centenary of Wilberforce's death with parades, church services, wreath-layings, and memorial lectures; a ceremony in his home city of Hull included twenty thousand spectators, Negro spirituals, a trumpet fanfare, the unfurling of the flags of fifty countries, and an aircraft fly-by. Several dozen biographies of Wilberforce have appeared since then, almost all of them by evangelicals, with such titles as *God's Politician, A Hero for Humanity, Statesman and Saint,* and *The Man Who Freed the Slaves.*

As with many myths, parts of this one are true. Wilberforce doggedly promoted the antislavery cause in Parliament for more than three decades. When the House of Commons banned the trade in 1807, it gave him a rare standing ovation, and he deserved it. From the accounts of his friends, he was a man of deep personal kindness and great charm: he sang magnificently and was a splendid mimic. He was famous for never having the heart to let an elderly servant go; one visitor counted thirteen of them tottering about his dining table, attending Wilberforce, his wife, and three guests. He gave away much of his money and lowered the rents of tenants on his land. And although deeply reactionary by modern standards—he felt that labor organizers belonged in prison and that the poor should accept "that their more

---

* Who has since, of course, gone on to higher office.

lowly path has been allotted to them by the hand of God"—his views were no worse than those of most of his fellow MPs. Otherwise, they wouldn't eventually have listened to him about slavery.

Today, however, we've come to see British abolition as involving far more than one man's personal virtue. In 1787 and 1788, during the heady period between the American and French Revolutions, a huge grassroots movement against the slave trade and slavery burst into life in Britain, startling abolitionists and slave traders alike. It lasted decades and sometimes included a solidarity across racial lines that often seems elusive in our own time. As the years passed, radicals began to point out similarities between the plights of slaves and British factory workers, some of whom in Yorkshire marched under a banner calling for "the immediate abolition of slavery both at home and abroad." Antislavery fervor spread quickly in Ireland, where people felt that they, too, knew something about oppression by the English. In 1792, more Britons signed petitions to Parliament against the slave trade than were eligible to vote. In the same year, more than three hundred thousand people refused to buy slave-cultivated West Indian sugar. This was the largest consumer boycott the world had yet seen, and it was driven by women, for they were the ones who did the household food shopping. British women had no vote, and the boycott was their first mass political act. Without boycott, petitions, and other popular pressure, Wilberforce could have done nothing in Parliament.

Leading the antislavery movement was an extremely imaginative, hardworking committee of activists who pioneered tactics that are still used by human rights groups today. Their movement created the first political logo—a kneeling slave in chains, surrounded by the legend, "Am I Not a Man and a Brother?"—and the first political poster: you've seen it, the often-reproduced top-down diagram showing how hundreds of bodies were crammed into a slave ship like rows of sardines. Indeed, the committee created the very prototype for the kind of political organization we take for granted today, with headquarters in a nation's capital and dozens of local chapters around the country. This was all virtually new at the time, as was the idea of members of different religious sects—primarily Quakers and Anglicans—working together for a secular end.

The committee's moving spirit and traveling organizer, Thomas Clarkson, was for much of his life a staunch radical who kept in his living room a stone he had proudly removed from the ruins of the Bastille a few weeks after its fall. Clarkson, who estimated that he covered thirty-five thousand miles by horseback in the movement's first half-dozen years, didn't get the full, scholarly biography he deserved until 1989. Historians now also give credit to the fiery Quaker pamphleteer Elizabeth Heyrick (1769–1831), who inspired the formation of some seventy women's antislavery societies, which were generally more outspoken than men's. Another important stimulus to popular feeling came from the eyewitness testimony of two former slaves living in Britain, Quobna Ottobah Cugoano and Olaudah Equiano, each of whom wrote books and traveled extensively throughout the country promoting them— Equiano for five years. Equiano's autobiography, a best seller in its time, has been rediscovered and is now often assigned in American college courses.

A further force behind the ending of British slavery, today widely recognized at last, was a long string of West Indian slave revolts, which intensified during the 1790s. The Haitian Revolution of 1791–1803 was the greatest slave uprising in history. First, the slaves successfully threw off their French masters. Two years later, Britain, at war with France, tried to seize for itself this most populous and lucrative of all Caribbean territories. After five years of hard fighting against the former slaves, British troops gave up and pulled out. Britain's army fought rebellions elsewhere in the Caribbean as well during this period, and several officers came home from these campaigns to write and speak (and, in one case, publish caricature drawings) against slavery. A later revolt by some twenty thousand slaves in Jamaica in 1831–32 was only barely contained by the British army after five weeks of fighting, and military officers and colonial and plantation officials testified before Parliament that more revolts were likely. It was no coincidence that in 1833 Parliament voted to free the empire's slaves.

· · ·

We might expect, then, that a new film released for the bicentenary of British abolition of the slave trade would reflect some of the new, broad-ranging research and awareness—in Europe, the United States, the Caribbean, and Africa—of these historical currents. Particularly since *Amazing Grace* is directed by the talented and accomplished Michael Apted, the creator of the superb *Up* series of documentaries that have sensitively followed the lives of a group of Britons at seven-year intervals for half a century. And Apted's scriptwriter was Steven Knight, author of the screenplay for *Dirty Pretty Things,* a memorably bold look at the gritty underside of immigrant life in today's London. The cast of the film, which opened to generally enthusiastic reviews, includes some of the finest British actors, starting with Albert Finney.

Amazing Grace is a visual treat. We see the familiar lush landscape of Jane Austen's England: grand country houses, mist-covered sheep meadows, formal gardens, wood-paneled rooms with roaring fires, frock coats for men and plunging lace-trimmed necklines for women. "It's pretty much all true, certainly in spirit and essence," Apted told the *New York Times* about his film. "It had to be very accurate or else it would have lost its power." But he is using, to say the least, a very Hollywood definition of accuracy. The wigs and stagecoaches may be authentic, but "in spirit and essence" the movie could have been made a hundred years ago. It gives the impression that William Wilberforce brought the slave trade to an end almost single-handedly. A biography published as the official companion to the movie calls Wilberforce "simply the greatest social reformer in the history of the world."

In years past, lionizers of Wilberforce have painted that rosy picture by simply leaving out other parts of the story, like the slave rebellions. *Amazing Grace* does so with far more subtlety and sophistication. It gives short glimpses of some of the other important people and events—Clarkson's epic travels, Equiano's book tour, the sugar boycott, the mass petition campaigns. But it implies, completely falsely, that Wilberforce orchestrated or supported all of these.

Much of the movie unfolds as flashbacks. This allows the film's Wilberforce, played appealingly by Ioan Gruffudd, to recount the beginnings of the antislavery movement to the young woman he is falling in love with, Barbara Spooner (Romola Garai). And so we see Thomas Clarkson (Rufus Sewell) galloping down a picturesque country lane, and we see Olaudah Equiano (the Senegalese singer Youssou N'Dour) selling copies of his book to eager buyers. Clarkson is also shown, oddly, somewhat drunk. But we are hearing Wilberforce's voice describing their work to his beloved, as if it were he who had dispatched them on their missions. At one point, when the antislavery movement revives after a hiatus, it is the film's Wilberforce who personally comes to fetch Clarkson, saying, "We need you back in London straight away."

In fact, the very sober Clarkson mounted his horse and set off on the first of his great organizing trips some two years before Wilberforce said a word against the slave trade in Parliament. Thirty-seven years later, in his sixties, Clarkson finished his last, thirteen-month trip around the country by stagecoach. And always on these journeys he was reporting to the largely Quaker abolition committee, not to Wilberforce. Early on, Clarkson bought some slave shackles at a ship chandler's shop on the Liverpool docks and displayed them to shocked audiences on his travels; in the film, it is Wilberforce who does this. And far from Wilberforce being a friend of Equiano (in the film the two have dinner and tour a slave ship together), there is no evidence that they ever met. Nor, as far as we can tell, did Wilberforce ever read Equiano's book; in his view, the proper role for freed slaves, he wrote in 1823, was to act as "a grateful peasantry."

In yet another misleading episode, Wilberforce, talking to his future wife, appreciatively mentions the sugar boycott and the way she is taking part in it. In real life, however, deeply uneasy with any uncontrolled expression of popular will, he opposed the boycott. He also believed women should obey their husbands and should have nothing to do with politics or the movement. The rise of women's antislavery societies dismayed him. "For ladies to meet, to publish, to go from house to house stirring up petitions," Wilberforce wrote to a friend, ". . . appear to me proceedings unsuited to the female character as delineated in Scripture."

In a similar reversal of reality, the film's Wilberforce dramatically unrolls a huge petition against the slave trade on the floor of the House of Commons and declaims to a pro-slavery MP, "No matter how much you shout, you will not drown out the voice of the people!" The real Wilberforce cared about many things, but the voice of the people was not one of them: he opposed all the various reform proposals that would have increased the less than 5 percent of the population, all male, eligible to vote. For him, government was strictly a matter for a small elite of well-born, educated men like himself. The Wilberforce of Apted's film does something else that would have shocked the real one: he includes ex-slaves and a woman in a planning session about parliamentary strategy. On one of the few occasions where we know Wilberforce was even in the presence of people of color, an 1816 dinner he chaired of something called the African and Asiatic Society, the handful of Africans and Asians present ate at one end of the room, behind a screen. This curious movie seeks to lionize Wilberforce by portraying him as something he decidedly was not: a modern liberal.

But not too liberal. Just to be sure we don't get any foolish ideas that the antislavery movement was an integral part of the age of revolutions, the film shows us a wise Wilberforce cautioning a hot-headed Clarkson about to head off to revolutionary France. Sounding like a proto-Leninist, Clarkson says, "We must fight! For a perfect order!"

Another character on the screen, the writer of the beloved hymn after which the movie is named, is distorted in a different way. In 1785, after Wilberforce's conversion to evangelicalism, he was trying to decide whether to remain in Parliament and went to consult the clergyman John Newton. Newton had been a slave-ship captain in his youth. In the traditional telling of the story, it is often implied that this great hymn and the many others Newton wrote were his atonement for a disgraceful past. Hollywood loves nothing better than repentant sinners, and so in the publicity material sent to film critics, the makers of *Amazing Grace* say: "Newton was captain of a slave ship for many years, until he underwent a dramatic religious conversion while steering his vessel through a storm. Repenting and regretting the misery he had inflicted on the thousands of human cargo he had transported across the Middle Passage . . . he devoted his life to the Church."

When the film shows Wilberforce coming to visit Newton, the minister is the very picture of repentance: he wears a monk's rough cloth robe and is cleaning the floor of his church, barefoot. Wilberforce says, "You told me that you live in the company of twenty thousand ghosts—the ghosts of slaves." Albert Finney, who plays Newton with a trembling passion worthy of a Best Supporting Actor nomination, then tells Wilberforce to fight the slave traders: "Do it, Wilber! Take them on! Pull their dirty filthy ships out of the water! The planters, sugar barons . . . do it! For God's sake!"

The reality was starkly, embarrassingly different. Most inconveniently for sin-and-repentance storytellers, John Newton was converted to evangelical Christianity *before* making four transatlantic voyages as a slave-ship officer, not afterward. He left the trade for reasons not of conscience but of health. And when he was later ordained a minister, he still had all his savings invested with his former employer, who had a fleet of slave ships on the ocean. Newton said not a word in public against the slave trade for more than thirty years after he left the sea, during much of which time he was the most famous evangelical preacher in England. There is no evidence whatever that he mentioned slavery when Wilberforce first came to see him. He spoke out on the subject for the first time only when a huge mass movement was under way and it was no longer possible for so prominent a former slave trader to be silent. He then wrote a pamphlet against the trade, testified twice at parliamentary hearings, mentioned the subject once or twice in sermons, and otherwise did not raise it again in public for the remaining two decades of his preaching and writing life. He devoted endless sermons, however, to what he believed was *"our* national sin"—blasphemy.

. . .

Amazing Grace is only one of many ways in which Britain marked the abolition bicentenary. Commemorative events were staged throughout 2007 by every conceivable institution from the House of Lords to the Socialist Workers Party. Prime Minister Tony Blair expressed his "deep sorrow" for the slave trade. Mayor Ken Livingstone of London declared, "The British government must formally apologize. . . . All attempts to evade this are weasel words." A special £2 coin commemorated the end of the slave trade and a new set of stamps honored both black and white abolitionists. Queen Elizabeth II attended a memorial service in Westminster Abbey. Virtually every major museum in the country mounted exhibitions. The archbishops of Canterbury and York posted a video on YouTube about their visit to a slave prison in Zanzibar. More than £20 million from the national lottery funded slavery-related projects organized by local governments. A group of Wilberforce admirers marched from Hull to London in yokes and chains.

By contrast, in 1907, not a single event commemorating the centenary made it into the London *Times* index for the year. But it is a different Britain today: more than 11 percent of the population of London, for example, is of African or West Indian descent. Traditionally, black Britons have voted Labour; the government was eager for anything to take people's minds off its embrace of the disastrous American venture in Iraq. Still, the immense attention lavished on the abolition bicentenary can't be seen as political expediency only. More and more Britons are aware that they are living in an increasingly multiracial society, in a country whose full history involves far more than kings and queens. Furthermore, some of the commemorative events were staged by members of the black community itself.

On a cold March afternoon in 2007, for instance, I was one of several speakers at a small ceremony to dedicate a bicentennial plaque in a park in Ealing, a part of London where many Caribbean immigrants and their descendants live. A borough councilor welcomed everyone, and some of the participants lit a candle and planted a tree—symbolically, a variety of palm that does well in northern climates. A minister poured a vial of salt water over the new plaque, for the tears that had been shed by those in bondage. Four children from a local school, two black, two white, read from William Cowper's "The Negro's Complaint," the most widely sung antislavery ballad of the 1780s. Its opening lines, "Forc'd from home and all its pleasures . . . O'er the raging billows borne," surely evoked for older West Indian immigrants assembled at the park their own journey across the ocean to a new and often difficult life in England. At the end of the proceedings, everyone scattered flowers in memory of those who died as slaves. Four municipal park workers in green safety vests, three of them white, one black, waiting to tidy up the grounds after the ceremony, had been standing nonchalantly off to the side in the manner of gravediggers at a funeral. Unexpectedly—and I found this moving—they came forward to scatter flowers as well.

In Britain's black press, there were occasional grumblings about the year's events as a "Wilberfest." But for the most part, people heard a more genuine story. Many of the year's more than two dozen special BBC programs having to do with slavery and abolition—documentary, drama, and hybrid— touched on subjects such as slave revolts, modern-day racism, and reparations. There were so many programs, the producer of one told me, because a group of black employees had gone to the BBC's director general to ask for extra air time for the bicentenary. Liverpool, the country's largest slave port, opened a new £10 million International Slavery Museum on August 23, 2007, the anniversary of the start of the great Haitian uprising. Anyone today in Britain who turns for information about slavery to a museum, a bookstore, or radio and TV will quickly find a far richer and more informed version of this history than was easily available a generation ago.

. . .

Why, then, does *Amazing Grace* revert to telling the story in such a determinedly old-fashioned way? The filmmaker's job is to entertain us, of course, not to stick to the minutia of history or to reflect the latest scholarship. But is there something else going on?

There is. The movie's principal financier, Philip Anschutz, is an American businessman who has long sought to fund a film about Wilberforce and who had been turned down by various big-name directors in the past. Anschutz is a tycoon with a vast empire of holdings in real estate, cattle, oil, newspapers, railroads, and sports teams, including the Los Angeles Lakers. In 2002, *Fortune* named him the country's "greediest executive" for selling more than $1.5 billion in shares of Qwest Communications, of which he had been chairman, before the company announced it had inflated its revenues and its stock price collapsed. A major backer of the evangelical Right, Anschutz has also been a significant donor to George W. Bush and to groups opposing everything from gay rights to abortion to the teaching of evolution.

Although he has not given a press interview since 1974, it's not hard to guess why Anschutz was so eager to make this film. Most important for all of Wilberforce's present-day political admirers on the Right like Anschutz and Pence is to celebrate him as someone whose Christian fundamentalism was central to his politics. *Amazing Grace* makes sure that we get this message. We see, for instance, Wilberforce having his ecstatic moment of evangelical conversion in a bucolic meadow. "You found God, sir?" a servant asks him. Wilberforce replies, "I think he found me." Later, over a dinner table, Clarkson says to him, "Mr. Wilberforce, we understand you're having problems choosing whether to do the work of God or the work of a political activist." The evangelical writer Hannah More (played by Georgie Glen) quickly adds, "We humbly suggest that you can do both."

This is the message the film wants us to carry away: that God's work is best done by a wealthy, virtuous man like Wilberforce, who is against slavery and various forms of sin but questions nothing else in the social and political order. But just what is the work of God? Almost all believers might agree that it is a matter of opposing slavery. But is it a matter of opposing abortion, and gay and women's rights as well? Or, is it a matter of fighting to narrow the gap between rich and poor? President George W. Bush, who hosted a special screening of *Amazing Grace* at the White House, has several times suggested that God told him to invade Afghanistan and Iraq. More than a century ago, President William McKinley said that "God Almighty" told him to annex the Philippines. People hear God say very different things, many of which have to do with advancing somebody's interests here on earth. All of which speaks for great wariness when politicians claim to be doing God's work.

Did Philip Anschutz closely control the way Wilberforce's story was presented in this film? Perhaps he didn't have to do so with too heavy a hand. If you want to downplay or ignore the slave rebellions and a sometimes unruly grassroots movement and emphasize the politics of pious, from-the-top-down benevolence, it is enough to simply tell the story of this pivotal moment through the character of Wilberforce. But when history now allows us a far deeper and richer look at British abolition, it is a pity that artists of the caliber of Michael Apted and Steven Knight have lent their talents to such a tamely traditional and misleading film. Although Apted claims its slippery distortions are "accurate," he is in fact presenting no more than a Sunday-school version of one of history's great liberation movements.

2007

America

FIGURE 6. Mark Twain.

TWENTY

Pilot on the Great River

MARK TWAIN'S NONFICTION

SOME GREAT WRITERS LIVED LIVES that seem limited to only a small slice of human experience—Proust, Austen, Dickinson—but nonetheless they saw far and deep. The lives of others—Cervantes, Tolstoy, Dostoevsky— far overflowed what they were able to get between the covers of their books. Mark Twain is among the overflowers. His work does not begin to contain the breadth, contradictions, and tragedies of his life.

It was a large and restless one, which stretched from the era when doctors bled their patients to that of the automobile and the airplane, from the boundless freedom of his childhood (read the passage in his autobiography about skating on the frozen Mississippi under moonlight, as ice floes break up and separate him from land) to crossing the country by stagecoach, sleeping atop mailbags, in the aftermath of the California Gold Rush. As a young man, he heard Charles Dickens read *David Copperfield* aloud from a New York stage; as an old one, he played miniature golf with a college president who had not yet gone into politics, Woodrow Wilson. He began as Sam Clemens in the riverside town of Hannibal, Missouri; as Mark Twain he traveled the world as the most renowned American author of his time, received by princesses and presidents, explorers and emperors, even the admiring shah of Persia. The young Kipling made a pilgrimage to meet him; Sigmund Freud came to hear him speak. Yet, amid these triumphs, Twain saw his beloved wife and three of his four children die before him.

He denounced the love of money and helped coin the phrase "Gilded Age" but hobnobbed happily with Andrew Carnegie and other robber barons, vacationed on the 227-foot yacht of one of them, preferred the fanciest of hotels, and lived in a palatial mansion with Tiffany furnishings, a marble-floored entrance hall, and a staff of seven. Hankering after still greater wealth, he spent himself deep into debt by investing money, his own and borrowed, in a long string of muddleheaded inventions. The most disastrous was one whose failure could have been predicted by a mechanically minded teenager: a typesetting machine with eighteen thousand separate parts. Into this hopeless dream the ever-optimistic writer poured the equivalent of well over $3 million in today's money. It would take another Twain to get all of this into a novel.

His work, like his life, was of volcanic proportions. An editor entitled one anthology *Mark Twain in Eruption.* In addition to the more than thirty books he published during his lifetime, Twain wrote thousands of newspaper articles and left behind some fifty notebooks and six hundred unpublished or unfinished manuscripts. Over his seventy-four years, it is estimated, he wrote at least fifty thousand letters. The eruptions never ceased. On April 13, 1897, after working on his travelogue *Following the Equator,* he wrote triumphantly in his notebook, "I finished my book today." Five weeks later came another entry, "Finished the book *again.* Addition of 30,000 words."

On top of all this material, Twain left behind, largely unedited, some half million words of recollections about his life. The more famous he became, the more often people pressed him to write his autobiography. But he claimed that all written memoirs were fraudulent; instead he would create the first truly honest one by dictating his, to be published in full only after his death. "If I should talk to the stenographer two hours a day for a hundred years," he declared, "I should still never be able to set down a tenth part of the things which have interested me." Between 1906 and 1909, the year before he died, he made a good start on the hundred years, dictating bountifully in 242 sessions.

Rambling from one corner of his life to another, free-associating, embroidering stories he had once written, mixing fanciful anecdotes, personal experience, and pungent opinions with news items and half-finished sketches, Twain's dictated eruptions most resemble a genre that would not be named for nearly another century: blog posts. This mountain of proto-blogging, sometimes with earlier bits of autobiographical writing mixed in, has been repeatedly reshaped by different editors since his death, depending on whether the compiler wanted to present an apolitical, avuncular Twain, an autobiography at manageable length, an all-inclusive colossus, or Twain's life in chronological order rather than in the meandering fashion in which he actually recounted it.

No matter which version of the autobiography you read, it is not one of the great literary memoirs. It digresses wildly, drops famous names, has patches of mawkishness, and assumes (true for readers then, but not necessarily now) that we already know a good deal about his life. There are many pages about billiards and bowling. The whole thing could use a careful rewrite. Nonetheless, it yields sudden stretches of great beauty, like shafts of sun falling on a mountainside, as when he describes childhood visits to his uncle's farm: "I can call back the solemn twilight and mystery of the deep woods, the earthy smells, the faint odors of the wild flowers, the sheen of rain-washed foliage, the rattling clatter of drops when the wind shook the trees … the snap-shot glimpses of disturbed wild creatures skurrying through the grass."

One of the fascinations of the dictated autobiography is that we can see some of the sources for his greatest work of fiction, *The Adventures of Huckleberry Finn*. Not just the boyhood figures who were to some degree the models for Huck, Tom Sawyer, and others, but the spirit of that boyhood: the universe of woods, fields, caves, and islands to be explored in an age without supervised after-school activities; the pervasive acceptance of slavery; the small town where everyone knew everyone else's business; the great river coursing past, as ceaseless as the flow of time itself. And in his recollections we can also see Twain's knowledge of the wider world beyond Hannibal: its chicanery, its illusions, its lust for gain, and its cruel gulf between rich and poor. Without the experience of all this he never could have imagined into being, in his childhood landscape, an outlaw like Huck.

· · ·

Another crucial part of Twain's nonfiction, perhaps more so than for most other writers, is his letters, for the window they provide onto his soul is less mediated and controlled by Twain than the dictated autobiography. Through the letters we can feel his thrill at seeing new countries, his enjoyment of his growing fame, and his perpetual dreams of making a fortune through a magically successful investment. We see his immense gratitude when his friend the novelist and editor William Dean Howells gives him the greatest gift any writer can give another, which is to mark up a manuscript, in this case *The Adventures of Tom Sawyer*. Although Twain was startlingly willing to let his wife, Howells, and others prune material out of his writing, almost everyone else was so in awe of him that he received too little of the tough, intelligent, critical feedback that could have benefited his more ragged and loquacious books.

Nonetheless, he did have another way of testing the effect of his words, integral to honing his prose. During the course of his lifetime, he gave well over five hundred lectures, readings, commencement addresses, or after-dinner speeches, more than 140 of them just on one exhausting, round-the-world, 53,000-mile speaking tour he undertook to pay off his huge debts. "I know a great many secrets about audiences," he says in one letter, "secrets not to be got out of books, but only acquirable by experience." He learned to speak in a way that would appeal equally to the 25-cent customers in the balconies and those in evening dress in the front row. He was wearied by this endless round of performing, but at the same time he reveled in it, noting carefully which lines worked and which didn't, learning the value of a drawl and a calculated pause.

This part of his life made him a shrewd and interested judge of other performers. His best work all seems born to be read aloud—which usually it was, first to an audience of his wife and daughters and then on stage. It is this side of Twain that the actor Hal Holbrook brought to life by staging constantly changing versions of his one-man show, *Mark Twain Tonight!* on Broadway, on television, on recordings, around the country, and across the world for more than sixty years. This talented imitator of Twain has himself had many imitators.

To return to the letters: above all, they let us feel with Twain what lay behind his statement that "the source of all humor is not laughter but sorrow." He feels responsible for the agonizing death of his brother, lethally scalded when a boiler exploded on the steamboat where Twain had gotten him a job. The blows that would come later in his life help account for the darker tone of the writing from his final decade and a half. When spinal meningitis takes the life of his favorite daughter, the 24-year-old Susy, it is all the more painful because it comes when he is away from her, in England finishing up that mammoth international lecture tour. "She that had been our wonder and our worship," he calls her. "It is one of the mysteries of our nature that a man, all unprepared, can receive a thunder-stroke like that and live." Some weeks after the news of her death, still deep in mourning, he writes to his friend Rev. Joseph Twichell that "she was my superior in fineness of mind, in the delicacy & subtlety of her intellect . . . I know her better now; for I have read her private writings & sounded the deeps of her mind; & I know better, now, the treasure that was mine than I knew it when I had it . . . And now she is *dead*—& I can never tell her."

Another daughter, Jean, years later would die horribly on Christmas Eve, while visiting her father, when an epileptic seizure caused her to drown in a bathtub. She was twenty-nine. But perhaps nothing surpassed Twain's grief at the loss of his wife, Livy, in Italy, where they had gone in search of the respite and climate that might aid her heart disease and difficulty in breathing. One evening he came to her "to say the usual good-night," as he writes Howells, "& she was dead!" To his friend Twichell he describes how he sat with her body for the next twenty hours "till the embalmers came at 5; & then I saw her no more. In all that night & all that day she never noticed my caressing hand—it seemed strange." It is all the more poignant to read that side by side with an early love letter to her, where he speaks of her "eyes that are dearer to me than the light that streams out of the Heavens."

. . .

It would take tens of thousands of words to cover all of Twain's nonfiction, but there is no question which book is at its summit: *Life on the Mississippi.* Who among us, as a child, has not dreamed of driving or piloting or captaining something greatly faster and more powerful than ourselves: a ship, a train, an airplane? I used to think this was a boy's dream, but judging from the number of women in airline cockpits these days, many girls must have it too. Twain evokes his version of this dream in the marvelous passage where he first describes the "dead and empty" summer day in Hannibal: "the white town drowsing in the sunshine of a summer's morning; the streets empty . . . one or two clerks sitting in front of the Water Street stores, with their splint-bottomed chairs tilted back against the wall, chins on breasts, hats slouched over their faces, asleep . . . a sow and a litter of pigs loafing along the sidewalk."

But then: "A film of dark smoke appears . . . instantly a negro drayman, famous for his quick eye and prodigious voice, lifts up the cry, 'S-t-e-a-m-boat a-comin'!' and the scene changes! The town drunkard stirs, the clerks wake up . . . and all in a twinkling the dead town is alive and moving. . . . The people fasten their eyes upon the coming boat as upon a wonder they are seeing for the first time." And a wonder it is: two tall chimneys belching black smoke, a roaring furnace where you can see the flames, a glass pilot house on the highest deck, and within it the figure that every boy in Hannibal wants to become, the steamboat pilot. "Your true pilot," Twain writes later in the book, "cares nothing about anything on earth but the river, and his pride in his occupation surpasses the pride of kings."

Part of the pleasure of reading *Life on the Mississippi* is that it verifies that childhood dream. Twain grew up to become a steamboat pilot, and, for those magic few years, his pride did surpass that of kings. He takes us into the intricacies of this trade: the rituals, the hierarchy, the sense of comradeship among the members of this elite fraternity, the danger they face of having a boiler blow up. And he makes us feel, without ever saying so directly, that learning the river—the bends, the shallows, the hidden sandbars, the eddies and currents, the sunken trees that could poke a fatal hole in your hull—and learning which of these things, like the sandbars or the course of the river in flood, will be constantly changing, is a metaphor for finding one's way through life. It is even more challenging than life itself, because you have to learn to navigate this treacherous waterway in both directions, by day, by night, and in fog. Unlike so much of Twain's other supposed nonfiction, here there are few tall tales: when he is writing about an extraordinary profession at the height of its glory, he had no need to make anything up.

Something else that makes the book so unusual is that it is one of the very few American classics about work. As we hear pilots talking, we hear the language of this craft:

> "Jim, how did you run Plum Point, coming up?
> "It was in the night . . . started out about fifty yards above the wood pile on the false point, and held on the cabin under Plum Point till I raised the reef—quarter less twain—then straightened up for the middle bar till I got well abreast the old one-limbed cotton-wood in the bend, then got my stern on the cotton-wood and head on the low place above the point, and came through a-booming—nine and a half."

When you think about our best-remembered works of literature, whether *The Scarlet Letter, The Great Gatsby, The Sun Also Rises,* or countless others, very few show us a line of work from the inside. In the second two, the very subject matter is people at leisure; reading the first, you wonder how the citizens of Puritan Massachusetts got any work done at all when they were so busy persecuting adulterers. (The shining exception among great American novels, of course, is *Moby-Dick,* written just a few years before Twain took to the river.) Other writers throughout history have taken pen names, but who besides Twain took one from work that he loved?

One word of warning for anyone picking up *Life on the Mississippi* for the first time: don't read the whole thing. Encountering many a work by Twain is like exploring a new city: some sights are to be savored, other neighborhoods skipped entirely. Here you should start with chapter 4 and end with chapter 21. These are the loving pages about being a young pilot on the river—the book's emotional and aesthetic core. The rest is mostly fluff and could be boiled down to a quarter of its length. As with so much of his other writing, Twain could have used a good editor. He takes three chapters to warm up and then many more to cool down—largely a collection of stray bits of history and lore, plus an account of coming back to the river years later. The only moving part in these later pages is his sadness about what he finds as a much older man: steamboats have largely been replaced by trains, and for those still plying the water, dikes, beacons and powerful electric searchlights have made steamboating safer but less of an art. It is as if the Wright brothers had returned to the air today, to see how commercial flights all have to follow air traffic controllers' orders and almost all of the time are flown by autopilot.

. . .

Newspaper articles, humorous sketches, speeches, diatribes, essays, and pamphlets flowed from Twain's pen throughout his life. But just because there are various anthologies of his nonfiction, don't assume that this word describes the contents. Many of these pieces may have some actual event as a kernel, around which Twain then spun a tale at least as fanciful as anything Tom Sawyer could have invented. "Mark Twain took a democrat's view of fact and fiction," his biographer Ron Powers writes; "he ... let them mingle in his work without prejudice." If he had lived long enough to write for the *New Yorker*, little of his supposed reportage could have gotten past its fact-checking department unscathed.

His shorter pieces cover a spectrum from those that seem embarrassingly flat or eccentric today to a few like "A Telephonic Conversation" that can still make us burst into laughter, as we hear him describing the frustration of overhearing one end of a call:

> Pause.
> Perhaps so; I generally use a hair-pin.
> Pause.
> What did you say? [*Aside*] Children, do be quiet!
> Pause.
> Oh! B *flat!* I thought you said it was the cat!
> Pause.
> Since *when?*
> Pause.

Why, *I* never heard of it.
Pause.
You astound me! It seems utterly impossible!
Pause.
Who did?
Pause.
Good-ness gracious!
Pause.
Well, what *is* this world coming to? Was it right in *church?*
Pause.
And was her *mother* there?
Pause.

In the vast miscellany of his sketches and articles for newspapers and magazines can be found enough ammunition to supply either side in the famous argument between the critics Van Wyck Brooks and Bernard DeVoto over whether or not this son of the frontier was lethally tamed by his mother, his wife, his wealth, and his long years in the more genteel culture of the East Coast. They show us a Twain who fluctuates between the daringly subversive and the conventional prejudices of his time (about American Indians, for example), and also a Twain who had some decided quirks—a fascination with clairvoyance, for one thing, and the conviction that someone other than Shakespeare wrote those plays.

But these writings also show us something deeper: a man becoming keenly aware of the injustices of his age. From the young Sam Clemens whose father and uncle owned slaves and who even briefly joined a unit of Confederate irregulars (an episode he considerably embellished in "The Private History of a Campaign that Failed"), he grew into the Mark Twain who felt that slavery was America's original sin. *Huckleberry Finn* is surely the most eloquent expression of that feeling in all our literature, a portrait all the more slyly powerful because Huck believes he will be doomed to hell for helping the enslaved Jim—Miss Watson's lawful property—escape down the Mississippi toward freedom.

Twain understood, more clearly than most white Americans, that the Civil War had changed too little and that for former slaves, the United States could still be a place of lynchings and terror. One act of generosity he made would reverberate decades after he was dead. He supported the studies of a number of black students, among them one of the first men of color to enter Yale Law School. Twain met him only briefly and may have forgotten his name, but he told the school's dean that he would help pay the expenses of "this young man"—who was working odd jobs on the side to make ends meet—until he graduated. The student was Warner T. McGuinn, who became a respected lawyer and Baltimore city council member and who, decades later, himself mentored and referred cases to a grateful young black attorney just starting out on his career. *That* lawyer was Thurgood Marshall, who argued the successful Brown v. Board of Education case that ended legal school segregation in America and who became the first black justice of the United States Supreme Court. We can imagine the smile that would have brought to Twain's face.

As Twain aged, he came to see that the racism so intertwined with American slavery took other forms around the world—and it was a world he saw as much or more of than almost any other American writer of his day. As he puts it in one article, "I think I have no color prejudices nor caste prejudices nor creed prejudices. All that I care to know is that a man is a human being—that is enough for me; he can't be any worse." While staying in Vienna in the late 1890s, he presciently observed—unlike virtually any foreign journalist of the time—just who were always the first victims of ethnic nationalist demonstrations. "In some cases the Germans [were] the rioters, in others the Czechs," he wrote in *Harper's,* "and in all cases the Jew had to roast, no matter which side he was on."

Although he had spoken as early as 1867 about the harmful impact of American "civilization" on Hawaii and had noticed how brutally Chinese immigrant laborers were treated in California, it was mostly during the last fifteen years of his life that Twain's ire focused on the worldwide drive for colonies, fueled by "the white man's notion that he is less savage than the other savages." When he circled the globe on his lecture tour in 1895 and 1896, he encountered evidence at almost every stop. In Australia he saw how British settlers had displaced and almost exterminated the Aborigines and how they had put South Sea islanders to work in harsh conditions on the sugar plantations. In India he noticed how a white man punched his servant in the face, and he sensed the deep desire of many Indians for self-rule. His reaction to South Africa was different from that of almost all Americans and Europeans of this time, who saw the territory just through the lens of the conflict over land and mineral wealth between white Britons and white Afrikaners, or Boers, which would culminate in the Boer War of 1899–1902. Twain, however, felt that the underlying crime was that both groups "stole the land from the . . . blacks."

He was appalled when, in the treaty ending the Spanish-American War, the United States acquired a colony of its own by buying the Philippines from

Spain, for $20 million. "I am opposed," he declared in an interview, "to having the eagle put its talons on any other land." This didn't stop him, however, from thoroughly enjoying the company of the great imperialists of the age, whether the explorer Henry Morton Stanley, the bellicose Kaiser Wilhelm II of Germany, or the young Boer War hero Winston Churchill.

The purchase of the Philippines led to one of the most shameful episodes of American imperialism. Not surprisingly, Filipino nationalists who had fought for independence from Spain had no wish to see themselves colonized anew by the United States. The brutal Philippine-American War that broke out in 1899 was one of naked conquest that saw American troops use widespread, systematic torture. The war spurred Twain's "To the Person Sitting in Darkness." He took his ironic title from the Gospel according to St. Matthew, which refers to "the people which sat in darkness" as those not yet enlightened by Christ's good news. There had been much talk about how it was America's duty to bring Christianity to the backward Filipinos. President William McKinley, for instance, ignoring the fact that millions of Filipinos were already Catholics, declared that he wished "to educate the Filipinos, and uplift and civilize and Christianize them."

Against Washington's claim that it was fighting this war on the other side of the world only for the most high-minded of motives (does that sound familiar?) Twain lumped the new American imperial venture with the seizure by Britain, France, Germany, and Russia of territory in Africa and China. He followed up his widely reprinted pamphlet with "To My Missionary Critics" and several other articles. In Massachusetts, the *Springfield Republican* called him "the most influential anti-imperialist and the most dreaded critic of the sacrosanct person in the White House." In 1901, succeeding the assassinated McKinley, Theodore Roosevelt became that person. When Roosevelt, who ardently craved an American colonial empire, heard a crowd cheering for Twain, he angrily muttered that anti-imperialists like him should be skinned alive.

Soon Twain spoke out for another anti-imperial cause. Artfully outflanking larger European countries, King Leopold II of Belgium had made himself an early beneficiary of the rush for African colonies. The deadly forced labor system Leopold devised for extracting the Congo's vast wealth in rubber and ivory attracted the attention of a brilliant young British journalist, Edmund Dene Morel, who mounted against Leopold the biggest international human-rights campaign of its time. Morel came to visit Twain in 1904 and persuaded him to make three trips to Washington to lobby President Roosevelt and the

State Department to bring pressure on the king and to write about the Congo. The result was "King Leopold's Soliloquy," which the author's usual publishers found too acid for their taste. Twain gave it, and the royalties from it, to the American branch of Morel's Congo Reform Association, which published it as a pamphlet in 1905. Although the king's soliloquy is imaginary, it is based on real events and has quotations from eyewitness testimony. Morel's campaign tools included a slide show of atrocity photographs, some of which were included in "King Leopold's Soliloquy." Twain's Leopold rages against "the incorruptible *kodak* . . . The only witness I have encountered in my long experience that I couldn't bribe." The pamphlet clearly stung its target; the king's formidable public-relations apparatus issued a 47-page response entitled "An Answer to Mark Twain."

Remarkably, for decades after Twain died, such pieces of his writing largely disappeared from new editions of his work. "King Leopold's Soliloquy" and several other attacks on imperialism were not republished until more than half a century after his death. Sanitizing Twain's legacy were his authorized biographer and literary executor, Albert Bigelow Paine, and the author's one surviving child, his daughter Clara, who lived to the age of eighty-eight. They were eager to have the public remember only Twain the humorist, the sage of Hannibal, the kindly white-suited figure with the big mustache and flowing mane of white hair. The Twain who had been the strident opponent of colonial conquest they shoved out of sight.

In the various volumes of the writer's speeches, letters, notebooks, and other work that he edited, Paine downplayed, greatly condensed, or simply omitted many of Twain's comments on events like the Philippine War. In his three-volume biography, he never even mentioned that Twain was a vice president of the Anti-Imperialist League. When Paine edited a collection of the letters, for example, one sentence where Twain had written "I am going to stick close to my desk for a month, now, hoping to write a small book, full of playful and good-natured contempt for the lousy McKinley" ended simply with "hoping to write a small book." Paine's versions of various Twain texts were long accepted as authentic by later editors, who had no idea that they had been bowdlerized. Happily, by the late 1960s scholars had discovered and undone enough omissions for opponents of the Vietnam War to be able to use his prophetic work in support of their cause. What greater testimony to Twain's subversive side could there be than that he was censored for so long after his death?

2016

TWENTY-ONE

A Literary Engineer

THE NEW JOURNALISM OF THE 1960S AND 1970S from Tom Wolfe, Gay Talese, Hunter Thompson, and others made the biggest collective splash in recent American nonfiction and certainly enlarged our idea of what the genre could do. But will people still be enthralled by Thompson's psychedelic ramblings or the early Wolfe's strings of italics and exclamation marks fifty or a hundred years from now? More lasting, I think, a grand pointillist mural of our time and place, as expressed in the lives of an encyclopedic range of people, will be the work of John McPhee.

For one thing, there is more of it. McPhee has written more than thirty books, while some of the most notable New Journalists lapsed into silence. Truman Capote never published another substantial piece of nonfiction after *In Cold Blood,* nor did Michael Herr after his remarkable reporting of the Vietnam War in *Dispatches.* McPhee, however, has steadily averaged close to a book a year. Some of us for whom it is a struggle to get a one out every five or six years feel he should be prosecuted under the Fair Labor Standards Act.

McPhee's choice of subjects is driven by certain personal predilections. Among other things, he is drawn to geology (four books), practitioners of ancient arts (*The Survival of the Bark Canoe*), eccentrics (*The Headmaster*), the American wilderness (*Coming into the Country*), and people obsessed by unusual technology, as with the blimp enthusiasts of *The Deltoid Pumpkin Seed.* He also has found wonderfully fertile terrain by simply doing things that small children dream of. For what other thread connects his flying with a bush pilot, traveling the seas on a merchant ship, crossing the country in the cab of a railway engine, and going on maneuvers with the Swiss Army? In an age besotted by celebrities, the people McPhee has chosen to bring alive on the page are not presidents, singers, or movie actors, but country doctors, pinball players, produce sellers in a farmers' market, aid workers in Africa, a long-haul trucker, and the man responsible for grooming the grass at Wimbledon.

Like so many of the people he writes about, McPhee is a consummate craftsman. There are many aspects of his craft that a fellow writer can envy, from his keen ear for the quirks and rhythms of American speech, to his arsenal of tools for nimbly hopping about in time—including shifts of tense you only notice on the second reading. But I'm here to talk about his engineering.

A few years ago I was talking with a college student who told me she was majoring in civil engineering. "I've never really understood," I asked her. "What's the difference between an architect and an engineer?"

"An architect plans what the skyscraper is going to look like from the outside," she said. "An engineer makes sure it doesn't fall down."

When we write, we often pay too much attention to the architecture and not enough to the engineering. We focus on the skyscraper's outside— images, metaphors, bits of description, the sparkle of prose—and not enough on the framework of trusses and beams: the structure, the plot (something that applies as much to nonfiction as to fiction), the careful doling out or withholding of information to create suspense, all of which, in the long run, ultimately determines whether or not someone keeps on reading. A piece of writing can sparkle aplenty from one paragraph to the next, but if the inner engineering isn't there, the reader's attention wanders; the building falls down. This is all the more important when someone writes, as McPhee usually does, about unknown people, of whom, unlike celebrities, we have no knowledge to begin with. For a writer, this sets the bar higher.

Much of McPhee's ability to make us care about his vast and improbable range of human subjects lies in his engineering. From the pilings beneath the foundations to the railing of the roof-top observation deck, he is the master builder of literary skyscrapers. Other writers may have more glittering prose or weave more elegant metaphors, but few have built such an interesting and varied array of structures. With many authors of narrative nonfiction, I often feel that structure is almost an afterthought: an array of lively scenes is arranged more or less chronologically, with one that seems to wrap things up placed at the end. But when McPhee picks up his pen, I sense a writer thinking long and shrewdly about structure before he even puts a word on paper.

Consider, for example, his portrait of the late Thomas Hoving as director of New York's Metropolitan Museum of Art. A less imaginative writer might have followed Hoving around for a time and interwoven that material with background information about his childhood and comments that others made about him. But McPhee does it differently. He assembles a dozen or so scenes from Hoving's life: some from the present (Hoving answering the mail; talking with his wife; hunting art for the museum in Europe) and some from the past (getting into trouble in high school; working in a clothing store and realizing this was not for him). Almost all involve closely observed or reconstructed interplay and dialogue between Hoving and other people. And then McPhee arranges them, just as one might find an artist's work on the walls of a museum, not in chronological order. The headline on the article? "A Roomful of Hovings." (It is the title piece in one of McPhee's many collections.)

Similarly imaginative structures underlie almost all his books. *Levels of the Game,* for instance, is built around a single tennis match, between Arthur Ashe and Clark Graebner at Forest Hills in the 1960s. It begins with the opening serve and ends with the final point. But into this one match are woven portraits of two players who differ radically by style of play, politics, background, race, and approach to life. In an article, "In Search of Marvin Gardens," McPhee uses the Monopoly board, whose street names all come from Atlantic City, as his starting point to explore the real Atlantic City, right down to the jail. The city, of course, turns out to be a far shabbier place than the one conjured up by the landing places on the Monopoly board. The structure reinforces the impact of the piece; as McPhee put it in a *Paris Review* interview, "Structure is not a template. It's not a cookie cutter. It's something that arises organically from the material." But I think he understates his point, for surely in the Atlantic City article, and in many others, he must have had an engineering blueprint in mind in order to decide what kind of material to gather.

Some of the structures McPhee uses are ancient ones. In "A Forager" (another piece in *A Roomful of Hovings*), he spends an entire week with his subject, Euell Gibbons, an expert in edible wild plants, gamely joining Gibbons in munching on dandelions, watercress, ground cherries, chicory greens, and the like along the way. A week in the life of someone or something is the oldest narrative structure there is, going back to the Book of Genesis. Layered on top of that is another classic structure, at least as old as *The Odyssey,* for McPhee and Gibbons spend that week on a journey, by canoe and foot, eating their way along the Susquehanna River and then a portion of the Appalachian Trail.

Sometimes McPhee devises a framework of columns and beams entirely his own, as in one of his most anthologized pieces, about another journey, "Travels in Georgia." Here he follows a man and a woman on a strange trek across that state, telling us in great detail how they poke about in streams, swamps, and roadside ditches, make notes on clipboards, and collect an odd variety of stuff, including the carcasses of small animals that have been struck by cars. Who *are* these people, we wonder, and why on earth are they doing this? That's what keeps us reading. We're nearly half way through the piece before we learn that the pair work for an obscure state agency that designates protected areas for endangered plants and animals. All good narrative writers purposely withhold some information for a while, but I've never seen one bold enough to withhold the very profession of the people he is profiling.

. . .

To my mind, McPhee's engineering masterpiece is his *Encounters with the Archdruid,* the text of which, like almost all of his books, first appeared in the *New Yorker.* A portrait of the environmental activist David Brower (1912–2000), it is structured like no other biography or profile. Brower was a militant, not a deal-maker, and his passionate, lifelong defense of the American wilderness against any threat left his enemies enraged. And so the book is arranged around three prolonged encounters between the "evangelical" Brower, as McPhee calls him, and people who detest everything he believes.

The first is a prominent mining geologist named Charles Park, whose entire life has been devoted to targeting deposits of valuable minerals, wherever they are found. He was a man who believed, McPhee says, "that if copper were to be found under the White House, the White House should be moved." How does McPhee bring him together with Brower? He takes the two of them camping and hiking for a week in Washington State's Glacier Peak Wilderness. The setting is shrewdly chosen: Glacier Peak is a federally designated wilderness area, "not to receive even the use given a national park, not to be entered by a machine of any kind except in extreme emergency, not to be developed or lumbered—forevermore." But there's a key exception: mining claims, including a huge one held by Kennecott Copper, remain valid, and new claims could still be made. To display two political enemies in combat, McPhee could not have picked a better battleground. Park chips away at rocks with his geologist's tools, curious about what metals here could feed the American economy; Brower praises the beauty of the mountains, still unravaged by men like Park. Almost any other writer, doing a story like this, would have elicited these rival points of view by interviewing the two men separately. McPhee, however, brings them together, where, with spectacular scenery in the background, their fierce arguments provide him with writer's gold: dialogue.

The second encounter McPhee sets up, again for what appears to be a week or so, is between Brower and a businessman who wants to build a vast housing development on a wild island off the coast of Georgia, complete with an airport suitable for private jets. Compared to the first encounter, the conversation between the two antagonists is much more polite. However, the businessman, Charles Fraser, has great contempt for environmentalists, calling them "druids." He tells Brower, "I call anyone a druid who prefers trees to people" (hence the book's title).

The third encounter is the most dramatic, and threaded through it, providing its narrative backbone, is one of the more spectacular journeys anywhere: going down the Grand Canyon by raft. In the 1950s and '60s some of the fiercest American environmental battles were over the building of dams. As McPhee puts it, to environmentalists, at

> the absolute epicenter of Hell on earth ... stands a dam. Conservationists who can hold themselves in reasonable check before new oil spills and fresh megalopolises mysteriously go insane at even the thought of a dam.... the reaction to dams is so violent because rivers are the ultimate metaphors of existence, and dams destroy rivers.

David Brower regarded failing to stop the Glen Canyon Dam, which blocked the Colorado River to form Lake Powell, upstream from the Grand Canyon, as "the greatest failure of his life," McPhee says. But after losing that battle, he went on to furiously wage and win several others, stopping Bureau of Reclamation plans to build two more large dams in the Grand Canyon itself. His arch-enemy in this prolonged warfare, the proud builder of the Glen Canyon Dam, defeated in the later struggles, was Floyd Dominy, longtime commissioner of the Bureau of Reclamation. Dominy, in effect, was chief dam-builder for the U.S. government.

McPhee's swift brush strokes etch him: "He appears to have been lifted off a horse with block and tackle. He wears blue jeans, a white-and-black striped shirt, and leather boots with heels two inches high. His belt buckle is silver and could not be covered over with a playing card. He wears a string tie that is secured with a piece of petrified dinosaur bone. On his head is a white Stetson."

"Dave Brower hates my guts," he tells McPhee, who goes to see Dominy in his office.

> "I can't talk to preservationists. I can't talk to Brower because he's so Gad-damned ridiculous. . . . I had a steer out on my farm in the Shenandoah reminded me of Dave Brower. Two years running, we couldn't get him into the truck to go to market. He was an independent bastard that nobody could corral. That son of a bitch got into that truck, busted that chute, and away he went. So I just fattened him up and butchered him right there on the farm. I shot him right in the head and butchered him myself. That's the only way I could get rid of the bastard."
>
> "Commissioner," I said, "if Dave Brower gets into a rubber raft going down the Colorado River, will you get in it, too?"
>
> "Hell, yes," he said. "Hell, yes."

In the very next paragraph, in one of McPhee's adroit leaps in time and space, all three men are on the river, approaching a set of rapids at Mile 130.

In this section of the book, as in the first panel of the triptych, the heart of the story is verbal combat. The repartee has all the more drama because it takes place in front of an audience—a boatload of tourists who had no idea that these two longtime enemies would be aboard when they signed up for a few days of rafting down the Grand Canyon. At Mile 144.8, triumphantly brandishing a map,

> "We are entering the reservoir," Brower announces. "We are now floating on Lake Dominy."
>
> "Jesus," mutters Dominy.
>
> "What reservoir?" someone asks. Brower explains. A dam that Dominy would like to build, ninety-three miles downstream, would back still water to this exact point in the river.
>
> "Is that right, Commissioner?"
>
> "That's right."
>
> . . . The other passengers are silent, absorbed by what Brower has told them.
>
> "Do you mean the reservoir would cover the Upset Rapid? Havasu Creek? Lava Falls? All the places we are coming to?" one man asks Dominy.
>
> Dominy reaches for the visor of his Lake Powell hat and pulls it down more firmly on his head. "Yes," he says.

Their argument continues when McPhee takes the two of them for a boat ride on Lake Powell—which covers much of what had once been Glen Canyon:

Brower pointed to strange striations in jagged shapes on the opposite canyon wall. "That is hieroglyphic, written centuries ago by God Himself," he said. "Yeah? What does it say?" said Dominy. "It says, 'Don't flood it.'"

A few additional little touches—the kind of thing that too hasty a reader might let pass by—make McPhee's tripartite structure more sturdy, like rebar hidden in concrete. In each of the three sections, for example, a bulldozer appears. McPhee and his subjects encounter one as they walk out of the Cascades: "Half submerged, its purpose obscure, it heaved, belched, backed, shoved, and lurched around on the bottom of the Suiattle [River] as if the water were not there. The bulldozer was stronger than the river." In the middle section, the developer Charles Fraser talks cheerfully about moving sand dunes out of the way with a bulldozer. And in the final section, "on a shelf behind Dominy's desk, in the sort of central and eye-catching position that might be reserved for a shining trophy, was a scale model of a bulldozer."

Encounters with the Archdruid is not a perfect work: the middle panel of the triptych is weaker than the other two, and McPhee skims too lightly over Brower's darker side, which included, but was by no means limited to, his tendency to tangle with friends as well as enemies. But as an imaginative feat of structure—and as a case where a writer has deliberately brought his characters together on a succession of brilliantly chosen stages—it is unmatched.

After being awed by this engineering, I found it a revelation to learn that in McPhee's mind the idea for this book's structure preceded his choice of subject matter. In that same interview, he describes how, many years ago, he got bored with doing profiles of a single person and wanted to write pieces about people in relationships: "A dancer and a choreographer. . . . A baseball manager and a pitcher." Out of this came *Levels of the Game.* Then "I got ambitious. I decided to escalate, and I had the idea of writing a triple profile— a three-part piece in which three people would be separately profiled as they related to a fourth person. . . . So I wrote on my wall: ABC over D. I stuck it on a three-by-five card, in big letters. ABC over D. That's all I knew."

Eventually, McPhee settled on Brower as D. "Now, who were going to be the three others?" He knew only that they had to be people who hated everything Brower stood for. After Brower agreed to the idea, McPhee and a friend "and various other people in Washington got together a list of seventeen possibilities." They were scattered around the country and the world, and after many months of negotiations, the list was finally narrowed down to three.

An alert reader will notice one small graphic survival of McPhee's three-by-five card, ABC over D, in the finished book. On the title page—and repeated on the title pages of each of the three parts—is a black line with three small black triangles above it and one beneath it. This was truly a case where the engineering of a skyscraper came before the decision about what the building was to contain. But like the beams in a brick-and-mortar skyscraper, and the structural bones in all good pieces of writing, that engineering is invisible to the casual reader. The line through the cluster of little black triangles is its only remaining symbol; like an artist's name in the lower right-hand corner of a canvas, it is the signature of a literary engineer extraordinaire.

2012

TWENTY-TWO

A Nation of Guns

"WELCOME, PATRIOTS! GUN SHOW TODAY," says a big sign outside the Cow Palace in Daly City, California, just south of San Francisco, the building where the Republican National Convention nominated Barry Goldwater for president in 1964. Inside the Palace, past the National Rifle Association table at the door, a vast room, longer than a football field, is completely filled with rows of tables and display cases. They show every conceivable kind of rifle and pistol, gun barrels, triggers, stocks, bullet key chain charms, Japanese swords, telescopic sights, night-vision binoculars, bayonets, a handgun carrier designed to look like a briefcase, and enough ammunition of every caliber to equip the D-Day landing force. Antique guns on sale range from an ancient musket that uses black powder to a Japanese behemoth that fires a bullet 1.2 inches in diameter.

Also arrayed on tables are window signs, bumper stickers, and cloth patches you can sew onto your jacket: 9–11 WAS AN INSIDE JOB; THE WALL: IF YOU BUILD IT THEY CANT COME; and HUNTING PERMIT UNLIMITED LIMIT *[sic]* FOR ISIS. Perhaps 90 percent of those strolling the aisles are men, and at least 98 percent are white. They wear enough beards and bushy mustaches to stuff a good-sized mattress. At one table a man with a gray crew cut is selling black T-shirts that show a map of California, in red, with a gold star and hammer and sickle. Which means? "This state's gone Communist. And I hate to say it, but it was Reagan that gave it to them. The 1986 amnesty program." (This granted legal status to some 2.7 million undocumented immigrants.)

· · ·

If reason played any role in the American love affair with guns, things would have been different a long time ago. Almost everywhere else in the world, if you proposed that virtually any adult not convicted of a felony should be allowed to carry a loaded pistol—openly or concealed—into a bar, a restaurant, or a school classroom, people would send you off for a psychiatric examination. Yet many states allow this, and in Iowa, a loaded firearm can be carried in public by someone who's completely blind. Suggest, in response to the latest mass shooting, that still *more* of us should be armed, and people in most other countries would ask you what you're smoking. Yet this has been the NRA's answer to the massacres at Orlando, Las Vegas, Newtown, Connecticut, and elsewhere, and after the high school killing spree at Parkland, Florida, President Trump suggested arming teachers. One bumper sticker on sale here shows the hammer and sickle again with GUN FREE ZONES KILL PEOPLE.

Nor, when it comes to national legislation, do abundantly clear statistics have any effect. In Massachusetts, which has some of America's most restrictive state firearms laws, three people per 100,000 are killed by guns annually, while in Alaska, which has some of the weakest, the rate is more than seven times as high. OK, maybe Alaskans need extra guns to fend off bears, but that's certainly not so in Louisiana, another weak law state, where the rate is more than six times as high as in Massachusetts. All developed nations regulate firearms more stringently than we do; Americans are ten times more likely to be killed by guns than are the citizens of twenty-two other high-income countries.

A Congress terrified of the NRA ignores such data and has not only shielded gun manufacturers and dealers from any liability for firearms deaths but prevented the Centers for Disease Control from doing any studies of gun violence. The top ten recipients of direct or indirect NRA campaign funds in the U.S. Senate have received a total of more than $42 million from the organization over the past thirty years. Funneling a river of money to hundreds of other members of Congress as well, the NRA has certainly succeeded in getting what it pays for.

After each horrendous mass shooting, like the one at the Sandy Hook Elementary School in Newtown, Connecticut, in December 2012, not only does the NRA once again talk about good guys with guns stopping bad guys with guns, but gun purchases soar. By the way, only a tiny fraction of the more than thirty thousand Americans killed by guns each year die in these mass shootings. Roughly two-thirds of the deaths are suicides; the rest are more mundane homicides, and about five hundred are accidents. Some eighty thousand more people are injured by firearms each year. All these tolls would be far less if we did not have more guns than people in the United States and guns were not so freely available to almost anyone.

The most powerful single lobbying organization in Washington, the NRA for decades has pursued a two-faced strategy. It presents itself to the public as willing to consider "reasonable" restrictions on firearms and touts its courses in gun safety, but at the same time it tells its members that almost any kind of gun control whatever would be the first step to taking everybody's guns away. This technique worked under President Franklin D. Roosevelt in the 1930s and it works today. With five million members to mobilize and an annual budget of more than $300 million, the NRA makes sure that Congress never passes any meaningful gun control. Some states may tighten regulations in the years ahead—Florida did, very slightly, after outspoken campaigning by the high school students who survived the shooting in Parkland—but don't expect sweeping changes at the national level any time soon. Because the NRA so reliably turns out right-wing voters on election day, the Koch brothers have been major financial backers. Supporting the NRA has a curious side benefit for the Kochs and their ilk as well: it encourages the illusion that the key source of political power in America is gun ownership, rather than, say, great wealth.

Guns were a major part of our early history, but as the frontier disappeared the deep American mystique about them only grew. In the 1800s, Winchester rifles were advertised in utilitarian terms, but by the early 1900s the tone had changed. Guns develop "the study manliness that every real boy wants to have," read one ad. "Perfect freedom from annoyance by petty lawbreakers," wrote the magazine *Sports Afield* in 1912, "is found in a country where every man carries his own sheriff, judge and executioner swung on his hip." In 2017, someone who would dearly love to wield such powers against his enemies became the first sitting president to address the NRA in more than three decades. "The eight-year assault on your Second Amendment freedoms has come to a crashing end," Donald Trump told the group's annual convention. "You have a true friend and champion in the White House."

Over more than a century, the NRA has argued with its opponents over the meaning of that amendment: "A well regulated Militia, being necessary to the security of a free State, the right of the people to keep and bear Arms, shall not be infringed." Gun enthusiasts and lawyers marshaled by the NRA claim that this protects almost anyone who wants to carry a rifle down the street or a pistol to church and that gun control therefore violates the Constitution. Liberals, on the other hand, maintain fervently that the rights granted by the Second Amendment refer only to a "well regulated Militia," such as those that fought the redcoats at Lexington and Concord or the National Guard today. Yet something feels sterile about this dispute over what the Founding Fathers had in mind. It is tragic that we should still have to battle over what that assembly of men in their frock coats and powdered wigs intended when, all around us, the carnage from gun violence continues. In the past fifty years alone, more people have been killed by firearms in the United States than have died in uniform in all the wars in American history.

Roxanne Dunbar-Ortiz's *Loaded: A Disarming History of the Second Amendment* offers a blast of fresh air on this subject so endlessly argued over. She is no fan of guns, or of our absurdly permissive laws surrounding them. But she does not get to this point by merely taking the liberal side of the familiar debate. "Neither party," she writes of that long squabble, "seems to have any idea of what the Second Amendment was originally about." Of course the amendment was written with militias in mind, she says, but, during and after the colonial era, just what *were* those militias? They were not merely upstanding citizens protecting themselves against foreign tyrants like King George III. They also searched for runaway slaves—and seized land from Native Americans, often by slaughter.

Loaded quotes the former Wyoming senator Alan Simpson: "Without guns, there would be no West." But in this sense, the West began at the Atlantic seaboard, where settler militias were organized from the seventeenth century onward. Before long, members could collect bounties for the heads or scalps of Native Americans—an early case, incidentally, of the privatization of warfare. When the thirteen colonies declared their independence, one grievance was the king's Royal Proclamation of 1763 by which the British, fretting over the expense of sending troops across the Atlantic to fight endless Indian wars, placed land beyond the Appalachian-Allegheny mountain range off-limits to white settlement.

Many well-armed settlers, however, thirsted for that land and crossed the mountains to take it. Among them was the eager young George Washington, who went on to make a fortune speculating in land far to the west of the Virginia coast where he had been born. As settlement expanded across the Great Plains, U.S. Army troops took over the job of suppressing the doomed Native American resistance, but militias had long preceded them.

The militias also kept slaves in line. Dunbar-Ortiz cites a North Carolina legal handbook of 1860 on such duties: "The patrol shall visit the negro houses in their respective districts as often as may be necessary, and may inflict a punishment, not exceeding fifteen lashes, on all slaves they may find off their owner's plantations. . . . [and] shall be diligent in apprehending all runaway negroes." If a captured slave behaved "insolently" the militia could administer up to thirty-nine lashes. Some militias, such as the Texas Rangers, did double duty, both seizing land and hunting down escaped slaves. After the Civil War, when the South was still awash in guns and ammunition, militias morphed easily into the Ku Klux Klan—and into private rifle clubs; by 1876 South Carolina alone had more than 240.

. . .

Cleansed of its origins, some of this history has been absorbed into our culture, in the form of romantic stories of bandits like Jesse James, said to be American Robin Hoods. Those who believed such tales included Woody Guthrie and Pete Seeger, both of whom recorded an 1882 ballad,

> Oh, they laid poor Jesse in his grave, yes, Lord
> They laid Jesse James in his grave
> Oh, he took from the rich and he gave to the poor
> But they laid Jesse James in his grave.

But who was Jesse James? He was a veteran of a particularly brutal militia, in which he had fought for the Confederacy in the Civil War. The records of men like Daniel Boone and Davy Crockett, Dunbar-Ortiz points out, have been sanitized in a different way, and they are remembered not as conquerors of Native American (and, in Crockett's case, Mexican) land but as frontiersmen roaming the wilderness in their fringed deerskin clothing—and as skilled hunters. This has powerful resonance with many gun owners today, who hunt, or once did, or at least would like to feel in themselves an echo of the hunter: fearless, proud, self-sufficient, treading in the footsteps of pioneers. One of those fringed leather jackets, incidentally, (although not deerskin, the salesman acknowledges) is on sale at the gun show, as is a huge variety of survival-in-the-wilderness gear: canteens, beef jerky, buffalo jerky, bear repellent, and hundreds of knives, many of them lovingly laid out on fur pelts: coyote, beaver, muskrat, possum, and, the softest, badger.

The early militias are one strand of the ancestry of gun enthusiast groups like the NRA that *Loaded* identifies. Another is the legacy of America's wars—not those with defined front lines, like the two world wars and Korea, but the conflicts in Vietnam, Central America, Iraq, and Afghanistan. In those wars the distinction between friend and enemy was (and is) often unclear. Massacres of civilians have been common, and many a military man has evoked the days of the Wild West. General Maxwell Taylor, Lyndon B. Johnson's ambassador to South Vietnam, for instance, called for more troops so that the "Indians can be driven from the fort and the settlers can plant corn."

One of the greatest predictors of American gun ownership today is whether someone has been in the military: a veteran is more than twice as likely to own one or more guns than a non-veteran. Among the bumper stickers and signs at the gun show are JIHAD FREE ZONE and I'LL SEE YOUR JIHAD AND RAISE YOU A CRUSADE; the latter shows a bloody sword. Many a vet is strolling the aisles, happy to talk about fighting in Iraq or Afghanistan. Several of them—sufferers from PTSD?—are accompanied by service dogs. The first of the chain of mass shootings that have bedeviled the United States over the past half century or so was by the ex-Marine Charles Whitman from atop a tower at the University of Texas at Austin in 1966, just at the time of indiscriminate mass killings by Americans in Vietnam.

The passion for guns felt by tens of millions of our people also has, of course, deep social and economic roots. The fervor with which they believe liberals are trying to take all their guns away is so intense because so much else *has* been taken away. In much of the South, in the Rust Belt along the Great Lakes, in rural districts throughout the country, young people are leaving or sinking into addiction and jobs are disappearing—outsourced to distant, low-wage parts of the world or lost forever to automation. These hard-hit areas have not shared the profits of Silicon Valley and its offshoots or the prosperity of coastal cities from Seattle to New York. Even many of his supporters know in their hearts that Trump can never deliver on his promises to bring back coal mining and restore those once abundant manufacturing jobs. But the one promise he, and other politicians, *can* deliver on is to fight for every imaginable kind of right to carry arms.

People passionate about guns often show a sense of being under siege, left behind, pushed down, at risk. One of the large paper targets on sale at the gun show shows a scowling man aiming a pistol at you. On bumper stickers, window signs, flags, is the Revolutionary era DON'T TREAD ON ME, with its image of a coiled rattlesnake. At one table, two men are selling bulletproof vests. For $500 you can get an eight-pound one whose plates—front, back, side—are made of lightweight compressed polyethylene. "They used to use it to line the bottom of combat helicopters." For only $300, you can get one with steel plates, but it weighs twenty-three pounds. Also on sale is a conceal-able vest that goes under your clothing: medium, large, and x-large for $285; xx-large and xxx-large for $315.

Who buys these? I ask.

"Everybody—who sees the way the world is going."

. . .

The most belligerent descendants of the American militias of centuries past are the forces that go under the same name today. We have seen a lot of these camouflage-clad men (and the occasional woman) in the past few years: they strode through Charlottesville, Virginia, in 2017 with their rifles and walkie-talkies under Confederate flags; they travel in convoys with gun barrels vis-ible through the windows of pickup trucks and SUVs to camp near the Mexican border and watch for immigrants slipping across; and, most often, they have tangled with U.S. Forest Service or other federal officials in theatri-cally orchestrated stand-offs over the use of federal land in the Far West. Four hundred armed militiamen were on the scene in 2014 at the height of a stand-off in Nevada, a hundred appeared at another in Montana the next year, and three hundred at one in Oregon the year after that. Similar armed confronta-tions have taken place in New Mexico, Texas, and California, and a militia leader from Utah was arrested in 2016 after apparently trying to bomb a Bureau of Land Management outpost in Arizona. Between 2010 and 2014 alone there were more than fifty attacks on BLM or Forest Service employees, including two by snipers.

Genuine grievances lie behind these Western land occupations, however alien the ideology of the occupiers may feel. The Endangered Species Act, for instance, has thrown both loggers and ranchers out of work, and even though there are good reasons for limiting grazing on federal land (such as prevent-ing erosion or the pollution of drinking water), a new restriction can push a struggling small sheep farmer into bankruptcy. And so people focus their ire on federal control of vast tracts of land. But those who will really benefit from any privatization of this territory are not the militiamen with their "Ranchers' Lives Matter" yard signs but those who have the capital to exploit the land's riches: agribusiness, big mining companies, oil and gas drillers. It's no surprise that many of those interests enthusiastically support the militia occupations.

There are rivalries aplenty between various militia groups, but one undercurrent in almost all of them, whether spoken or denied, is white nationalism. The first attempt to plant a private militia on the Mexican border was made by David Duke of the Ku Klux Klan. Cliven Bundy, patriarch of the family behind several of the Western land standoffs, has said of African Americans, "I've often wondered, are they better off as slaves, picking cotton . . . ?" Two of Bundy's sons were among those who occupied federal buildings at the Malheur National Wildlife Refuge in southeastern Oregon; one of their collaborators had recently aired a video that showed him wrapping pages of the Koran in bacon and setting them on fire. The Malheur occupiers rifled through a collection of Native American relics; the site of a nearby archeological dig containing more artifacts they turned into a latrine. It is not hard to see the continuity with the militias of two hundred years ago.

American right-wingers in uniform have been around, of course, since the Nazi and blackshirt groups of the 1930s. Later militias have been more heavily armed, and a new wave of them was spurred by the election of Barack Obama in 2008. Their ideology tends to echo that of others on the crackpot Right: the New World Order and its chief conspirators (Barack Obama— born in Kenya, of course—, "crooked" Hillary Clinton, George Soros, most people in Hollywood, and many others) are conspiring to flood the United States with immigrants and refugees, favor the spotted owl over loggers and ranchers and black people over white, patrol the skies with black helicopters, install United Nations rule and Sharia law, and seize guns from their rightful owners. *As long as I'm alive and breathing,* sings the country and western artist (and Trump supporter) Justin Moore, *You won't take my guns.* One bumper sticker on sale at the gun show says, AMERICA HAS BEEN OCCUPIED BY GLOBALIST FORCES. Militias go farther than other right-wing groups, of course, in that they promise to resist this imposition of the New World Order with arms. "When the ballot box doesn't work," says John Trochmann, founder of the Militia of Montana, "we'll switch to the cartridge box."

Some of this, of course, is hot air. The number of active militia groups actually fell by 40 percent from 2015 to 2016, according to the Southern Poverty Law Center, which monitors the movement closely. One "key factor" was that when the brothers Ammon and Ryan Bundy and their followers seized buildings at Malheur in early 2016, the federal government hung tough, shooting dead one militia leader when he tried to pull a gun on officers at a roadblock, arresting many more, and indicting them on serious charges.

There has been, of course, one huge change since then: the election of Donald Trump. Several years before, during an earlier stand-off, Trump voiced qualified support for Cliven Bundy, father of the two brothers. (He was uneasy about the occupation and suggested Bundy cut a deal with Obama, but said, "I like him, I like his spirit, his spunk and the people that are so loyal . . . I respect him.") Several friends of the Bundys or supporters of their Malheur occupation became prominent Trump backers, and one, the oilman Forrest Lucas, was on the president's shortlist for secretary of the interior. A judge's recent declaration of a mistrial was the latest in a series of setbacks the government has had in prosecuting the Bundys. Since the election, militia members have been increasingly visible around the country, providing "security" for right-wing demonstrators and speakers. One such speaker has been Cliven Bundy, newly released from jail. And, in contrast to their decline as Obama cracked down on the land occupations, under Trump the number of armed militia groups in the United States has soared ominously, from 165 in 2016 to 273 in 2017.

What happens with them next? I see two dangers. The first is that the next militia standoff over a federal land occupation in the West may end differently. It is hard to imagine Trump's Justice Department firmly enforcing the law against people who so represent the concentrated essence of his base. Does that mean that the armed seizure of some National Forest land, say, might be unhindered and become permanent? And might that not, in turn, encourage dozens of similar land grabs? The rural areas of Western states are full of people—including thousands of county sheriffs' deputies and other state and local office-holders—who believe no one has the authority to tell them where they can't graze their cattle, hunt game, cut down a tree, or dig for gold. And hey, what right do the feds have to all that land, anyway? Promoting oil drilling in National Parks, Trump clearly feels the same way.

The second danger is this. Trump will probably be forced out of office—by defeat in 2020 if not by other means before then. If that occurs, we know it will be a stormy process, in which he will try in every possible way to inflame and rally his supporters, with dark charges of "rigged" voting if he loses the election. To anyone on the far Right, his defeat or removal will be virtual proof of a conspiracy to impose the New World Order. Will these gun-toting men in boots and camouflage flak jackets accept his departure from the White House quietly? And, if they can't prevent it, will they somehow take revenge?

2018

The Continent of Words

FIGURE 7. The author at the ruins of the Butugychag prison camp, Russia.

TWENTY-THREE

You Never Know What's Going to Happen Yesterday

KEYNOTE ADDRESS TO THE NATIONAL COUNCIL ON PUBLIC HISTORY

It's only in the past few years that I've been aware of the meaning of "public history." I feel grateful to be in a whole roomful of people practicing it, because now, at last, I know what to call myself. I've always felt uncomfortable when people introduce me as a historian, since I don't teach in a history department and what interests me is writing history, not for other historians but for ordinary people. Now I feel like that character of Molière's who was thrilled to discover that all his life he'd been speaking prose. When anyone asks me my profession, I can now say it's public history.

I thought I would talk about a couple of my experiences in this craft of ours. They all follow the same pattern. When I was a student, I thought of history as unchangeable. It was what had happened in the past, so it couldn't be undone. The historian's job was to know what those events were and to understand why they happened. But the longer that I work with the past, the more I realize that it's not unchangeable at all. What we see when we look at something that happened, say, two hundred years ago is very different from the way people remembered exactly the same thing fifty or a hundred years ago. These shifts take place not because previously hidden sources of information are newly discovered but because of events in the ever-changing present.

I first started thinking about this when I noticed how different the American history my children were learning in school was from the American history I had studied. When I went to high school in the 1950s, I learned that there had been slavery in the United States but that it was mainly important because it caused the Civil War. I never read a slave narrative; I never read a description of an American slave's daily life. But when my children went to school in the 1980s, they learned who Frederick Douglass was, they read the extraordinary slave narratives gathered by the Federal Writers Project in the 1930s, and they learned a great deal about what life was like in the slave quarters and fields of a plantation. This transformation was due, of course, to the upheavals and victories of the 1950s and '60s in the long American struggle for civil rights.

You can see another reflection of that change at one of the great public history sites in the United States, Colonial Williamsburg. If you had visited this collection of carefully restored buildings before about 1970, you would have seen no indication whatever that roughly half the population of the original Williamsburg were slaves. But if you visit today, you can see slave quarters, hear lectures about the slave trade, see black "reenactors" working in the fields, and see a host of other exhibits and demonstrations about the life and labor of a Williamsburg slave of several hundred years ago.

So, as I came to study other countries for the books that I've written, I've always been intrigued by how a nation's lens on its past changes—often quite radically—over time. And sometimes these changes show up more quickly and dramatically in museums, films, pageants, and other public history sites than they do in monographs or scholarly journals. Let me take you to several such times and places.

. . .

I want to begin by talking about Russia, because there has seldom been a more spectacular example of tight control, for an amazingly long period of time, over what people were allowed to see in the past. From the 1920s until the late 1980s, history officially involved the glories of Soviet communism and the shortcomings of every other system. Furthermore, during the murderous Stalin era, there were constant changes to the official historical record as various leading communists were abruptly arrested and dispatched to the Gulag or the execution cellar. Historically speaking, they ceased to exist. Several times a year, librarians all over the Soviet Union received new pages that were to be immediately inserted into the *Great Soviet Encyclopedia*, a vast compendium that eventually ran to some fifty volumes, in place of other pages that were to be torn out or pasted over. The joke in Soviet days when you spoke with people who were trying to study history was "You never know what's going to happen . . . yesterday."

When I traveled to Russia as a journalist in the 1960s, '70s, and early '80s, I was always fascinated by the discrepancies between private and public discussions of history. If someone trusted you, over the family kitchen table he or she might talk about a grandfather, an uncle, or aunt who had been sent to a Siberian prison camp or shot during the 1930s. But in school textbooks and newspapers, in museums, or on TV, there was never any mention of the fact that this country endured deaths on a genocidal scale in the quarter-century during which Joseph Stalin was dictator. Even today, historians are still unsure how many million perished during that time in man-made famines, far-flung prison camps, or execution sites. After Stalin's death the mass murder ended, but, except for a brief and partial "thaw" under Khrushchev, there was no open discussion of that time. In the later editions of the *Great Soviet Encyclopedia*, the biographical entry on Stalin was very short: just a page and a half, with a bare-bones listing of posts he held and the dates he held them—and a cryptic remark that "certain of his character traits had negative repercussions."

Then Mikhail Gorbachev came to power in the mid-1980s. And by the end of that decade, enormous changes were in the works. The one that interested me most was that now at last it became possible to speak openly about the past, not just with friends in your home but in lecture halls, on the radio, in the press, in museums, in new history books. I lived in Russia for the first half of 1991, to look at that experience first-hand and write about it. What was it like to be in a country where free study of history had been totally forbidden for more than sixty years and now, so suddenly, was allowed?

The historians who were doing the most exciting work, I found, were generally not in university history departments, since these were mostly filled with tenured party hacks who had no interest in a searching reexamination of the past. Rather, the most interesting scholars were usually people who had day jobs doing something else. Many were affiliated with a national society called Memorial—in Russian the stress is on the last syllable—which had sprung up under Gorbachev, headquartered in Moscow with branches throughout the country. Some members were human rights activists, some were elderly survivors of the Gulag, some were younger people who had grown up haunted by stories of family members who had disappeared during the Stalin years. All of them were fiercely dedicated to looking at that previously off-limits history and examining it deeply.

One group of historians in Memorial was constructing a comprehensive map of where all the hundreds of prison camps had been. Others were researching writers who had perished during the 1930s and after. One man was studying camp rebellions. Memorial put on lectures, film showings, exhibits, and conferences; its members spoke on radio and TV and wrote articles for newspapers. It was public history at its best.

Who were these people? Of those who were descendants of Stalin's victims, I found, the sons and daughters had often spent their childhoods in such fear that they didn't want to rock the boat; Memorial researchers were more likely to be from the next generation, the grandchildren. A surprisingly high percentage of Memorial activists made their living as scientists. Why? Because during the Soviet years, science was an area where you could be free to do research with few restrictions. I remember, for example, sitting in the apartment of a Moscow physicist who had become fascinated by a set of old prison camps along an abandoned railway line in the Arctic. He had first glimpsed their ruins years before, when working as a deckhand on a Siberian riverboat one summer while a student. The camps were for prisoners building the railway: Stalin had a penchant for grand railways and canals and had ordered the construction of this one despite the fact that engines and freight cars kept sinking into swamps. The work was stopped when he died. The physicist had returned to the area several times, taken photographs, and gone through the ruins of these buildings, now deserted and crumbling away in the wilderness, to collect old file cards on prisoners and other paperwork, which he spread out on his kitchen table to show me.

It was another scientist, active in his local chapter of Memorial in the Siberian city of Krasnoyarsk, who took me to my first mass grave. In the late 1980s and early '90s, Russians began excavating dozens of such sites around the country. The one in Krasnoyarsk was on a hillside, with a view out over the city, the Trans-Siberian railway line, and the Yenisei River. You could reach down and pick up from the ground one earth-stained skull after another with a bullet hole through the forehead. For a moment, more than half a century was collapsed, and I was holding history in my hand.

Sadly, in Russia today the free study of history has become, once again, as risky as other forms of free speech. Vladimir Putin said recently that history books in schools "should cultivate in young people a feeling of pride" in their country. The curriculum has become much more restrictive, and some innovative textbooks are no longer allowed. In 2008, the St. Petersburg office of Memorial was raided by police in camouflage uniforms and ski masks. What did they take? Eleven computer hard drives containing documents, letters, oral histories, and the like, primarily relating to events that happened seventy or eighty years ago. It's a reminder that in many parts of the world practicing public history is a dangerous business.*

. . .

I now want to switch continents and centuries and talk about another piece of history that has changed shape as time has passed. The Scramble for Africa that took place between 1870 and 1910 as Europe divided up the continent was a pretty bloody affair. One of the most brutal parts of it was the seizure and colonization of the area that today is the Democratic Republic of Congo. Formerly, it was the Belgian Congo, and before that, from 1885 to 1908, it was the personal, private possession of King Leopold II of Belgium.

During the time that Leopold owned the Congo, he made a huge fortune from it, primarily by harvesting rubber. Sparked by the invention of the inflatable bicycle tire, a worldwide rubber boom began in the early 1890s. The demand for rubber only increased with the automobile, with rubber's many uses in industry and with the spread of rubber-coated telephone and telegraph wires across the world. A plantation of new rubber trees takes some fifteen years to reach maturity, but this valuable commodity grew wild throughout the great equatorial African rainforest, which covered about half of Leopold's Congo.

This rubber came not from trees but from vines that were scattered through the forest, twining around palms and other trees upwards towards the sunlight. Leopold developed his notorious forced labor system to harvest it. The king's private army of nineteen thousand officers and men would send units into village after village, holding the women hostage—there are photographs of them in chains—until the male villagers had gone into the rainforest for days or weeks at a time to gather a monthly quota of wild rubber. As the process continued, sometimes they had to walk for days to find rubber vines not yet drained dry. And as the price of rubber went up, the quota increased. Many women hostages starved, and many of the male forced

---

* In Russia it has become still more so. In 2017, Russian police arrested the Memorial activist Yuri Dmitriev on an implausible array of trumped-up charges: pornography, child endangerment, and possesion of illegal firearms. Dmitriev's real crime was to have identified more than 9,500 victims from many countries buried in a mass grave in 1937 and 1938 northeast of St. Petersburg and to have helped organize an annual international memorial meeting at the site.

laborers were in effect worked to death. When you have women held hostage and men doing forced labor, there is nobody left to plant and harvest crops, to hunt, to fish, and to do all the things through which a community feeds itself, and so people ran short of food. And in famine or near-famine conditions, people often succumb to diseases they otherwise would survive. In addition, tens of thousands of people were shot down by soldiers when they rose up in rebellions against the regime. Finally, hundreds of thousands fled to avoid getting conscripted as forced laborers, but the only place they could go was deep in the rainforest where there was little food and shelter—and they died. Not surprisingly, the population shrank by the millions.

After about 1920—by this point, Leopold was long dead and the territory had become the Belgian Congo—the system became much less murderous, in large part because Belgian colonial officials realized that if they continued with the forced labor system as harsh as it had been, they would soon have no workers left. You can actually find alarmed colonial bureaucrats saying this on paper.

But the territory remained a colony. By the mid-1950s, it was clear that independence was in the offing, in one way or another, for colonial Africa. Soon came the first stirrings of such a movement in the Congo itself, and the Belgians began reluctantly preparing for independence, although they assumed it was still decades away. One of the things they did was to construct a small Congo university. How did they deal with the study of history there? What would students think if they looked at the Holocaust-level loss of life in the territory under Leopold II, for instance? The colonial authorities had a simple solution: the new university had no history department.

After the Congo became independent in 1960, how was the colonial period remembered in Belgium itself? Until very recently, in Belgian schools and in officially sponsored public history institutions like museums, the colonial period was as whitewashed as anything the USSR did in trying to ignore or sanitize the Stalin era. A spectacular example for many years is on the outskirts of Brussels, the Royal Museum for Central Africa, which is, so far as I know, the largest museum in the world specifically focused on Africa. It was started by Leopold with some of his Congo profits and is filled with an extraordinary wealth of African art, not to mention tools, plants, stuffed animals, and more. Its twenty large exhibit halls and vast archives contain seventy thousand maps, eight thousand African musical instruments, six hundred thousand photographs, and six million insect specimens. Up through the late 1990s, there was nothing on exhibit in this museum, not one single display case, that gave any indication whatever that during the time that this magnificent array of African art and artifacts was being brought back to Belgium, millions of Congolese were being worked to death as forced laborers. The exhibits even included a rubber vine, but no information about those who died harvesting rubber. As late as 2005, a special temporary exhibition that purported—falsely—to at last tell the truth about the colonial days made no mention whatever of the hostage system.

The Belgian government whitewashed that history in other ways as well. For years, for example, it has funded an institution called the Royal Academy of Overseas Studies, formerly the Royal Academy of Colonial Studies. Among other things, the Academy has published an eight-volume biographical encyclopedia mostly devoted to Belgians who worked in the Congo in colonial days. It also publishes a series of historical monographs in English, French, German, and Dutch, well over a hundred volumes, which you can find in many university libraries. I can recall only two that even mention the forced labor system. In 1959—just a year before the Congo became independent—the Academy refused to publish two papers by one of its members, a missionary priest and scholar named Edmond Boelaert who had been interviewing Africans about their memories of the Leopold-era forced labor system—the only researcher to do anything like this for decades.

In school textbooks, the situation is much the same. Here's a short quote from one that was in use in Belgium as of four years ago: "When the Belgians arrived in the Congo, they found a population that was a victim of bloody rivalries and the slave trade. Belgian civil servants, missionaries, doctors, colonists, and engineers civilized the black population step by step." Not a word about forced labor or the massive number of deaths. Until the past dozen years or so, when the Royal Museum for Central Africa began at last to make some timid changes—e-mails from a dissident staff member first alerted me to behind-the-scenes tensions there—the subject of forced labor in the colonial Congo simply did not appear in Belgian public history.

Unless it absolutely has to, no country likes to pay much attention to painful, difficult, embarrassing periods of its own past. Look again at the United States: where in any American museum or public history site can you find much mention of the dozens of U.S. military interventions in Central America or the Caribbean over the twentieth century? Where will you find anything about the war we waged against Philippine independence just over a hundred years ago? Belgium is not alone in ignoring parts of its past.

Countries only treat the past differently when someone or something forces them to do so. Belgium has not experienced anything comparable to the civil rights movement in the United States or to the large postwar immigration of Africans and West Indians to Britain, events that have forced public history to deal differently with slavery in both those countries. The black population of Belgium is, by comparison, small and politically powerless.

. . .

I want to end by talking about one more country that I've had some experience with, South Africa, because when it comes to public history, it is one of the most interesting places in the world today.

You know, I'm sure, the basic history: South Africa was built by a long series of colonial conquests and then, for almost all of the twentieth century, saw the right to vote in national elections and many other rights restricted to the very small percentage of the population who were white. Only since 1994 has the country enjoyed full political democracy, and the new president elected that year, Nelson Mandela, was himself able to vote for the first time in his life. You can easily imagine how the power of the old regime was reflected in school classrooms and in the public history displayed by museums, historic sites, and much else. One tiny reflection of it that always struck me when I traveled there before 1994 was that in a country whose population was more than 85 percent people of color, I don't think I ever saw, in a town square, park, museum, public building, or anywhere else, a statue of anybody who was not white. This, and much more, has now started to change dramatically.

Since 1994, there has been an explosion of historical documentary films reckoning with the apartheid years. An Apartheid Museum has opened in Johannesburg. The prison on Robben Island, in the sea off Cape Town, where Nelson Mandela and his comrades were jailed for many years, is now a UNESCO World Heritage Site, visited by hundreds of thousands of people a year. Historic sites elsewhere in the country have been reinterpreted. The list could go on far longer.

The most spectacular example of new public history I've seen in South Africa is in architecture. I'm referring to the building in Johannesburg that houses the country's Constitutional Court, which has the ultimate authority in interpreting the post-apartheid constitution. The building's outer and inner walls are largely of glass, so you can see who is walking where and who is going into which office—a visual representation of transparency. The room in which the Court meets is unlike any courtroom I've seen anywhere in the world: a bowl-shaped auditorium, which means that the judges of this high court sit below the audience rather than above it. Besides skylights, the room has one long window, which is maybe a hundred feet long and eighteen inches high, and it looks out, level with the ground, at a pedestrian plaza outside. The reason it is constructed that way is because virtually all you can see of the people walking by are their shoes and socks. And, when you see only the bottom twelve or eighteen inches of a person, you usually can't tell if he or she is rich or poor, black or white. The law applies to everybody equally.

And where does public history come in? The building is built on the site of one of the most notorious prisons of the old regime, a jail in which Gandhi, Mandela, and thousands of others spent time over the years. And it is built, in part, out of the actual bricks of that prison. To me, that is public history at its best: taking the bricks of the past and using them to build something solid for the future.

2010

TWENTY-FOUR

Practicing History without a License

SOMETIMES WHEN I MEET ACADEMIC HISTORIANS, I feel like a plumber who, by accident, has found himself among heart surgeons, for I've had no graduate training, in history or anything else. And often people assume that authors like me who write history for the general public and historians inside the academy belong, like plumbers and heart surgeons, to two separate professions. Each has its place, perhaps, but with an unbridgeable gulf between them.

Writers of history for the public (sometimes called popular historians), the assumption goes, skip over complexities and prefer heroic subjects. Sometimes, like Doris Kearns Goodwin or the late Stephen Ambrose, they get caught borrowing others' words without attribution. Or sometimes they simply invent details or conversations, as did Edmund Morris in his biography of Ronald Reagan. Academic historians, on the other hand, deal in subtlety and paradox and are meticulously careful, but their writing is often dust-dry and pedantic.

This assumption about the two cultures of history writing surfaces in odd ways. Sometimes people presume that if a book is lively enough to draw them in, it has to be made up. From time to time I get letters or e-mails telling me how much someone has enjoyed my novel. When I answer, I have to prune out the exclamation marks. "No!!!" I want to say. "There are more than eight hundred source notes! Look at the bibliography! I didn't invent anything!" Or, the nonspecialist reader assumes that anything written by a professor of history is likely to be deadly dull, and so "academic" becomes a term of opprobrium.

Not so long ago, all history was written for the general public. The Greeks felt that historical writing should be of a piece with good writing generally, and so they had a muse of history, Clio, who reigned over our field just as her fellow goddesses reigned over the arts of music, tragedy, comedy, and epic poetry. Clio is often pictured with a trumpet, so she clearly expected us to broadcast history far and wide. She might blanch at some of today's monographs, but I think she'd be pleased that there's more museworthy writing by university historians than by professors in any other academic field. If the Greeks were still inventing muses today, I don't think they'd have one for economics or linguistics. And they certainly wouldn't have one for literary criticism, with its talk of tropes and discourses and privileging essentialist paradigms.

The idea that the historian's craft includes outreach to a wider audience has lasted over the millennia. In the eighteenth century, David Hume wrote, "The first quality of an historian is to be true and impartial; the next is to be interesting." The great American historians of the next century, like Francis Parkman and Henry Adams, were certainly writing for an audience far beyond their own fellow scholars, who were few: in 1895, there were only about a hundred full-time history teachers at U.S. colleges and universities. When Thomas Babington Macaulay was writing his *History of England,* he said he would only be satisfied if, for a few days, it displaced the latest novel from women's tables.

It's only for little more than a century that the United States has seen a parting of the ways between those writing history for the public and those writing for their fellow scholars. This began when the number of historians who could write for each other mushroomed. In history, as in so many other fields that also followed the example of German universities, it was the last quarter of the nineteenth century and the first few years of the twentieth that saw the founding of a professional society (the American Historical Association, or AHA, in 1884), an academic journal (the *American Historical Review,* in 1895), the growth of the idea that there were certain standards to be followed, and a rapid expansion of Ph.D. programs.

Ever since, we have seen periodic outbursts of concern about the bifurcation of the audience for history. In 1920, concerned by the "general protest of a large portion of the public against the heaviness of style characteristic of much of the history now being written," the AHA appointed a committee to study the problem. In one chapter of the resulting report, John Spencer Bassett of Smith College asked, "Can writers devoted to research and filled with the scientific spirit be true to their purposes, and at the same time write history that has the charm of literature?"

In the late 1930s, the historian Allan Nevins (who taught at Columbia but came from the world of journalism) let loose a blast against the academic who writes only for other academics. Such a person, he said, "at long intervals . . . prints an unreadable paper in some learned periodical. He may once in a decade excrete a slender, highly specialized, and . . . quite exhausting monograph. Apart from this his literary production is confined to an occasional spiteful review." More such fusillades followed, even after Nevins, later in his life, was elected president of the AHA.

Peter Novick, in his *That Noble Dream: The "Objectivity Question" and the American Historical Profession,* traces a further "inward turn in the profession" in the years after the Second World War. Universities were expanding dramatically because of the GI Bill, foundations were passing out more generous grants, and so historians no longer needed to earn extra money by writing or lecturing for the public. Those who wrote history outside the academy, like William L. Shirer or Barbara Tuchman, were regarded by "most professional historians . . . as the equivalent of chiropractors and naturopaths." According to Walter Prescott Webb, an AHA president in the 1950s, too many academics believed that "there is something historically naughty about good writing."

Another recent salvo in this sniping was fired by Sean Wilentz, a professor of history at Princeton who also has written for nonacademic venues, from *Salon* to *Rolling Stone* to Bob Dylan's web site. In the course of an excoriating 2001 *New Republic* attack on David McCullough's biography of John Adams, he took aim at many other targets. Among them were the "pleasantly weathered baritone" with which McCullough and others have narrated various TV history shows, the "crushingly sentimental and vacuous" Ken Burns PBS series *The Civil War,* and PBS itself for staging the "egregious advent of the 'presidential historian,' a hitherto unknown scholarly species whose chief function is to offer television viewers anodyne tidbits of historical trivia." When it came to books, Wilentz blasted "costume-drama Americana," and biographies like those by McCullough, a "genre of spectatorial appreciation . . . a reliable source of edification and pleasant uplift" filled with "pieties."

. . .

What are we, plumbers and heart surgeons both, to make of all these years of harsh accusations? Unfortunately, some of the charges fired in each direction are true. Whether they are truer now than fifty or sixty years ago I doubt, because the past saw plenty of overspecialized pedantry, on the one hand, and uplifting popular pieties, on the other.

What are the forces that have so long pushed the two types of history writers in opposite directions? In the academic world, of course, promotions and tenure largely depend on getting published: for articles, that means scholarly journals, and for books, almost always university presses. Knowing that such work is peer reviewed may encourage high standards of care and accuracy but all too often leads to the kind of writing that cites previous scholars of the subject in every other paragraph. After all, you never know: several of them may be among your peer reviewers; heaven forbid that you failed to mention their names. Graduate students in history are often further trained to write—unnecessarily—for a small audience. In choosing a subject for a Ph.D. thesis, for example, they are often encouraged to find a phenomenon, a trend, a group or person that no one has fully examined before. Should that be the only criterion? Why not take up a subject that until now has been dealt with only by specialists writing for each other but whose moral or intellectual significance merits a wider readership—and then write it for that audience? Isn't that as worthy a challenge as looking at some angle of nineteenth-century tariff reform that no one has studied before?

"To produce a mighty book," Melville wrote in *Moby-Dick*, "you must choose a mighty theme. No great and enduring volume can ever be written on the flea, though many there be who have tried it." Too often, the pressures in the academic world push Ph.D. candidates and other historians towards writing books about fleas rather than whales.

People writing for the general public face different dangers. To begin with, it's an extremely difficult way to earn a living. If you want to attract enough readers to pay the rent, you usually have to write narrative history, and to do that you have to bring characters alive. But that often leads to the temptation to go overboard and imply that Abraham Lincoln single-handedly freed the slaves, that Eisenhower alone won the Second World War, or that it was the wisdom of Washington and Jefferson that created the American nation and has guided us beneficently to the present day.

Similarly, the narrative arc needed to carry a reader through a story also has its fatal seductions, one of which is happy endings. It makes for a much better story if the history of some tyranny describes how after Nazism, South African apartheid, or American slavery came to an end, the surviving victims all saw their lives dramatically improved. But that, of course, is seldom the case. Every system of oppression is tenacious and all too often reorganizes itself into something similarly nasty under a different name. Lawrence Langer has written insightfully about the way many people, including the popular historian Martin Gilbert, are eager to see the testimony of Holocaust survivors as showing "the triumph of the human spirit," when their words, if listened to carefully, usually tell a much darker story.

The greatest danger of all in writing history for the general public is a more hidden one: letting popular taste, or publishers' beliefs about popular taste, determine your subject matter. This can bar the door to worthwhile writing even more firmly than the conventional image of what a Ph.D. thesis should be. Big publishers can be very small-minded. When I was looking for a publisher for my book on the conquest of the Congo by King Leopold II of Belgium, nine out of the ten publishers who received the book proposal turned it down. African history? Belgium? Forget it! Nobody would be interested: why, there isn't even an African history shelf in most bookstores. If historians wrote for the public only on subjects with a strong record of popular interest, 90 percent of all history books would be about the Founding Fathers, the Civil War, or the Second World War.

As it is, sometimes it seems that 90 percent of nonacademic history books already *are* about these Big Three subjects. The interlibrary electronic catalog lists more than fifty-four thousand books on the Civil War, for instance; as Drew Gilpin Faust has pointed out, that's more than a book a day since Appomattox. The Big Three have long reigned in American popular taste; when Barbara Tuchman first tried to get her book on the Zimmermann Telegram published in 1955, an editor told her that this was the "wrong war"—the public only wanted the Civil War and the Second World War. Looking just now at the selections available on the History Book Club web site, I note a total of 166 volumes on the Big Three subjects, compared to a mere 19 for all of Africa and the Middle East. It makes me want to demand a moratorium on new books about the Big Three.

But I will make exceptions to my moratorium for books that challenge our traditional picture of these events, such as Simon Schama's *Rough Crossings: Britain, the Slaves and the American Revolution* (2005), which makes the provocative case that many wavering white Southerners joined the rebel side in the American Revolution because Britain had so enraged them by granting freedom to the slaves of rebel masters. Or Giles MacDonogh's *After the Reich: The Brutal History of the Allied Occupation* (2007), with its disturbing revelations of cruel British and American treatment of German POW's at the end of Second World War, in camps that make Guantanamo look like a health resort. But except for rare volumes like these, the torrent of books on the Big Three find so many readers mostly because they are reassuring: the Founding Fathers were brilliantly farsighted; the Civil War was tragic, but the country reunited; the good guys of the Greatest Generation won the war against the Nazis. It's no surprise that our most prolific interpreter of history for the public, the filmmaker Ken Burns, has exhaustively filmed two of the Big Three—all three, in fact, if you count his three-hour documentary on Thomas Jefferson.

. . .

If we put aside these pitfalls, both forms of history writing have tremendous merits. The craft of history inside the academy is immeasurably more rigorous, more accurate, and more thoughtful and wide-ranging than it was a century ago. It is no longer a history merely of presidents and kings but of ordinary people, of women, of the dispossessed. It makes use of the tools of statistics, sociology, anthropology, and more. Refereed scholarly journals and university presses have produced an enormous wealth of sophisticated and reliable material that had few equivalents in the nineteenth century.

At the same time, the writing of history for the general public has become, at its best, more sophisticated and careful as well. And more accurate: as any writer who has been through the process can testify, seeing an article go under the magnifying glass of fact checkers at the *New Yorker* or at a few other magazines is as potentially humbling an experience as being peer-reviewed by a scholarly journal or university press. We know that if we write, "Marie Antoinette felt gloomy as she woke up on that fateful morning" we'd better be able to show the fact checker a diary entry for October 16, 1793, that says, "feeling gloomy today."

There are plenty of times when it is perfectly legitimate to write not for the public but for your fellow scholars, and such work can advance the field. But outside the circle of professional practitioners of history, there are clearly millions of men and women with an appetite for reading it. Academic historians ignore the audience beyond their institutions' walls at their peril. Because if they cannot, at least some of the time, write and speak about history in a way that reaches out to the nonspecialist, they risk being poor teachers of undergraduates. And this, in turn, risks making the proportion of U.S. college students who major in history drop even farther than it already has— from some 5 to 2 percent in the past thirty years.

I am convinced that deep in the heart of many a historian in the academy is someone who would like to write for a wider audience—and who is more capable of doing so than he or she thinks. Here's a curious little example from my own experience. When I finished a draft of my *Bury the Chains*, about the antislavery movement in the British Empire, I wrote to half a dozen scholars in this field, whose work I had learned much from, to ask if they would be willing to read my manuscript. Despite my fears that they would resent an unlicensed interloper in territory they had been working in all their lives, all of them generously said yes.

But the interesting thing was that they did far more than what I had hoped for, which was to save me from dozens of factual errors. Even though these were people who hold university posts, write for academic journals, and for the most part do not think of themselves as addressing the general public, they knew that this was what I was doing—and they responded in that spirit. Beyond the factual and interpretive corrections, several of them offered thoughtful literary critiques of my manuscript. "You make a lot of this particular character later on; don't you think you should introduce him earlier?" Or: "It would be more suspenseful if you switched the order of Chapters Four and Five." To get valuable feedback in this realm, as well as about accuracy and interpretation, greatly touched me. It made me feel that university history departments are rich in people who are eager and able to address the wider audience that Clio, with her trumpet, had in mind for us.

•   •   •

What, then, is required for a synthesis of these two types of writing? To write in a way that reaches beyond the academy's walls but at the same time has intellectual depth? How can it avoid intimidating the general reader but also add to the body of human knowledge?

To reach that wider audience, I think, historians who know their subjects deeply must also learn to wield the tools of those inspired by two of Clio's fellow muses, Melpomene and Thalia: the dramatists. The historian's job is to use the classic narrative devices of plot, character, and scene-setting to tell a story—but without getting so seduced by the tools themselves that the story gets distorted. Like those who write for the stage, historians have to keep a close eye on the audience. "I am very conscious," wrote Tuchman, "of the reader as a listener whose attention must be held if he is not to wander away. In my mind is a picture of Kipling's itinerant storyteller of India, with his rice bowl, who tells tales . . . to a circle of villagers by firelight. If he sees figures drifting away from the edge of the circle in the darkness . . . he knows his rice bowl will be meagerly filled."

Beyond using the storyteller's traditional tools skillfully, there's one other thing we need to do to keep readers in that circle of firelight. We need to pay more attention to Melville's advice about writing about whales and not fleas.

Some of the most interesting moments in history, for instance, are when there seems to be a sudden leap of empathy. Unexpectedly, mysteriously, whole new groups of people who had not been seen that way before are looked at as human beings. The late 1780s saw the birth of an amazingly vigorous antislavery movement in Britain. In fact, you can even pinpoint the very month this idea caught fire: February 1788, when, after decades in which the subject had seldom come up, suddenly half the debates staged by London debating societies had to do with slavery or the slave trade. Four years later, several hundred thousand Britons had signed petitions against the trade and were boycotting slave-grown sugar from the Caribbean. Where did this upsurge of feeling come from, when there had been so few signs of it before? Why did it become a huge, lasting popular movement in Britain and not in any of the other half-dozen European countries with slave colonies? I'm far from the first writer to ask those questions, and I don't think any of us have figured out all the answers. The general reader has an appetite for books on subjects like this, which writers and publishers too often ignore. When I began doing research on this topic, I found a wealth of brilliant specialized scholarship, often with marvelous quotations or human details buried in the footnotes, but very little written for the wider public.

I am also attracted to those times when, with equal mystery, human empathy seems to shrink, something that has taken me to Franco's Spain and Stalin's Russia. How could Russia, which in the nineteenth century gave the world Tolstoy, Chekhov, Dostoyevsky, and Turgenev, in the twentieth give us the Gulag? Why were tens of millions of Russians, people who devoured the best poetry and fiction the way the rest of us breathe air, so quick to denounce friends, teachers, or co-workers as spies and saboteurs? I'm not sure any of us has fully figured out that one either, but I've had no more riveting research experience than traveling across Siberia, walking through the snowy, desolate ruins of Gulag camps, looking at secret police interrogation transcripts, and interviewing survivors of the Stalin era, both victims and perpetrators.

There are plenty of other paths toward harpooning Melville's whale, taken by first-rate writers both inside and outside the academy. We still read Tuchman's *The Guns of August* today, not only because it is a beautifully written account of the moment the world went mad in 1914 but also because it has echoes for our own time: it shows how countries can blithely slip into a devastating war. We read Taylor Branch and David J. Garrow on Martin Luther King Jr., not just because he was a major figure in American history but for clues about how social movements awaken a national conscience. We read Jared Diamond's *Guns, Germs, and Steel* because (even though I don't agree with all his conclusions) he boldly goes after one of the biggest whales of all: the question of why some societies develop economically far more than others. Most unusually, by the way, he reached a huge audience with a book that is not a chronological or biographical narrative.

There is no reason why most history can't be written in a way that offers thought-provoking analysis and at the same time reaches well beyond an audience of fellow scholars. Plenty of people span both worlds. Tuchman and Branch both came from my first trade, the world of journalism; historians from the academy who write with exceptional grace, like Schama of Columbia and Jill Lepore of Harvard, can be regularly found in the pages of the *New Yorker*. Lepore, incidentally, has taught one of the all-too-few university courses in the art of writing history.

These two types of history writing already nourish each other more than we might imagine. A group of historians from southern California universities gathers at the Huntington Library each month to talk about writing history as a craft, sometimes hearing from writers outside the academic world. And when I see some scholar tackling a subject I have written about, but with analytic insights that escaped me (something that happens dismayingly often), I vow to dig deeper next time.

The British historian Peter Burke, describing his wish to see these two ways of writing combined, compares a lively account of the Indian Mutiny by Christopher Hibbert, perhaps the most widely read popular historian in England, with Eric Stokes's trenchant collection of scholarly essays, *The Peasant and the Raj: Studies in Agrarian Society and Peasant Rebellion in Colonial India* (1978). "If one reads the two books one immediately after each other," he writes, "one may be haunted, as I was, by the ghost of a potential third book, which might integrate narrative and analysis." He suggests that historians turn to novels and film for examples of vivid storytelling, pointing out that the models to be found there don't necessarily require oversimplification: narrative in art can have multiple viewpoints, as in *Rashomon*.

How many other such ghosts of potential books are there? Where we can imagine combining two writers: one who writes with a novelist's flair, one who is an expert scholar? There are several pairs of books on my shelves, each set of which I wish I could shred, mix well, and bake into one. In making such matches, I'd take Burke at his word in his reference to fiction and combine a thoughtful academic historian with a novelist. Let Chinua Achebe and John Thornton write the history of Africa. Toni Morrison and David Brion Davis could do slavery and abolition. Pat Barker and Niall Ferguson could handle the First World War. We could use the superb British novelist Barry Unsworth, whose historical fiction is set in a wide variety of times and places, as a utility infielder, dispatching him to be coauthor as required to anywhere from ancient Greece to the Spanish Inquisition. The books I'm imagining are not hybrids of fact and fiction but pure history, pathbreaking, opening up new vistas, where everything is well documented. They are written, however, in such a way that the reader is absolutely forced to turn the page. We can all imagine such books, and it is the job of all of us—plumbers and heart surgeons alike—to write them. It can be done. The tools are there for the using, and there are plenty of whales at sea.

2008

TWENTY-FIVE

On the Road Again

SOME DOOMSAYERS THESE DAYS CLAIM that the printed book will soon be eclipsed by the magic of virtual reality and still newer technologies we cannot yet even imagine. They're wrong—but only about the kind of doom involved. What will replace the book is something else: the book tour. It's already happening.

Even as the number of independent bookstores has fallen over the decades and as the amount of time Americans spend reading serious books continues its long, slow decline, 367 authors have "events" scheduled this fall, according to *Publishers Weekly,* and publishers are still making bookings. Just in the San Francisco Bay Area, where I live, a recent Sunday newspaper listed 143 author events for the following week, from a group reading of new European poetry, with translations, to a chance to meet the author of *Reaching for Reality: Seven Incredible True Stories of Alien Abduction.* More preachers of the written word than ever are filling the pulpits, it seems, while the believers ebb away. Our planet's Last Reader, fossilized in the act of turning the page by a sudden spike in global warming, will not be someone in a cozy armchair at home. It will be an author on tour, declaiming his or her own words in an empty bookstore.

Many of us still writing books today feel somewhat the way a blacksmith must have felt around 1920. It's a wonderful trade, but. . . . I have to admit, however, that for me one consolation of the extended twilight of the book has been the book tour. I've never completely believed writers who say they find book tours totally wearisome. Can anything be wearisome when you're the center of attention all day long?

Also, traveling around talking about what you've written, you meet people who are connected to the story. In the course of touring for my book on the conquest of the Congo, I met a Congolese whose grandfather was worked to death as a porter; Belgians who grew up on tales of heroic missionaries; and the Paris real estate agent for Mobutu Sese Seko, the country's late kleptocrat dictator. He described how Mobutu and his entourage would inspect properties very early in the morning, so as not to attract attention. I wish I could have put these stories into my book—an argument, incidentally, for having the book tour precede the writing of the book, an idea I will return to in a moment.

In addition, while on the road you get to discuss your book with the country's best talkers. Intelligent American radio talk shows really came into their own around the same time that the book tour did, in the 1980s, and it's been a happy marriage. It would be hard to find better conversationalists than Terry Gross of National Public Radio's *Fresh Air* or local talk show hosts like Milt Rosenberg in Chicago and Michael Krasny in San Francisco—both college professors who moonlight on the radio.

The less highbrow interviewers have their own appeal. A well-known nighttime right-wing host in New York once interviewed me while drunk. His swaying from side to side in his chair would have caused problems on television, but did not do so on radio. And the most colorful was Ed Schwartz, a popular liberal in Chicago whose show at WGN-AM went on the air at midnight and who billed himself at the time as "The World's Largest Talk Show Host." He weighed, he said, 550 pounds, "slimmed down from 650," and he wheezed painfully with every breath: "We have with us—eeeeeeesss!—tonight a man who has written a book about—eeeeeeeesss! . . . " Already groggy from the hour, I sat across a table from him, watching him push his vast bulk on a wheeled desk chair past tiers of dials and switches, rolling into unlighted corners of the room during commercial breaks and then reappearing phantasmagorically, like a shadowy mountain emerging out of the darkness.

Schwartz claimed a million listeners, and the phone lines lit up with their calls: truck drivers on the Interstate near Omaha, insomniacs in Indianapolis, night shift workers in Duluth. Did any of them read books? I don't know. But a million of them heard my voice, from midnight until I staggered away at 2 a.m., and perhaps that counts for something.

Book tours are far more civilized in Europe. There are even certain hotels where publishers traditionally put visiting writers. I discovered this inadvertently when, coming downstairs one morning in Amsterdam, I found several television crews, not on my schedule, waiting in the lobby. Ha!—clearly an unexpected surge of Dutch media interest in me. But it turned out they were waiting for a Japanese novelist. When I checked out, the desk clerk asked for a copy of my book to add to their shelves. In London you can find similar shelves at Hazlitt's Hotel, which incorporates the one-time home of the essayist William Hazlitt, and in Paris at the Hôtel Sainte-Beuve, named after the famous critic, situated on the Rue Sainte-Beuve. Can you even imagine an Edmund Wilson Street in the United States?

The French, in fact, were the most civilized of all. This I realized at the Paris studio of an all-news radio network. In the United States, the interviewer would glance at the press release, talk to you for five minutes, then later quickly edit the recording down to two minutes for broadcast. In Paris, a well-spoken man in a three-piece suit introduced himself and began asking me questions. I soon noticed that he was taking very careful notes, in an almost diagram-like format—and that he hadn't turned the recording equipment on. He stopped and explained: "We only have two minutes. However, I don't like to edit. *Ce n'est pas élégant.* I prefer a conversation. But we will plan our conversation very carefully, so you can get all your major points across." We spent half an hour planning. Then he turned the tape recorder on for two minutes. When he turned it off, we spent more time discussing his belief that one could say a lot in a short time. I inscribed my book, "*à l'homme des deux minutes.*"

The other nice thing about the French is that they have no literary incest taboo. The *New York Times Book Review,* for example, will not assign you to review a book if the writer has ever reviewed a book of yours, if you share a publisher, or if you are friends. In Paris, by contrast, the publisher takes you to lunch with the reviewer. Who says, "What an interesting book, Monsieur!" while the publisher orders another bottle of Côtes du Rhône. Incestuous? Yes—but how many times, in reviewing a book myself, have I wanted to ask the author something: why did you include X and ignore Y? What did you mean by that passage on page 174? It might have made for a better review.

As an art form, the book tour is evolving faster than the book itself. When Knopf sent the Gothic novelist Anne Rice on the road for her *Vampire Armand,* she combined bookstore appearances with a blood drive. Stores were paired with hospitals and people who had given blood got to the head of the book-signing line. When Ann Mariah Cook took to the road to promote her book *Running North,* about dog sledding in Alaska, she traveled between two New Hampshire bookstores by dog sled and brought the huskies to the book signings. Representative Peter T. King, Republican of New York, once went on book tour to promote a novel—and simultaneously to test the waters for a Senate run. Governor Jesse Ventura of Minnesota was on the road at the same time promoting his own book, with three bodyguards in tow. And why shouldn't we have political campaigns by book tour? A Terry Gross interview is far more revealing than a sound bite.

Finally, back to the question of sequence. Once you've been on tour awhile and have described your book a few dozen times, you realize what makes people sit up and what makes their eyelids droop, and you find better ways of telling your story. And then you regret that you didn't use these fine images and turns of phrase in the book itself. Why not, then, have the book tour precede the writing of the book? Publishers might object—but of course when the book tour comes to replace the book itself, that won't matter.

Anyone who doubts that writers will still tour even when no one reads our books any more should consider this story from the novelist and historian JoAnn Levy, writing in the Internet magazine *Spotlight:* "In San Antonio . . . a Barnes & Noble store asked 23 authors from a Women Writing the West conference to sign books at their store. Employees picked us up at our hotel, had a huge horseshoe of tables, backed with 23 chairs, and 23 stacks of books next to place cards with our names in calligraphy. Plus a big spread of cookies and coffee. Not one person came! Not one. . . . After an hour we started buying each other's books and then we ate all the cookies."

1999

TWENTY-SIX

Books and Our Souls

FOR THE FIRST TIME, some American school and college students are being issued electronic books instead of printed textbooks. Their arrival feels to me not like technological progress but like the first notes of a death knell. In a society in which relatively few people read books for pleasure to begin with, still fewer will do so if they do not encounter books—real books—as students.

There are many reasons to love the old-fashioned paper book: the subtle differences in how different kinds of paper smell, for instance, and that promising, virginal crackle of the spine as you open a new hardcover for the first time; the sense of accomplishment as you look at the shelves of what you've read, and of humility as you look at the shelves of what you haven't.

I have been feeling sad about the imperiled state of printed books for an additional reason: what books tell us about the person who owns and loves them. In this way, books give a small measure of immortality not just to writers but also to readers.

Each year my wife and I spend time in what was once the summer home of her late parents, and the room where I work is lined with her father's books. He was a career Foreign Service officer, a staunch Cold War liberal and a man who believed that the best of human virtues were incarnated in Puritan New England. His picture of the United States was far rosier than mine; particularly during the Vietnam War, we argued furiously, although he was a good man and we eventually made our peace. But whatever the limits of his worldview, what strikes me now is how much of it I can still see, in the books on his shelves. They are a portrait of his mind.

There are books about the various places where he served as a diplomat— Ghana, New Zealand, Israel, Tunisia—for, each time he was sent to a new

268

country, he read up on it enthusiastically, looking for upbeat parallels to the New England experience. There are books by the hundred about the United States, for the most part portraying it as a country where everything works as wondrously as the Founding Fathers planned. Their titles alone tell the tale: *This Glorious Burden, Chance or Destiny, The First New Nation, This Is the Challenge, The Pilgrim Way, The Discipline of Power.* Sometimes a slip of paper marks a passage he especially liked.

Some of his books are from a phase when he read biographies and memoirs of the famous—no dissidents or women but many presidents, great writers, and Supreme Court justices. He was trying, he once told me, to figure out what were the early life experiences that made people into Great Men. But that interest must have been a resurfacing of an earlier one, for here in another section of the shelves I can see a row of dusty biographies in a series called American Statesmen, which perhaps were passed on to him by his parents, for they were published in the 1890s, the decade before he was born.

Another group of books reflects his ardent Unitarianism and the writings of a minister, A. Powell Davies, he knew and admired. Other volumes clearly represent less what he actually read than what he would like to have read, for books also form portraits of our unfulfilled ambitions: an ancient leather-bound set of Blackstone's *Commentaries on the Laws of England* (perhaps a graduation present when he finished law school), a huge family Bible, Gibbon's *Decline and Fall of the Roman Empire*, and Emerson's *Complete Writings*. None of them have the creased spines of books that have been frequently opened. It is also revealing what is not among these more than a thousand volumes: not a single book about business.

Finally there is his beloved collection of books on New England, including the 795-page *Genealogical Dictionary of Maine and New Hampshire*, which I pull out every summer to try to imagine the mysterious controversy alluded to in its preface. This acknowledges the contributions to the volume made by one Charles Thorton Libby, who "acted as a consultant in problems in which he was known to have a personal interest, but his deep-seated conviction that the book should not be published at all did not make for an entirely happy situation."

The point is this: I can look around the room and see a landscape of my father-in-law's passions, quirks, and beliefs. His four grandchildren, one born after his death, will be able to do this for years to come. Collections of books, large and small, transcend time. Sometimes the collection is as carefully preserved as the library of the great seventeenth-century diarist Samuel Pepys, which sits at Magdalene College, Cambridge, on the shelves that the naval official Pepys had built for him by dockyard carpenters. Sometimes it is just the shelf of books over a bed: How many times, as a guest in someone else's house, staying in the room of a son or daughter no longer at home, have I looked through a bookshelf for clues to the tastes and dreams of the person who once slept here?

Such voyeurism is not a forbidden one but one to be celebrated. It is not just the writing of books that expresses who we are but also the freedom to collect them, to arrange them, and to enjoy the collections of others. Once a man who had recently been released from many years as a political prisoner in Pakistan was visiting our house. Sitting in our living room talking, at one point he paused, jumped up, and began running his hands over the books on our shelves. "You must excuse me," he apologized. "I have not been able to do this for years."

Technology now lets us put a twenty-volume encyclopedia on a DVD, with movies and music as well; before long, I'm sure, we'll be able to get the contents of a Barnes & Noble superstore on a microchip. But when we're gone, will someone ever be able to look at the chips and disks we used and clearly see, as one can through a collection of books, some glimmer of the shapes of our souls?

1999

ACKNOWLEDGMENTS

Over the course of more than two decades, many people kept my spirits up, helped with the articles that compose this book, and had a hand in its final form. Every writer knows that honest criticism is the greatest gift he or she can receive, and I've been lucky to have reaped much of that. My thanks to the editors of the various books and magazines where these pieces first appeared; particularly helpful in improving them at that stage were Anne Fadiman of the *American Scholar,* Monika Bauerlein of *Mother Jones,* and the late Robert Silvers of the *New York Review of Books.* Mark Danner, Zachary Shore, Elizabeth Farnsworth, Robert F. Worth, Michael Meyer, and an anonymous reviewer for the University of California Press all read the whole collection and gave me their feedback, for which I'm most grateful. Naomi Schneider and her colleagues at the Press have helped midwife this book into the world. A particularly low bow to its copy editor, Peter Dreyer, who corrected not only errors of grammar and syntax but some of historical fact as well.

My literary agents, Georges and Anne Borchardt, have steered me skillfully through the waters of the book world for more than thirty years. And, for almost that long, I've been fortunate to be able to teach at the Graduate School of Journalism of the University of California at Berkeley and to enjoy the company of talented colleagues and students in that community. Many of the people in these pages are activists who've worked to make this a more just world. Harriet Barlow, to whom this book is dedicated, is model of how to be one today, and has taught me and many others more about fighting the good fight than she will ever know.

My wife, Arlie Russell Hochschild, was with me on the trips to India and Russia that I report on here, and on many more for which there weren't room, all the while writing remarkable books of her own. Always my best critic, she edited all of these pieces before they were first published, and then again once they were collected and revised for this volume. I have learned so much from her over more than fifty years that it's impossible to imagine this book, or my life, without her.

In slightly different form and usually under different titles, these articles appeared in the following publications:

"Lessons from a Dark Time," "Hoover's Secret Empire," "Prison Madness," "The Listening House," "Sunday School History" and "A Nation of Guns" in the *New York Review of Books;* "The Father of American Surveillance," "All That Glitters" and "The Brick Master" in *Mother Jones;* "Students as Spies" and "The Impossible City" in *Harper's;* "A Showman in the Rainforest" in the *New Yorker;* "Heart of Darkness: Fiction or Reportage?"—introduction to *Heart of Darkness* by Joseph Conrad, Penguin Classics; "On the Campaign Trail with Nelson Mandela" in the *Village Voice;* "India's American Imports" in the *American Scholar;* "Palm Trees and Paradoxes" in the *San Francisco Examiner Magazine;* "Our Night with it Stars Askew"—foreword to *Memoirs of a Revolutionary* by Victor Serge, New York Review Books; "Shortstops in Siberia" in the *Times Literary Supplement;* "A Homage to Homage"—foreword to *Homage to Catalonia* by George Orwell, Mariner Books; "On Which Continent Was the Holocaust Born?"—introduction to *The Dead Do Not Die* by Sven Lindqvist, New Press; "Pilot on the Great River"—introduction to *Collected Nonfiction, Volume 1* by Mark Twain, Everyman's Library; "A Literary Engineer" in *Understanding the Essay,* edited by Patricia Foster and Jeff Porter; "You Never Know What's Going to Happen Yesterday" in the *Public Historian;* "Practicing History Without a License" in *Historically Speaking;* "On the Road Again," in the *New York Times Book Review;* "Books and Our Souls" in the *Los Angeles Times Book Review.* Reprinted by permission.

PHOTO CREDITS

Cover photo by Alexander Togolev.

Figure 1: Photo by Paul Weinberg, Wikimedia Commons.

Figure 2: Author's personal collection.

Figure 3: Photo by Marcus Bleasdale.

Figure 4: Photo by Soman, Wikimedia Commons.

Figure 5: Getty Images.

Figure 6: Photo by A. F. Bradley, Wikimedia Commons.

Figure 7: Photo by Alexander Togolev.

ALSO BY ADAM HOCHSCHILD

Half the Way Home: A Memoir of Father and Son
The Mirror at Midnight: A South African Journey
The Unquiet Ghost: Russians Remember Stalin
Finding the Trapdoor: Essays, Portraits, Travels
King Leopold's Ghost: A Story of Greed, Terror and Heroism in Colonial Africa
Bury the Chains: Prophets and Rebels in the Fight to Free an Empire's Slaves
To End All Wars: A Story of Loyalty and Rebellion, 1914–1918
Spain in Our Hearts: Americans in the Spanish Civil War, 1936–1939